Bloom's Modern Critical Views

African-American
  Poets: Volume 1
African-American
  Poets: Volume 2
Aldous Huxley
Alfred, Lord Tennyson
Alice Munro
Alice Walker
American Modernist
  Poets
American Women
  Poets: 1650–1950
American Women
  Poets: 1950 to the
  Present
Amy Tan
Anton Chekhov
Arthur Miller
Asian-American Writers
August Wilson
The Bible
The Brontës
Carson McCullers
Charles Dickens
Christopher Marlowe
Contemporary Poets
Cormac McCarthy
C.S. Lewis
Dante Alighieri
David Mamet
Derek Walcott
Don DeLillo
Doris Lessing
Edgar Allan Poe
Émile Zola
Emily Dickinson
Ernest Hemingway
Eudora Welty
Eugene O'Neill
F. Scott Fitzgerald
Flannery O'Connor
Franz Kafka
Gabriel García
  Márquez
Geoffrey Chaucer
George Bernard Shaw

George Orwell
G.K. Chesterton
Gwendolyn Brooks
Hans Christian
  Andersen
Henrik Ibsen
Henry David Thoreau
Herman Melville
Hermann Hesse
H.G. Wells
Hispanic-American
  Writers
Homer
Honoré de Balzac
Jack London
Jamaica Kincaid
James Joyce
Jane Austen
Jay Wright
J.D. Salinger
Jean-Paul Sartre
John Donne and the
  Metaphysical Poets
John Irving
John Keats
John Milton
John Steinbeck
José Saramago
Joseph Conrad
J.R.R. Tolkien
Julio Cortázar
Kate Chopin
Kurt Vonnegut
Langston Hughes
Leo Tolstoy
Marcel Proust
Margaret Atwood
Mark Twain
Mary Wollstonecraft
  Shelley
Maya Angelou
Miguel de Cervantes
Milan Kundera
Nathaniel Hawthorne
Native American
  Writers

Norman Mailer
Octavio Paz
Oscar Wilde
Paul Auster
Philip Roth
Ralph Ellison
Ralph Waldo Emerson
Ray Bradbury
Richard Wright
Robert Browning
Robert Frost
Robert Hayden
Robert Louis
  Stevenson
The Romantic Poets
Salman Rushdie
Samuel Beckett
Samuel Taylor Coleridge
Stephen Crane
Stephen King
Sylvia Plath
Tennessee Williams
Thomas Hardy
Thomas Pynchon
Tom Wolfe
Toni Morrison
Tony Kushner
Truman Capote
Twentieth-Century
  British Poets
Victorian Poets
Walt Whitman
W.E.B. Du Bois
William Blake
William Faulkner
William Gaddis
William Shakespeare:
  Comedies
William Shakespeare:
  Histories
William Shakespeare:
  Romances
William Shakespeare:
  Tragedies
William Wordsworth
Zora Neale Hurston

Bloom's Modern Critical Views

ROBERT FROST
New Edition

Edited and with an introduction by
Harold Bloom
Sterling Professor of the Humanities
Yale University

BLOOM'S
LITERARY CRITICISM
An imprint of Infobase Publishing

Bloom's Modern Critical Views: Robert Frost—New Edition
Copyright © 2011 by Infobase Learning
Introduction © 2011 by Harold Bloom

Bloom's Literary Criticism
An imprint of Infobase Learning
132 West 31st Street
New York NY 10001

Library of Congress Cataloging-in-Publication Data
Robert Frost / edited and with an introduction by Harold Bloom. — New ed.
    p. cm. — (Bloom's modern critical views)
    Includes bibliographical references and index.
    ISBN 978-1-60413-872-6 (hardcover)
    1. Frost, Robert, 1874–1963—Criticism and interpretation.   I. Bloom, Harold.
    PS3511.R94Z91595 2011
    811' .52—dc22
                                        2010039856

Contributing editor: Pamela Loos
Cover designed by Takeshi Takahashi
Composition by IBT Global, Troy NY
Cover printed by IBT Global, Troy NY
Book printed and bound by IBT Global, Troy NY
Date printed: January 2011
Printed in the United States of America

10 9 8 7 6 5 4 3 2 1

Contents

Editor's Note   vii

Introduction   1
    Harold Bloom

Frost and Nature   9
    Cleanth Brooks

"If It Had to Perish Twice": Robert Frost
    and the Aesthetics of Apocalypse   25
    Edward J. Ingebretsen

"Assorted Characters"   41
    George F. Bagby

Inscription and the Burden of Judgment in "Directive"   59
    Lewis Klausner

Robert Frost's Oven Bird   73
    John Hollander

The Echo of Frost's Woods   85
    David Hamilton

"By Pretending They Are Not Sonnets":
    The Sonnets of Robert Frost at the Millennium   93
    Richard J. Calhoun

Rationalist Ethics   111
     John H. Timmerman

Another Look at Robert Frost's "Birches"   141
     Marie Borroff

Quarreling Frost, Northeast of Eden   153
     Kenneth Lincoln

Chronology   169

Contributors   173

Bibliography   175

Acknowledgments   179

Index   181

Editor's Note

My introduction explores some elements of Emerson's influence on Frost, particularly their shared gnosis of "the American Religion." Cleanth Brooks provides a suitable opening to the volume in tackling that monolithic topic, Frost and nature, while Edward J. Ingebretsen makes a case for the poet's apocalyptic aesthetics.

George F. Bagby returns to the natural realm, taking up the congruence between psyche and phenomena in the poems, after which Lewis Klausner examines Frost's greatest piece, "Directive," and its interplay of poetic fact and fiction.

John Hollander turns his attention to "The Oven Bird" and Frost's reinvigoration of the avian trope in poetry, while David Hamilton looks to the woods and considerations of echo and closure in "Stopping by Woods on a Snowy Evening."

Richard J. Calhoun traces Frost's critical rehabilitation and provides a millennial reading of the sonnets, after which John H. Timmerman discusses the poet's classical leanings and an ethics of rationalism informing the work.

Marie Borroff revisits "Birches" and its collision of effort and resistance. The volume concludes with Kenneth Lincoln's assessment of Frostian metrics, tonalities, and syntax.

HAROLD BLOOM

Introduction

I

Frost—at his frequent best—rivals Wallace Stevens as the great American poet of the twentieth century. He does not much resemble Stevens, ultimately for reasons that have little to do with the "essential gaudiness" of much early Stevens, or even with the austere clairvoyance of the later Stevens, poet of "The Auroras of Autumn" and "The Rock." Both of those aspects of Stevens rise from a powerful, barely repressed influence-relationship to Whitman, a poet who scarcely affected Frost. Indeed, Frost's uniqueness among modern American poets of real eminence partly stems from his independence of Whitman. Eliot, Stevens, Pound, Hart Crane, W.C. Williams, Roethke— all have complex links to Whitman, covert in Eliot and in Stevens. Frost (in this like Whitman himself) is the son of Emerson, of the harsher Emerson that we begin only now to recover. Any deep reader of Frost understands why the poet of "Two Tramps in Mud Time" and "Directive" seriously judged Emerson's "Uriel" to be "the greatest Western poem yet." "Uriel's voice of cherub scorn," once referred to by Frost as "Emersonian scorn," is the essential mode of irony favored throughout Frost's poetry.

"Uriel" is Emerson's own irreverent allegory of the controversy set off by his "Divinity School Address." There are certainly passages in the poem that seem to have been written by Frost and not by Emerson:

> The young deities discussed
> Laws of form, and metre just,
> Orb, quintessence, and sunbeams,
> What subsisteth, and what seems.

One, with low tones that decide,
And doubt and reverend use defied,
With a look that solved the sphere,
And stirred the devils everywhere,
Gave his sentiment divine
Against the being of a line.
"Line in nature is not found;
Unit and universe are round;
In vain produced, all rays return;
Evil will bless, and ice will burn."

At the center of this is Emerson's law of compensation: "Nothing is got for nothing," as Emerson phrased it later, in the remorseless essay "Power" in his *The Conduct of Life*. The darker Emersonian essays—"Experience," "Power," "Circles," "Fate," "Illusions"—read like manifestos for Frost's poetry. Richard Poirier has demonstrated this in some detail, and I follow him here in emphasizing how pervasive and crucial the affinity between Emerson and Freud tends to be. If there is a particular motto that states the dialectic of Frost's best poems, then it is to be found in a formulation of Emerson's "Self-Reliance."

Life only avails, not the having lived. Power ceases in the instant of repose; it resides in the moment of transition from a past to a new state, in the shooting of the gulf, in the darting to an aim.

One thinks of the extraordinary early poem "The Wood-Pile" (1914), where the poet, "out walking in the frozen swamp one gray day," comes upon "a cord of maple, cut and split / and piled" and then abandoned:

I thought that only
Someone who lived in turning to fresh tasks
Could so forget his handiwork on which
He spent himself, the labor of his ax,
And leave it there far from a useful fireplace
To warm the frozen swamp as best it could
With the slow smokeless burning of decay.

That "slow smokeless burning" is the metaphor for Emerson's "instant of repose," where power ceases. Frost's restless turnings are his most Emersonian moments, American and agonistic. His Job, in *A Masque of Reason*, puzzling over God's Reason, deliberately relates Jehovah's dialectic to that of Emerson's "Uriel":

> Yet I suppose what seems to us confusion
> Is not confusion, but the form of forms,
> The serpent's tail stuck down the serpent's throat,
> Which is the symbol of eternity
> And also of the way all things come round,
> Or of how rays return upon themselves,
> To quote the greatest Western poem yet.
> Though I hold rays deteriorate to nothing:
> First white, then red, then ultrared, then out.

Job's last two lines here mark Frost's characteristic swerve away from Emerson, except that Emerson is the most difficult of fathers to evade, having been always so subtly evasive himself. Frost's authentic nihilism is considerable but is surpassed by "Fate" in *The Conduct of Life* and by a grand more-than-Frostian late entry in Emerson's journals, set down in the autumn of 1866, when the sage felt burned to the socket by the intensities he had experienced during the Civil War:

> There may be two or three or four steps, according to the genius of each, but for every seeing soul there are two absorbing facts, *I and the Abyss.*

Frost's religion, as a poet, was the American religion that Emerson founded. A latecomer exegete of that religion, I once offered its credo as *Everything that can be broken should be broken*, a Gnostic motto that eminently suits Frost's poetry, where God, whether in *A Masque of Reason, A Masque of Mercy,* or in "Once by the Pacific," is clearly animated neither by reason nor mercy but only by the blind necessities of being the Demiurge:

> It looked as if a night of dark intent
> Was coming, and not only a night, an age.
> Someone had better be prepared for rage.
> There would be more than ocean-water broken
> Before God's last *Put out the Light* was spoken.

A God who echoes Othello at his most murderous is himself also crazed by jealousy. Frost's celebrated negativity is a secularized negative theology,

almost wholly derived from Emerson, insofar as it was not purely tempera-
mental. Slyly aware of it, Frost used it as the occasion for lovely jokes, as in
the marvelous "Two Tramps in Mud Time":

> The water for which we may have to look
> In summertime with a witching wand,
> In every wheelrut's now a brook,
> In every print of a hoof a pond.
> Be glad of water, but don't forget
> The lurking frost in the earth beneath
> That will steal forth after the sun is set
> And show on the water its crystal teeth.

"Two Tramps in Mud Time" hymns the Emersonian negativity of
refusing to identify yourself with any work, in order instead to achieve the
Gnostic identity of the knower with what is known, when the sparks of the
Alien God or true Workman stream through you. A shrewd Gnostic, Frost
refuses to lament confusion, though he also will not follow Whitman in
celebrating it.

II

"Directive" is Frost's poem of poems or form of forms, a meditation whose
rays perpetually return upon themselves. "All things come round," even
our mental confusion as we blunder morally, since the Demiurge is nothing but a moral blunderer. Frost shares the fine Emersonian wildness or
freedom, the savage strength of the essay "Power" that suggests a way of
being whole beyond Fate, of arriving at an end to circlings, at a resolution
to all the Emersonian turnings that see unity and yet behold divisions:
"The world is mathematical, and has no casualty, in all its vast and flowing
curve." "Directive" appears to be the poem in which Frost measures the lot,
and forgives himself the lot, and perhaps even casts out remorse. In some
sense, it was the poem he always wrote and rewrote, in a revisionary process
present already in *A Boy's Will* (1913) but not fully worked out until *Steeple
Bush* (1947), where "Directive" was published, when Frost was 73. "The
Demiurge's Laugh" in *A Boy's Will* features a mocking demonic derision at
the self-realization that "what I hunted was no true god."

North of Boston (1914) has its most memorable poem in the famous
"After Apple-Picking," a gracious hymn to the necessity of yielding up the
quest, of clambering down from one's "long two-pointed [ladder] sticking
through a tree / Toward heaven still." Frost's subtlest of perspectivizings is the
true center of the poem:

I cannot rub the strangeness from my sight
I got from looking through a pane of glass
I skimmed this morning from the drinking trough
And held against the world of hoary grass.
It melted, and I let it fall and break.

The sheet of ice is a lens upon irreality, but so are Frost's own eyes, or anyone's, in his cosmos. This supposed nature poet represents his harsh landscapes as a full version of the Gnostic *kenoma*, the cosmological emptiness into which we have been thrown by the mocking Demiurge. This is the world of *Mountain Interval* (1916), where "the broken moon" is preferred to the dimmed sun, where the oven bird sings of "that other fall we name the fall," and where the birches:

shed crystal shells
Shattering and avalanching on the snow crust
Such heaps of broken glass to sweep away
You'd think the inner dome of heaven had fallen.

Mountain Interval abounds in images of the shattering of human ties and of humans, as in the horrifying "Out, Out—." But it would be redundant to conduct an overview of all Frost's volumes in pursuit of an experiential darkness that never is dispelled. A measurer of stone walls, as Frost names himself in the remarkable "A Star in a Stoneboat," is never going to be surprised that life is a sensible emptiness. The demiurgic pattern of "Design," with its "assorted characters of death and blight," is the rule in Frost. There are a few exceptions, but they give Frost parodies, rather than poems.

Frost wrote the concluding and conclusive Emersonian irony for all his work in the allegorical "A Cabin in the Clearing," the set piece of *In the Clearing* (1962), published for his eighty-eighth birthday, less than a year before his death. Mist and smoke, guardian wraiths and counterparts, eavesdrop on the unrest of a human couple, murmuring in their sleep. These guardians haunt us because we are their kindred spirits, for we do not know where we are, since who we are "is too much to believe." We are "too sudden to be credible," and so the accurate image for us is "an inner haze," full kindred to mist and smoke. For all the genial tone, the spirit of "A Cabin in the Clearing" is negative even for Frost. His final letter, dictated just before his death, states an unanswerable question as though it were not a question: "How can we be just in a world that needs mercy and merciful in a world that needs justice." The Demiurge's laugh lurks behind the sentence, though Frost was then in no frame of spirit to indulge a demiurgic imagination.

Frost would have been well content to give his mentor Emerson the last word, though "content" is necessarily an inadequate word in this dark context. Each time I reread the magnificent essay "Illusions," which concludes and crowns *The Conduct of Life*, I am reminded of the poetry of Robert Frost. The reminder is strongest in two paragraphs near the end that seem to be "Directive" writ large, as though Emerson had been brooding on his descendant:

We cannot write the order of the variable winds. How can we penetrate the law of our shifting moods and susceptibility? Yet they differ as all and nothing. Instead of the firmament of yesterday, which our eyes require, it is to-day an eggshell which coops us in; we cannot even see what or where our stars of destiny are. From day to day, the capital facts of human life are hidden from our eyes. Suddenly the mist rolls up, and reveals them, and we think how much good time is gone, that might have been saved, had any hint of these things been shown. A sudden rise in the road shows us the system of mountains, and all the summits, which have been just as near us all the year, but quite out of mind. But these alternations are not without their order, and we are parties to our various fortune. If life seem a succession of dreams, yet poetic justice is done in dreams also. The visions of good men are good; it is the undisciplined will that is whipped with bad thoughts and bad fortunes. When we break the laws, we lose our hold on the central reality. Like sick men in hospitals, we change only from bed to bed, from one folly to another; and it cannot signify much what becomes of such castaways,—wailing, stupid, comatose creatures,—lifted from bed to bed, from the nothing of life to the nothing of death.

In this kingdom of illusions we grope eagerly for stays and foundations. There is none but a strict and faithful dealing at home, and a severe barring out of all duplicity or illusion there. Whatever games are played with us, we must play no games with ourselves, but deal in our privacy with the last honesty and truth. I look upon the simple and childish virtues of veracity and honesty as the root of all that is sublime in character. Speak as you think, be what you are, pay your debts of all kinds. I prefer to be owned as sound and solvent, and my word as good as my bond, and to be what cannot be skipped, or dissipated, or undermined, to all the *éclat* in the universe. This reality is the foundation of friendship, religion, poetry, and art. At the top or at the bottom of all illusions, I set the cheat which still leads us to work and live for appearances, in spite of our conviction, in all sane hours, that it is what we really are that avails with friends, with strangers, and with fate or fortune.

III

Line in nature is not found,
Unit and universe are round;
In vain produce, all rays return;

An Emersonian spiritual ferocity always remained Frost's. It is there in the early "The Trial By Existence" (from *A Boy's Will*, 1913) and abides still in "A Cabin in the Clearing" (from *In the Clearing*, 1962). Valor reigns, though existence strips us of pride, and we end in pain and mystification. That is the argument of "The Trial by Existence" and prevails in "A Cabin in the Clearing," where all of us "are too sudden to be credible." Poems, being momentary stays against confusion, are also too sudden to be credible.

Frost's most famous poems may be "The Road Not Taken" and "Stopping by Woods on a Snowy Evening." They owe their popularity to a palpable exquisiteness but probably are misread by most of their public. Frost remarked of "The Road Not Taken" that: "It's a tricky poem, very tricky," while "Stopping by Woods on a Snowy Evening" is a rather dangerous poem, tempting the poet (and the reader) with a freedom that would also be destruction. So tricky is "The Road Not Taken" that the alternate routes are presented as though there were no pragmatic difference between them, and yet taking the one supposedly less traveled by has made a total difference in the speaker's life. As allegory or irony, this is open-ended: Was it a choice of the poetic vocation or of one woman rather than another? The final stanza, too sudden to be credible, is overtly the least trustworthy in the poem.

"Stopping by Woods on a Snowy Evening" (to me the superior poem) teases us with a near-nihilism and then reaccepts the world of continuities and obligations, whose emblem is the tingle of harness bells. Tempted by the dark loneliness of deep woods, speaker and reader share in the easy sweep of the wind and snowfall, intimating a solitary quest, where there can be no promises. When Frost observed that a poem was a momentary stay against confusion, he slyly played on the finer edges of the word *confusion*, as he did again in his late poem "Directive" (to me his best), where the traveler, having reached his waters and watering place, is commanded to "Drink and be whole again beyond confusion." Frost's "confusion" is inherited from Emerson's "Uriel," where the heavens come apart after Uriel's rhapsodic affirmation that "Evil will bless, and ice will burn":

The balance-beam of Fate was bent;
The bounds of good and ill were rent;
Strong Hades could not keep his own,
But all slid to confusion.

Both students of language, Emerson and Frost seem to have known that the
Indo-European root of "confusion" originally signified the pouring of a liba-
tion to the gods. To be whole again beyond confusion is to have transcended
such worship. Frost's poetic religion, like Emerson's, was *Self-Reliance*, a
lonely doctrine:

> That thought, by what I can now nearest approach to say it, is this.
> When good is near you, when you have life in yourself, it is not by
> any known or accustomed way; you shall not discern the footprints
> of any other; you shall not hear any name;—the way, the thought,
> the good, shall be wholly strange and new.

This Emersonian insistence on unprecendentedness was Frost's poetic
gospel. Formally, Frost remained a traditionalist, totally unaffected by Emerson's greatest disciple, Walt Whitman. But the poetic argument of Frost's
work, in "Directive," "The Oven Bird," "Design," "Birches," and so many other
triumphs, is extraordinarily individual. Frost was a severe poet, savage and
original in his primal vision, and as much an Emersonial fulfillment as Whitman had been, or as Wallace Stevens and Hart Crane proved to be in Frost's
own era.

CLEANTH BROOKS

Frost and Nature

It is easy for most readers to think of Frost as a typical nature poet. He clearly knew nature intimately—that of his New England in particular—and in poem after poem he described it lovingly, with a keen eye for its detail and with an evident joy in its plangent beauty. I hardly need remind the audience that I see before me poems such as "A Prayer in Spring," "Mowing," "After Apple Picking," "The Wood Pile," "Range Finding," "Nothing Gold Can Stay," "To Earthward," "Spring Pools," "Two Tramps in Mud Time," and dozens and dozens more. There can be no question as to Frost's knowledge of the natural scene, his love for it, and a yearning to find in nature a solace and comfort for human ills.

Though Robert Frost regarded Matthew Arnold as one of the finest poets, in some respects his favorite poet, he was to disagree sharply with what Arnold had said about man and nature in one of his sonnets, "In Harmony with Nature." The poem is addressed, as the subtitle indicates, "To a Preacher." Since the poem is not very well known and since it will serve as a good introduction to my topic, I shall read it.

In harmony with Nature? Restless fool,
Who with such heat dost preach what were to thee,
When true, the last impossibility—
To be like Nature strong, like Nature cool!

From *Robert Frost: The Man and the Poet*, edited by Earl J. Wilcox, pp. 1–17. Copyright © 1989 by UCA Press.

Know, man hath all which Nature hath, but more,
And in that more lies all his hopes of good.
Nature is cruel, man is sick of blood;
Nature is stubborn, man would fain adore.

Nature is fickle, man hath need of rest;
Nature forgives no debt, and fears no grave;
Man would be mild, and with safe conscience blest.

Man must begin, know this, where Nature ends;
Nature and man can never be best friends,
Fool, if thou canst not pass her, rest her slave.

If it is necessary to spell out Arnold's message in bolder detail, we can prosify the last two lines thus: "You are a fool to think that you can strike up a close friendship with nature. Though as a man you are a natural creature, nevertheless, if you can't surpass Nature, then you are bound to remain enslaved to Nature."

In his poem "New Hampshire" Frost expatiates on the sonnet. A certain city man who thought the only decent tree was a tree reduced to lumber— "educated into boards"—attacks a whole grove of trees with an axe. But he doesn't have the courage to carry out his tree murder and soon drops his axe and runs away, quoting Arnold's line: "Nature is cruel, man is sick of blood."

Frost goes on to comment further on this faint-hearted piece of urbanity by writing:

He knew too well for any earthly use
The line where man leaves off and nature starts,
And never overstepped it save in dreams.
He stood on the safe side of the line talking—
Which is sheer Matthew Arnoldism,
The cult of one who owns himself "a foiled,
Circuitous wanderer" and "took dejectedly
His seat upon the intellectual throne. . . ."

As we now know, it was to Goethe that Arnold is referring in those concluding lines, and not, as Frost evidently supposed, to himself. What prompted Frost's bitter reference to Arnold? Frost's biographer, Lawrance Thompson, suggests that it was Arnold's attacks on Puritanism, a subject on which Frost was sensitive and defensive since he claimed to be a Puritan himself. Thompson's suggestion does not satisfy me, and I remain puzzled, all the more so since I mean to argue in what follow that Frost, in poem after poem, shows that he knew very well where Nature ended and humanity began, and that he himself recognized that the limit is all but an unbridgeable chasm. Maybe Frost simply didn't like Arnold's primness of tone or his didactic manner. Certainly Frost found his own, and to my mind, much more satisfying way to describe the man-nature relationship. But I don't apologize for beginning with the Arnold sonnet, for it has the virtue of putting bluntly—even flat-footedly—this matter of the relation of nature to human nature, one of Frost's most significant themes.

Frost's beautiful poem "Two Look at Two" may seem to present an exception to Frost's usual attitude toward nature. You will remember that this poem relates how two lovers on an evening walk up the mountain slope stop at a ruinous stone wall. On the other side of the wall stands a doe. To their surprise and delight, she does not take alarm and bolt. She gazes at the human pair with what seems to them an almost friendly curiosity and finally moves on out of sight.

The human pair feel, as the poem tells us,

> A great wave . . . going over them,
> As if the earth in one unlooked-for favor
> Had made them certain earth returned their love.

This poem, almost alone among Frost's poems, suggests that nature does give some sort of answering response to the pulsations of the human heart, and it is clear that our poet would happily embrace this Wordsworthian belief. But "Two Look at Two" is the only poem of Frost's that comes even close to such an affirmation. And even here the belief takes the form of an aspiration rather than an article of faith. It is significant that the incident occurs at dusk, the time of illusions, that the experience occurs to a pair of lovers, prone to project their own tenderness upon the event and disposed to believe that the bond of love that unites them answers to that which links the buck and the doe; and finally, and most important of all, the experience of union is prefaced by the words "As if the earth . . . returned their love."

If we look at Frost's poems taken as a whole, we find the poet's essential position is put in quite other terms. Instead of the fond belief that "nature never betrayed the heart that loved her," Frost's more realistic view is that nature is not aware that the human world exists at all: nature is deaf and dumb to all human aspirations.

A classic example of Frost's typical stance is presented in his delicately phrased poem "The Need of Being Versed in Country Things." Frost, or at least the *persona* who speaks this poem, has, in the course of a walk, come upon what is left of a burned-down New England farm house. Somehow the barn had escaped the fire, but the house has been destroyed and the site abandoned. In fact, the only sense of life about the barn is that created by the phoebes that go in and out of the broken windows to the nests they have built in the barn loft. Frost vividly pictures the scene: there is still standing the central chimney of the house. He compares the burned-out house to a dead flower in which the petals have fallen away, leaving the pistil standing.

The comparison seems to be quite apt. Many years ago in New England, my wife and I heard one morning that an eighteenth-century house a few miles away had burned during the night. We hurried up to see it, for we hoped to buy from the owners any hinges, door-latch, or other early ironwork that could be retrieved from the ashes in order to use them in our own eighteenth-century house. We were not able to get any ironwork, but we did get the confirmation of the justness of Frost's simile.

But back to the scene that Frost has described. Other things that have survived the fire are the lilacs which have grown around what was once the ruined house; there is a "dry pump" that flings up "an awkward arm," and there are other relics of some family's disaster and the loss of their hopes. It is a scene of desolation, and the poet tells us that the murmur of the birds was "more like the sigh we sigh / From too much dwelling on what has been."

At this point in the poem, we stand where many a pre-Romantic of the middle- and late-eighteenth century stood. Such poets loved scenes of what they liked to call a "pleasing melancholy." Nature itself, through the voices of the phoebes, seems to make an appropriate response to the desolation of the scene and to express its sympathy for man's loss.

Then something quite remarkable happens in the poem. The pleasing melancholy of pre-Romantic vintage gives way to a very different attitude. The poet suddenly goes modern on us. He points out that there is no reason for the phoebes to be uttering anything like a human sigh for man's sorrow. Why should the scene seem in the least sad to them? After all, "for them the lilac renewed its leaf / And the aged elm, though touched with fire; / And the dry pump flung up an awkward arm; / And the fence posts carried a strand of wire." Since birds don't get their water from pumps, the fact that this one is out of order raises no problems, and since birds need only one strand of wire on which to perch, a fence with only one strand of wire is just as useful to them as a fence with three or four. Indeed, the poet goes on to say

> For them there was really nothing sad.
> But though they rejoiced in the nests they kept,
> One had to be versed in country things
> Not to believe the phoebes wept.

The poet is here really having it both ways. The scene does suggest to an observer that nature itself sympathizes with man's plight and mourns with him over the fragility of his existence. But the present observer is, after all, a hard-bitten modern. He is a man "versed in country things." He knows that the phoebes only sound mournful, and that they are sublimely indifferent to man's fate. For him, the notion that nature cares for man and speaks in sympathy to him is only an illusion.

Here is another example of the same theme; Frost's poem "Come In." The speaker begins his poem by telling us that at twilight, at the edge of a wood, he hears a thrush singing.

> Far in the pillared dark
> Thrush music went—
> Almost like a call to come in
> To the dark and lament

Again, the observer is almost deluded into believing that nature is here speaking through the voice of the thrush, and that she is inviting man to join her in her lamentation. But this observer is also a hard-bitten modern. In the concluding stanza, he does a complete *volte face*:

> But no, I was out for stars;
> I would not come in.

His original plan was an evening walk to look at the stars, not to enter the darkened woods to listen to thrush music, and he refuses the invitation, almost too sharply—for he obviously catches himself, evidently remembering his manners. After all, it would be presumptuous to assume that nature had issued any invitation for him to join her in her melancholy mood, and so with a new shift of tone, the speaker adds:

> I meant not even if asked,
> And I hadn't been.

The punch line of the poem is, of course, the last. The speaker knows that it is only what seems to human ears a sweet sadness in the thrush's song that has momentarily deceived him into thinking that nature has any word for him. The thrush itself does not know that a man out for a walk is passing by the wood in which it sings. It does not know, and nature does not know that man even exists.

In Frost's poems on this theme—and "Come In" is typical—nature, though beautiful and sometimes, heart-breakingly lovely, is quite indifferent to man. She commiserates with man no more than she commiserates with the dying elk or the lightning-stricken oak or the withered wild flower. Man, with his consciousness, is separated from the rest of nature by a barrier much more formidable than the wall across which the human pair looked at the mated buck and doe.

Frost, in short, is quite "unromantic" in his attitude toward nature, and if we are to understand his poetry and his art we must get this matter clearly in mind. Perhaps one of the best ways to enforce this point is to compare Frost to some of his modernist contemporaries. What I now shall proceed to do would not have been discouraged, I believe, by Frost himself. Frost, of course, liked his own way of putting things. He carefully cultivated his Yankee cranky conservatism, but he distinctly did not like to be considered an old fogey, inhabiting a backwater withdrawn from the mainstream of current poetry.

He had no desire to be regarded as a merely folksy, New England local colorist. The angriest I ever saw him was when some critic had remarked that his volumes were coffee-table stuff—the sort of thing that a couple who had made a little money and now lived in a fake New England saltbox house like to display in the living room along with the North Carolina-made cobbler's bench and a reproduction spinning wheel.

So the ghost of Robert Frost will not mind my placing him, on this issue at least, in the ranks of the modernist poets, poets such as Auden and Eliot. Suppose we begin with Auden. Consider, for instance, his poem entitled "The Fall of Rome." It is a poem written in crisp, almost staccato quatrains. The reader quickly discerns that though the poem is ostensibly about the fall of Rome, it is really about the fall of any civilization, including our own. Take the lines:

> Caesar's double bed is warm
> As an unimportant clerk
> Writes *I do not like my work*
> On a pink official form.

The "pink official form" belongs to the world of modern letterheads, memo pads, and business forms, and jars oddly—the poet, of course, means to do so—with the Roman Empire's civil service—which I suppose used the stylus and wax tablet.

As the poem opens, nature is gaining on the world of human kind:

The piers are pummelled by the waves;
In a lonely field the rain
Lashes an abandoned train;
Outlaws fill the mountain caves.

But if technology is going to pieces and needs repair, the inner lives of the citizens, including that of the upper classes, are a problem too.

Private rites of magic send
The temple prostitutes to sleep;
And the literati keep
An imaginary friend.

We don't have temple prostitutes—we have to make out with bunny clubs and massage parlors—but practices very like "Private rites of magic" abound. Every newspaper carries the daily astrological guide for the masses, and as for the elite, plenty of them are narcissistic, hypercivilized, and afflicted with various kinds of neurotic tics.

What to do? The problem is difficult. The Catos of the time always ask for a return to the good old days and extol the "ancient disciplines." But even if this could really serve to recall the more sober citizens to their duty, trouble breaks out elsewhere: the "muscle-bound Marines / Mutiny for food and pay."

The poem ends, however, with two stanzas which take us away from a world of economic and technological breakdown, and a narcissistic, physically damaged, and probably corrupt citizenry. The closing stanzas read as follows:

Unendowed with wealth or pity,
Little birds with scarlet legs,
Sitting on their speckled eggs,
Eye each flu-infected city.

Altogether elsewhere, vast
Herds of reindeer move across
Miles and miles of golden moss,
Silently and very fast.

Why should the little birds be endowed with pity anymore than with wealth? Nobody has ever taught them the uses of wampum or other currency, or pity either. Besides nature takes care of itself, can't help doing so—and is quite indifferent to what happens to men. Little birds will keep hatching out their young and the species will go on regardless of whether catastrophe overtakes Nineveh or Rome falls, or New York begins to totter.

With the last stanza we get even further from civilization: we are in Alaska now, or Siberia, and the reindeer, responding to their natural drives, set out on their annual trek in accordance with their seasonal timetables by simply following what nature has programmed into their nervous systems.

The world of nature is foolproof, by which I don't mean that human fools, by doing certain things to the environment, can't wipe out natural species. But left reasonably to themselves, and with a relatively undamaged environment, the creatures do pretty well take care of themselves. Natural laws cannot be broken. They can only be fulfilled. Yet the animals are at the mercy of their instinctual drives. Their power of choice is strictly limited. They also have very limited memories, and one supposes, a very limited notion of the future. In fact, they live in a virtual present like Keats's nightingale that was not "born for death"—was, that is, subject to no racking anxieties about the future, and could not imagine any other state than that which he now enjoyed. No wonder Keats called him an "immortal bird." The human being, of course, is not like that. He is a mortal creature, to be sure, obviously an animal like all the rest, with animal needs and desires. But man, with his self-consciousness, can feel forebodings and anxieties, memories of past failure and of guilt. But, of course, there is a positive side of the ledger. Man takes pride in his heritage and in past accomplishments and he has his hopes and plans and purposes to be realized in the future.

As Auden would put it, mankind inhabits the realm of *history*, which is the peculiarly human realm, whereas all the rest of the creatures live only in the world of nature. Man's world is a three-dimensional world from which the rest of the animal creation is barred out. Man has language—man is a symbol-using and symbol-making animal—and that makes all the difference.

In his various essays, Auden spells this out in his prose. Though Frost does not spell out these matters in Auden's terms, nevertheless the distinction between nature and history and the peculiar nature of man are implicit in nearly every poem that Frost ever wrote.

A great many other modern poets would concur. W. B. Yeats would clearly concur. I have remarked that Keats's nightingale died not knowing that it was ever going to die. But Keats himself was haunted by the knowledge that he would die, and after he began to spit blood, he knew that he would die very soon. Frost's phoebes, whose cry resembles a human lament, are also immortal birds—they do not know that they are mortal or that they do not inhabit a timeless world.

Yeats wrote a brilliant little poem on just this theme. His poem concerns the assassination of Kevin O'Higgins, an Irish politician for whom he had great regard. O'Higgins knew that his life was threatened and because he knew and yet defied his assassins, he showed that he rose superior to death. But here is the poem for your own inspection.

Nor dread nor hope attend
A dying animal;
A man awaits his end
Dreading and hoping all;
Many times he died,
Many times rose again.
A great man in his pride
Confronting murderous men
Casts derision upon
Supersession of breath;
He knows death to the bone—
Man has created death.

In the last line, Yeats may seem to claim far too much. How can he say that man has *created* death? But the statement is simply an exfoliation of what is implicit in the total context. The other creatures cannot conceive or imagine what it is to be dead. In a very real sense, then, man has created the notion of what it is to die and cease to be.

Man's consciousness—his sense of the past and of the future, and his consequent purposes and responsibilities—are indeed both man's glory and his bane. But—and this is the important matter—they involve his being more than simply a natural creature. Doing what comes naturally befits an animal; it is beneath the dignity of the truly human being.

Do I seem to have wandered far from the theme of nature's indifference to man? I do not think so. The indifference is bound up with the many ways in which the human being has to push beyond nature. This is not, of course, to say that man should not love nature. Frost clearly did; so did Auden and Yeats. But though man may properly love nature, he must not assume that nature loves him. Frost, I believe, never does make this assumption.

Let me invoke one further modernist poet, T. S. Eliot. Frost, it seems plain, felt a certain rivalry with Eliot, and certainly some of Frost's friends saw Eliot's poetry as implying a denigration of Frost's own. Actually, when Eliot and Frost finally met, we were told that they got on with each other very well. But their very differences—real or fancied—make Eliot a good choice for my purposes here.

In T. S. Eliot's unfinished play, *Sweeney Agonistes*, one of the characters, Sweeney, a rather raffish urban Irishman, is exchanging some banter with a girl by the name of Doris. They are at a party and he laughingly threatens to carry her to a "cannibal isle." He says to her:

Sweeney: You'll be my little stone missionary!
        I'll gobble you up. I'll be the cannibal.
Doris: You'll carry me off? To a cannibal isle?
Sweeney: I'll be the cannibal.
Doris: I'll be the missionary.
        I'll convert you!
Sweeney: I'll convert *you*!
        Into a stew.
        A nice little, white little, missionary stew.

Sweeney then proceeds to tell Doris what life is like on a "Crocodile isle." There are no telephones, motorcars, or any of the rest of the paraphernalia of civilization. On the island there is nothing to see "but the palms one way / And the sea the other way, / Nothing to hear but the sound of the surf." But the island really offers everything, for Sweeney declares that there are in fact only three things in life, and when Doris asks him what they are, Sweeney answers, "Birth, and copulation, and death, / That's all, that's all, that's all, that's all, / Birth, and copulation, and death." Then comes the following song:

SONG BY WAUCHOPE AND HORSFALL

Snow as Tambo. Swarts as Bones.

Under the bamboo
Bamboo bamboo
Under the bamboo tree
Two live as one
One live as two
Two live as three
Under the bam
Under the boo
Under the bamboo tree

  Where the breadfruit fall
And the penguin call
And the sound is the sound of the sea
Under the bam
Under the boo
Under the bamboo tree.

Where the Gauguin maids
In the banyan shades
Wear palmleaf drapery
Under the barn
Under the boo
Under the bamboo tree.

Tell me in what part of the wood
Do you want to flirt with me?
Under the breadfruit, banyan, palmleaf
Or under the bamboo tree?
Any old tree will do for me
Any old wood is just as good
Any old isle is just my style
Any fresh egg
Any fresh egg
And the sound of the coral sea.

Doris: I don't like eggs, I never liked eggs;
        And I don't like life on your crocodile isle.

SONG BY KLIPSTEIN AND KRUMPACKER

Snow and Swarts as before

My little island girl
My little island girl
I'm going to stay with you
And we won't worry what to do
We won't worry what to do
We won't have to catch any trains
And we won't go home when it rains
We'll gather hibiscus flowers
For it won't be minutes but hours
For it won't be hours but years
And the morning
And the evening
And noontime
And night
Morning
Evening

Noontime
Night

Doris: That's not life, that's no life
        Why, I'd just as soon be dead.
Sweeney: That what life is Just is
Doris: What is?
        What's that life is?
Sweeney: Life is death.

This account of life on a South Sea island is a rather jumbled affair—and one supposes that the poet satirically meant it to be so. The people singing about the delights of this simple life have evidently never been in the South Sea islands themselves, and they have added to the cliches of the earthly paradise some details that don't quite fit. For example, there are in fact no penguins found on a South Sea island and probably no banyan trees. One element in this muddled, composite picture comes from the old fashioned cartoon of lugubrious white missionaries sitting in great iron pots over a fire, with the cannibal chief now turned chef, presiding over the affair. Sweeney's South Seas paradise is obviously fake.

What Eliot has done is to present modern alienated man's confrontation with a nature which modernity has de-animated and neutralized. Even if the boredom incident to the meaningless routine of urban life may make nature seem for a moment an escape from the meaningless, a retreat into a healthful, rich, and organic world, the escape is illusory.

Man receives from nature finally only what he brings to it. Nature will prove just as boring as the world from which modern man seeks to escape. Man's attempt to shed his humanity by becoming simply a natural creature like a fruit-bat or a penguin won't work. For this maneuver to succeed he would have to give up the very consciousness that provides nature with its mystery and its beauty.

As Frost's poems make plain, he has no delusions that a mere relapse into nature can save us. Again, as we have seen, as a good modern, Frost is reconciled to the fact that nature is indifferent to man. But this acceptance does not leave him in despair. Man's life is not meaningless.

Perhaps this is as far as I ought to go in this lecture. But I think that it is as far as I need to go to set forth Frost's essential relation to nature. I shall leave it to others to speculate about Frost's ultimate metaphysical concerns. In any case, it is high time to return to Frost's own poems and to his own characteristic treatment of man's amphibious nature, a creature immersed in the world of nature and yet able, if not to step out of it, at least to hold his head above it.

Frost's poem "A Leaf Treader" is apt to my purpose here. The poem describes an autumn day in New England. All day the speaker has tramped back and forth in his woodlot. The brightly colored autumn leaves are falling all about him, and he has trodden many a leaf into the mire underfoot. In line 4 he explains—rather oddly, as it would at first seem—"I have safely trodden underfoot the leaves of another year." Why "safely"? Why this note of apprehension and fear? What has been worrying him comes out very clearly in the next stanza, though the tone of that stanza is whimsical and laced with a good deal of self-irony. The gist of the stanza is this: every autumn the speaker has come to speculate on whether he will end up on top of the autumn leaves or the autumn leaves will end up on top of him. Thus he observes:

> All summer long they were overhead, more lifted up than I.
> To come to their final place in earth they had to pass me by.
> All summer long I thought I heard them threatening under their
> breath
> And when they came it seemed with a will to carry me with them
> to death.

The leaves have been, then, threatening him throughout the summer months, but their power has resided in more than threat. As he tells us in the first lines of the last stanza:

> They spoke to the fugitive in my heart as if it were leaf to leaf.
> They tapped at my eyelids and touched my lips with an invitation
> to grief.

Thus there is something in man himself that responds to the pull of the seasons, something that yearns to give up the world of toil and anxiety and might even welcome a subsidence into the peace of death. The second line of this stanza has a realistic reference: the leaves blowing through the autumn wind do, some of them, tap at his eyelids or touch his lips, as if they were urging him to weep or to express his grief in words. At this point in the poem we are very close to the thrush's invitation in the fourth stanza of "Come In." The leaves' invitation cannot be dismissed in cavalier fashion. Man, like the leaves or the grass, is here today and gone tomorrow. Frost's speaker acknowledges that he is deeply involved in the processes of nature and is momentarily tempted to respond. But he pulls himself together and with a remarkable shift in tone concludes the stanza and the poem:

> But it was no reason I had to go because they had to go.
> Now up, my knee, to keep on top of another year of snow.

The special quality of tone of the third line is very important. It always reminds me of my own childhood when if the children next door were called in by their mother but I hadn't yet been summoned, I was tempted to express my good fortune by saying, "Well, I'm not going in. Just because you have to go in is no sign I have to." That some such tone is involved here is all to the good. This particular poem must not, at this point, take itself too seriously. And the poet proceeds to give the poem one further twist. With the last line, he remembers that his triumph over the autumn leaves may be short-lived. Man's effort never stops, soon the snowflakes will be coming down and the next pressing problem will be to stay on top of the snow rather than to allow the snow to provide a winter blanket for them.

There is another short poem of Frost, however, that puts more precisely the relationship of man to the brute creation, but also pays its respects to those men who pride themselves on their ability to calculate and reason. The poem to which I refer is the celebrated "Stopping by Woods on a Snowy Evening."

When the man in the sleigh pulls over to the side of the road to look at the snow falling in the woods, he indicates that he believes he knows the owner of the woods. He remarks rather pointedly:

> He will not see me stopping here
> To watch his woods fill up with snow.

Why does the speaker go to the trouble of saying this? It is hardly a criminal offense to stop and look at another man's property. Yet the speaker does hint that the owners of those woods might be suspicious. After all, why should anyone stop to look at woods on a snowy evening? Because he has some kind of land deal on his mind? Or because he is a little touched in the head? A man who stops just to look is scarcely acting like a rational man.

Now if the owner of the woods would find it queer that the man in the sleigh should stop to gaze at this property in a snowstorm, certainly the horse that pulls the sleigh thinks so:

> My little horse must think it queer
> To stop without a farmhouse near

Between the woods and frozen lake
The darkest evening of the year.

He gives his harness bells a shake
To ask if there is some mistake.
The only other sound's the sweep
Of easy wind and downy flake.

Actually, what the speaker surmises his little horse must "think" and what he surmises that the owner of the woods would think define the observer's own position. He is poised somewhere between the two. Neither pure practical calculation nor pure instinctive response can find a place for aesthetic appreciation. Neither horses, polar bears, nor nightingales are, so far as we can tell, aesthetic creatures. This is not to say that animals do not have their own sense of well-being and happiness, but that is different from detached contemplation indulged in for its own sake. The horse is clearly *not* enjoying the sight of the woods filling up with snow. But neither would the practical-minded property owner enjoy the sight of his woods or any other man's, filling up with snow.

I do not want to weight this rather charming little poem too heavily with moral and intellectual import. But, then, it is much more than a single-minded vignette of the New England landscape. I submit that it at least implies a definition of man. Man is the aesthetic animal, able to contemplate nature without reference to practical considerations. He is also the ethical animal. Yes, the poem touches on these considerations too. For the man in the sleigh, much as he would like to linger over the scene—perhaps he even feels an impulse to give up the human effort and simply sink back into nature, for the woods are indeed "lovely, dark and deep"—nevertheless drives on. Why? Because, as he tells us, he has promises to keep.

We are not told what these promises are. They may be weighty or trivial. But he feels a responsibility to fulfill them, to put matters in Auden's terms: the person who is truly human transcends the realm of nature and inherits the realm of history, for only there can he truly fulfill himself.

To sum up: Frost neither worships nature nor fears her. In a very real sense he belongs to her and is one of her children. He finds her infinitely interesting and lovely, but he knows how little he can ask of her. Nature is quite unconscious of his very existence. Man's gift of consciousness actually separates him from her and from his fellow creatures. But Frost is not tempted thereby to get above his raising. He doesn't let his own power of consciousness go to his head. Thus, he doesn't proclaim with Blake the supremacy of the imagination over nature, nor with Emerson declare that he "esteem(s) nature (to be a mere) accident and an effect (of spirit)." For Frost, man is indeed a peculiar being. But if I were forced to find a just analogue for Frost's definition of man, I think that I could do no better than to go back to Psalm 8, with its wonderful lines: "What is man, that thou art mindful of him? and the son of man, that thou visiteth him? For thou hast made him a little lower than the angels. . . ." But rather than recite the rest of the Psalm, let me simply conclude with the note supplied by the editors of the Jerusalem Bible. Their summary of the account of man given in Psalm 8 will very nearly fit the account implied by Frost's poems: "Man, frail yet made in the likeness of God, on the border between the spiritual and material worlds, rules the natural creation. . . ."

EDWARD J. INGEBRETSEN

"If It Had to Perish Twice":
Robert Frost and the Aesthetics of Apocalypse

"Yet like a Christian disciplined to bend
His mind to thinking always of the end."
—Robert Frost, "The Lesson for Today"[1]

I

Commentators as diverse as R. W. B. Lewis, Perry Miller, Sacvan Bercovitch, and Jacques Derrida note how extensively Christian themes shape
American culture. They point, in particular, to the apocalyptic quality of
American writings.[2] Douglas Robinson sharpens and extends the point in
American Apocalypses, where he remarks upon the "centrality of the apocalypse" (xi) in American literature.[3] If we also recall that Lionel Trilling
honored Robert Frost as "virtually a symbol of America" (154), these evalu-
ations make one hesitate. What connection can Frost, the writer of Currier
and Ives, New England miniatures—the poet most readers know—have
with apocalyptic literature, a genre that Robert Alter calls the "dark dream
passed down from the ancient world by religious and literary tradition" (47).
One would think not much. Nonetheless, a glance through his *Complete
Poems, 1949* suggests otherwise, since Frost's titles alone indicate his familiarity with popular versions of apocalypse as well as with more arcane variants: "Bursting Rapture," "Our Doom to Bloom," "Nothing Gold Can Stay,"
"It Is Almost the Year Two Thousand," "Fire and Ice," "Design." Thus,

From *Thought* 67, no. 264 (March 1992): 31–46. Copyright © 1992 by Fordham University
Press.

though Robinson's study mentions Frost only in passing, strong thematic echoes link Frost's verse to the genre of apocalyptic texts. In addition, Frost's verse itself is, in important ways, apocalyptic.

Frost's verse is apocalyptic, first, in the word's original sense of unveiling or uncovering, and, second, in its derivative sense of revelation. A major theme of Frost's verse—though appropriately enough, not always an obvious one—is textual secrecy: the secrets of the text that right reading reveals. When a Frost speaker says "I want you to understand me wrong" (510) Frost is, Herbert Marks suggests, playing on "the interaction of revelation and concealment—a theological commonplace" (Marks 125). Marks's comment brings to mind the historical and philosophical connections joining Frost to the wider tradition of American apocalyptic, especially as embodied and articulated by Emerson. In *Nature* (1836), in an effort to revitalize American Calvinism, Emerson argues that Nature constitutes the primary text through which God reveals himself and his designs. Emerson uses Scripture (specifically the Book of Revelation) as an analogue for nature. *Nature*, claims Alan Hodder, "grows out of the Bible, recapitulates its structure, and participates in its vision" (5).[4] Frost leaned heavily upon Emerson's poetic and philosophical example and took seriously the philosopher's lesson. Frost, too, discovered in nature an apt teacher with much to reveal about the ways of God (theology) and the ways of human beings (teleology). To the discerning eye nature revealed God's final meaning and life's definitive ends.

Frost echoes popular apocalyptic themes as much to control his own anxiety of endings as to parody the fears of others. Frost's preoccupation with the intricacies of form, in particular, was his response to anxieties that plagued him about other, less directly aesthetic aspects of life. To listen to Frost talk, life was merely a long, extended feat of prowess whose "form" he would come upon "later in the dark of life" (Cook 294). Life was a poem for which he needed only to find the last perfect line.[5] In "The Figure a Poem Makes" Frost directly compares life and the poem. The figure a poem makes, Frost says, like love, "begins in delight and ends in wisdom. . . . It has denouement. . . . It must be a revelation, or a series of revelations" (Cox and Lathem 18–19). The poem embodies and reflects life, and both are necessarily aesthetic: formed of connections, forms, relations. Finally and importantly, life and poem move to distinct and distinguishable ends, since the final rhythm or gesture confirms, or fails to confirm, the intended design. The grammar of a poem mirrors the grammar of experience; in both, the endings to which we come cast into high relief our intentions, successes, and failures: "Strongly spent is synonymous with kept" (Cox and Lathem 24). Knowing life's shape freed Frost to use its space more appropriately, as knowing the design shaping a poem helped him write better poems.

In "Design," for example, Frost considers the possibilities of ultimate revelation that one might divine from Emersonian "natural facts." The sonnet's octet asks what kind of cosmic order so arranged the conjunction of "dimpled" spider, moth, and "innocent" flower that traps the unwitting moth:

> What had that flower to do with being white,
> The wayside blue and innocent heal-all?
> What brought the kindred spider to that height,
> Then steered the white moth thither in the night?
> What but design of darkness to appall?—
> If design govern in a thing so small. (302)

Though the poem seems to argue for universal design as conventionally understood, the mounting tension caused by the sestet's series of unanswered interrogations undercuts the consolations typically associated with design and deistic order. If these interrogatives—"what had" and "what brought"—are more than rhetorical questions, then the more than rhetorical force of the poem's last interrogative catches the reader off guard. Looking for comfort, the reader finds none to be had as the sestet reveals universal design to conceal darker possibilities than first perceived. Finally, the closing couplet denies outright any rhetorical comfort that a design might offer.

The poem's conclusion suggests an apparently shattering, disruptive sort of revelation. It is apocalyptic in a traditional, though limited and derivative, sense of the word. The poem's intricate design traps the reader in despair as surely as the argument for design traps the spider. Lionel Trilling pointed to this poem as an example of Frost's "terrifying universe." Read it, Trilling comments, and see "if you sleep the better for it" (157). Nonetheless, "Design" actually is one of Frost's least terrifying poems. Though offered as proof of the "design of darkness to appall," "Design" proves the contrary, or at least offers a conclusion that points ambiguously toward another end: design, by indicating the presence of order at all, and by governing in a "thing so small" as a poem, must be construed as a sign of hope. The universe is *not* to be feared precisely *because*, and to the extent *that*, "design govern[s] in a thing so small." The thing so small, here, of course, is the verbal design of the poem, a design not so much predetermined as "believe[d] . . . into existence" beforehand (Cox and Lathem 45).

Frost himself warned readers against thinking him to be "undesigning," and in "Design" we can see why. On the one hand, Frost cleverly manipulates a discourse of fear, highlighting anxieties that are partly cultural and theological, but partly psychological in origin. On the other hand, "Design" does more than parody apocalyptic fears, since it is apocalyptic, revelatory, in a true sense. Though portending the ultimate collapse of human meaning, in the very last line the poem reverses itself and points forward to a new revelation, suggesting that appropriate design and form must govern human activity.

This is what Frost means in "Letter to *The Amherst Student*" when he says that anyone who has the "least form" to go with is "lost to the larger excruciations" (Cox and Lathem 106). In "Design" as elsewhere, Frost shows a preference for aesthetic metaphors of form over conventional religious or eschatological ones. For example, the concept of "design" as Frost uses it directs attention away from a divine agent who (or, more terribly, *that?*) creates a cosmos. Frost's use extends the word to mean a human agent, a writer, who designs a "cosmos" of words. The ambiguous doubleness of "cosmos" is suggestive; from its Greek root we derive both cosmology and cosmetic. Cosmology is a study, as one could say, of a design of beauty. It investigates a literal and symbolic place, at once world and word, in which human meaning reveals itself. Thus Frost goes Emerson's apocalypticism one better: the revelation of Nature is, rather, a revelation of the human spirit because Nature has less to teach us than we think. Frost put it most bluntly in "Kitty Hawk" (1962) "Nature's never quite / Sure she hasn't erred / In her vague design" till we tell Nature what "She's supposed to mean" (442).

Consequently, Frost's legendary concern about his talent—and his sometimes mean-spirited defense of it—will always seem borrowed from the reserves of a less focused and more private anxiety. The poetic moment arises, Frost said, out of a "background in hugeness and confusion, shading away from where we stand into black and utter chaos" (Cox and Lathem 107). Against the chaos the poet struggles for balance, drawing like anyone upon those resources of hand or heart that chance or talent make available. Frost, in particular, gained balance—righted himself—by writing himself, which is not to say that his poems simply provided windows into biography. They did not, as Frost rightly insisted. Order, Frost knew, is "everybody's sanity," and a need for order provides the major emotion organizing apocalyptic narrative. Life's logic, like that of a poem, must be somehow forward, though recognized backward: "more felt than seen ahead like prophecy" (Cox and Lathem 19). We tell apocalyptic stories, in the first place, because everyone, not merely poets, needs to know how the end turns out in order to live the rest.

II

Historically, spinning terrible narratives about collapsing worlds has been one way those excluded from power have gained power; apocalyptic narratives give rhetorical support, at least, to those needing help to survive life's periodic personal or social collapses. R. W. B. Lewis defines the apocalyptic mode as "another reanimating of those great archetypes by which western man has explained the full range of his condition and his fears" (206).[6] Nonetheless, as Nathan Scott observes, traditional apocalyptic texts reflect a "failure of confidence" in "the historical drama," a fear that it won't "attain any radical significance" (11). Derivatively apocalyptic texts thus resemble Edenic ones, in that their narrative strategies move toward closure *outside* time, offering illusory, inhuman solutions to human dilemmas.[7] Eden, like apocalypse, betrays a fear of time and historical process, the one seen as distantly past, the other as distantly future.

In histories derived from the Judaeo-Christian tradition, time's linear advance culminates in God's revelation (variously understood) breaking forth into history. This revelation is, at the same time, history's termination—and, consequently, the abrupt and disastrous ending of human affairs. Popular versions of apocalypse, of course, emphasize the novelty of such a moment: time's final gesture into the cosmic dark. The potential for melodrama in apocalyptic narrative accounts for the persistence of such lurid readings— or misreadings—of the end of the world. Fireworks, after all, are fireworks, regardless of who runs the show or in whose honor it is held. Although Frost was too deeply religious to take such narratives seriously, as a lifelong reader of Poe, Frost knew the value of an occasional Gothic pose.[8] He used Eden's blissful garden as well as the thunder of apocalypse to emphasize the need for human action, no matter how limited the context or inadequate the gesture. The point, for the poet, was not to end time but to "figure" its complexities for the *meantime*. Only in this way could the present moment—"too present to imagine" ("Carpe Diem" 336)—become accessible and meaningful, revelatory and apocalyptic in the truest sense.

Frost drew from a variety of apocalyptic sources as if to emphasize that everybody feels anxious about the way things end—or, put another way, about how things continue. Some examples: he borrows freely from Christian apocalyptic ("Fire and Ice" and "Bursting Rapture"); from classical—especially Virgilian—theories of the *Aevum* ("Nothing Gold Can Stay," "It Is Almost the Year Two Thousand"); from Stoic ideas of the world's final cleansing by fire ("Our Doom to Bloom," "It Is Almost the Year Two Thousand"). He even alludes to Greek, Sibylline texts ("Our Doom to Bloom"). Often the various images overlap in a single poem, as in "Nothing Gold Can Stay" (1923).[9] Christian apocalyptic themes, however, suited Frost's purposes best, since the Christian tradition resonated most naturally with the Yankee Farmer pose he adopted (or, as some critics contend, the pose that later co-opted him).

Like the post-Reformation apologists who read John's Book of Revelation as political document rather than as religious text, Frost makes the instinctive connection between apocalyptic texts and the real anxieties of life displaced by these cosmic psychodramas. For example, "Bursting Rapture"

(1949), like "It Is Almost the Year Two Thousand" (1942), employs millenar-
ian images in order to criticize attitudes Frost found disturbing in American foreign policy. "Bursting Rapture" aligns the development of the atomic
bomb with divine revelation, implicitly equating American imperialistic poli-
cies with the narrow-minded chauvinism of literalist Christianity, to whom
the bomb offered a politically expedient variant of God's will. With barely
concealed sarcasm the poem implies that ultimate authority for the use of
"a certain bomb" derives from the Book of Revelation. The bomb "was sent
to be" because the Rapture—according to the sacred texts, God's final judgment—comes upon the saved just like a bomb. Both culminate in a flash of
fire bringing relief from "mounting ecstasy."[10] The poem defines the apocalyptic mentality as need for comfortable solutions to uncomfortable problems, even if it means blowing everything up. In "Bursting Rapture" Frost's
speaker, a physician, explains:

> "There, there,
> What you complain of, all the nations share.
> Their effort is a mounting ecstasy
> That when it gets too exquisite to bear
> Will find relief in one burst. You shall see.
> That's what a certain bomb was sent to be." (398)

As these brief examples demonstrate, the melodrama and cosmic despair
of conventional apocalyptic narrative becomes something altogether different
and more positive in Frost's hands. The suggestively sexual connotations of
the images in "Bursting Rapture" show Frost's power of condensation. His
habit of "seeing doubly" enables him to compress philosophical, theological,
and biological significance into a word or phrase, which in turn gives his verse
its elliptic ambiguity. In Frost's parabolic, rarely undesigning way, behind the
collapsing worlds of rock and stone one senses symbolic and metaphoric
extensions, the more complex worlds of human forms, homes, and words.
Frost moves by way of analogy from a collapsing cosmos to the collapsing
world of human meaning. His verse is probably most complex where the
symbolic universe of human words and gestures collapses under pressure of
the fictional strategies designed to sustain it. Consider, for example, the deft
irony of "Fire and Ice" (1926):

> Some say the world will end in fire,
> Some say in ice.
> From what I've tasted of desire
> I hold with those who favor fire.

But if it had to perish twice,
I think I know enough of hate
To say that for destruction ice
Is also great
And would suffice. (220).

In this poem "fire" and "ice" sustain a variety of readings. Most literally, they describe the destruction that fire and ice can cause a world of real rock and stone—Frost, of course, alluding to religious and scientific narratives of the end-time. Frost sets the storied violence of Christian apocalyptic against the violence of a scientific—though equally simplistic—myth. The poem's deceptive whimsy becomes all the more serious as Frost's reader must decide which "reading" is, after all, the more horrible. Does one prefer the dangerous tyranny of a religious idea, one that leads as it often does to acts of violent despair? Frost plays out this scenario in "Bursting Rapture." Or perhaps one prefers the random, less culpable, inevitable violence of natural forces? Both readings—scientific and religious—fail, Frost implies, because in their haste to "end" time they stifle individual courage and responsibility, leaving humanity defenseless against the ravages of time and change.

In "Fire and Ice" Frost's reflections appear at first far distant from the everyday world's fiery passions and chilly hates. The indefinite pronoun serving as grammatical subject—"Some say"—dismissively suggests that the topic under discussion is hardly important—a matter maybe of a good story to kill some time or pass a moment or two. By poem's end, however, Frost strips the good story, not only of satisfying melodrama, but of comforting distance as well. He makes it human again. To talk about the end of the world is not, Frost suggests, a matter of killing a few minutes; rather, it is a matter of destroying all time by choking the imagination and threatening human hope. One's fictions—one's narrative frames, designs, bits of order, however come by and however kept—significantly shape how one lives. Consequently, they shape how one dies, as well. By eliminating hope, some fictions—Frost would include the apocalyptic and Edenic—serve only to "close a road, abandon a farm, / Reduce the births of the human race, / And bring back nature in people's place" ("The Times Table" 263).

R. W. B. Lewis reads "Fire and Ice" as a "poker-faced gloss on traditional apocalyptic theorizing" (186). Additionally, positioned against the political and social distress of the post–World War I years, "Fire and Ice" offers Frost's always pungent commentary on the art of the politically possible. Frost debunks the melodrama of apocalyptic "theorizing," criticizing those who invoke the authority of science, religion, or myth in order to be released from the burdens of history and time. "Fire and Ice" concludes that emotions—the casually human excesses of anger and desire—threaten life more than cycles of history, the metaphysics of religion, or the entropic dead-ends of scientific naturalism.

Robert Frost lived another forty years after publishing "Fire and Ice." His longevity is a metaphor in itself, a telling exemplum of the poet's will to live. As Frost endured first one major war, then another, and then another, one could imagine him in a darkened auditorium, pausing as he "said" "Fire and Ice." What had changed, if anything, in the passing years? The fatalism of deterministic answers, whether called evolution or God's Will, consoles those who cannot otherwise order their lives. Frost's brief poem suggests that the comfort of such designs is illusory, the human satisfactions minimal. That much had not changed, Frost knew. Fire or Ice; still the world aligns its passions with its political interests. Still, appropriately enough in a different kind of war, this is the way the world ends—not with fire, not with a bang, but with the cold and chill of ice.

III

If rewriting is revision, Frost's rewriting of apocalyptic materials significantly revised him—shaping his personal style and tightening his poetics. Frost's apocalyptic mode accounts for an eccentricity so pervasive in verse and personal style that, as we have seen, its presence gives rise to wider thematic concerns. In the words of Patricia Wallace, Frost's poems "curl away" from the reader. Robert Pack, honoring Frost at the centennial of his birth, called this quality the poet's "enigmatic reserve." Herbert Marks's phrase quoted earlier—an "interaction of revelation and concealment"—captures as well as any Frost's linguistic elusiveness. Frost's poems, if *about* anything, are finally about language—about its revelations and its obscurities, about the ends to which words move and the ends to which you can push language. Frost generally practices the art of veiling when he seems to be most unveiling; his verse always busily keeps the secrets it appears to give away. The revelations of his verse become, in the end, peculiarly unrevealing. Frost's verse implies that poetry itself is importantly apocalyptic: violent and revelatory, or violent *because* revelatory.

At the level of style Frost deflects the careless reader since the authentically revelatory moment in a poem—revelatory of life's risk and the need for human courage and craft—may be further disguised by what Richard Poirier calls a style of "posturing" (185). In "The Onset" (1921), the poem to which Poirier refers, the speaker confesses that the falling snow makes him feel "as" one who is "overtaken by the end" and who has "nothing done / To evil, no important triumph won" (226). But this speaker, like many others in Frost's

verse, only shows how thoroughly Frost disciplined personal fears by submit-
ting potential imaginative excesses to the final measures of verse. In "The
Onset," the world of analogy—signaled by the easily overlooked preposition
"as"—preoccupies the speaker more than the snowfall, its initiating cause. The
speaker's lack of interest in the snowfall alerts the reader that snow is, after
all, unremarkable and quotidian, and not generally threatening. But more
concerned with inner than with outer weather, the speaker transforms the
snowfall into something else, in the process giving himself a good scare with
thoughts of "last things":

> Always the same, when on a fated night
> At last the gathered snow lets down as white
> As may be in dark woods, and with a song
> It shall not make again all winter long
> Of hissing on the yet uncovered ground,
> I almost stumble looking up and round,
> As one who overtaken by the end
> Gives up his errand, and lets death descend
> Upon him where he is, with nothing done
> To evil, no important triumph won,
> More than if life had never been begun. (226)

One might observe that apocalyptic issues—fears of termination, the onset
of "final moments" or of inappropriate conclusions—unsettle the speaker's
balance. But the apocalypse here is consciously literary, and thus unliteral, in
the sense that words go where, and do what, bodies will not. The speaker's
allusive language betrays his artiness—never, to Frost's way of thinking, a
compliment—and the second verse reveals the poem's apocalyptic moment
to be a pose.

The enjambed cadences and elevated diction of the first stanza recall
Paradise Lost, John Milton's own bit of apocalyptic high drama and theorizing. Apocalyptic texts—Milton's *Paradise Lost* and Frost's "The Onset"
are two—share with Gothic texts a fascination with collapsing structures,
whether personal, social, or cosmic. Both genres work by voyeuristic displacement, inducing feelings of entrapment or terror in order, finally, to allay them.
Frost's occasional apocalyptic pose was not intended to deny that such anxieties plagued him since poem after poem reveals his susceptibility. Instead,
good craftsman that he was, Frost submitted his anxieties to the discipline
of words in order to control them, as he does in the second verse of "The
Onset." The first stanza establishes a fictional frame within which the speaker
indulges the limit of anxiety without succumbing to it. On the other hand,

the second verse reassures the speaker against the catastrophe that the first verse portends—perhaps pretends would be better—by establishing the fact that the earth's seasonal cycle naturally limits winter's force. The coming of spring ought to dampen any hysteria that a fertile imagination, literary or theological, might feel while considering how the world could end. Spring, as seasonal as winter, deflates winter's pretensions—if, of course, winter could have any, which as Frost's verse continually keeps before us, it cannot. Fictions, after all, are the rightful province of the human agent, who can use them negatively, as in "The Onset," or, more positively, as in "Stopping by Woods on a Snowy Evening."

"Stopping by Woods on a Snowy Evening" (1923) makes an interesting companion to "The Onset," especially since Frost intended them to be read together, placing the two poems on facing pages in *New Hampshire*. The settings in both poems are similar, if not identical, offering variations on what is practically a distinct subgenre in Frost's poetry—life imagined from the edge of the woods. The concerns of both speakers involve temporal issues; questions of time and how it is spent or kept prompt anxiety for both. Specifically, each reflects on a supposed or impending termination or conclusion. Though differing significantly in tone, each poem takes its energy from the pressure of the night and the presence of "dark woods." While the narrative voice in "The Onset" seems intent on scaring itself to death in a literary sort of way, the speaker in "Stopping by Woods" purposely distances himself from a fear which he cannot, apparently, yet articulate. Nonetheless, both speakers remain safely this side of the fears they imagine by shaping them into words. A small victory, perhaps, but a human one.

In "The Onset" the speaker works through his crisis by finally admitting the onset, not of winter, but of spring. This revelation differs from the arch and literary apocalypse of the first verse. Similarly, the speaker of "Stopping by Woods" turns from the "lovely, dark and deep" (224) solace of imaginative reverie to the mundane but nevertheless engaging commitments of quotidian life. The "darkest evening of the year" (224) will, after all, give way to a daylight world. In "The Onset" the speaker imagines the white "clump of houses with a church" (226) he will see when spring defeats winter. The other speaker recalls the "promises" he has yet to keep—importantly, the "promises" that *are* keeping *him* from indulging overmuch in the delicious inactivity at the edge of the silent woods. The social dimension in which these speakers exist rescues them from the trap of solitary imagination. Nowhere does Frost make clearer the social implications of the imagination, and thus of poetry, than in those poems where he explores the limits, edges, and the ends of anxiety, whether private or social. Frost is a poet of the imagined life not only because he knows its graces, but also because he was well acquainted with its nights.

He understands the terrors of an unrestrained imagination, the dangers of the world of the mind.[11]

Frost writes on the edges of language, creating meaning in the delicate pauses between the reader's sense of a word and the sense to which the word slides in the text. He writes in the silences that open between and around multiple contexts—as, for example, in the literary, religious, psychological echoes evident in the first stanza of "The Onset." Consequently, Frost's apocalypticism partially accounts for another persistent theme, questions of epistemology: how one knows and what one can know. Frost's verbal and narrative strategies demand that a reader follow him not only to the ends of time but almost to the limits of meaning.

Consider "For Once, Then, Something" (1920), which Frost placed between "The Onset" and "Stopping by Woods"; the three poems form a triptych considering various possibilities of language, time, and revelation. A speaker kneels along the edge of a well-curb trying to see into its depths. However, because of the angle of reflecting sunlight, the speaker "never see[s] / Deeper down" (225) below the surface images. That is, he can only self-reflexively view himself in the act of peering into the well. Images drift across the water's surface and once he thinks he sees something "more of the depths" (225). However, a drop of water agitates the surface and the observer realizes he actually does not know *what* he sees, whether reality, illusion, or a combination of both. The poem's evasive diction draws attention to the ephemeral nature of the speaker's perceptions: "I discerned, as I thought . . . / . . . a something white, uncertain, / Something more of the depths" (225). The speaker *does* see, in any case, that the water hides from sight what he wants to see. The water reveals to him, then, what he cannot, in the nature of things, see. Sight undermines and discredits vision; the poem focuses attention upon the observer's epistemological assumptions only to discredit them.[12] The poem achieves an ending in which initial desires remain unsatisfied, in which closure is only apparent and not real. Three rhetorical questions and a sentence fragment constitute the only revelation at hand.

"For Once, Then, Something" is not often anthologized, and one can see why. The poem appears to settle, if not for despair, then for intellectual quietism; Frost puts the reader in the unenviable position of being complicit in limiting what can be known. Yet "For Once, Then, Something" is typical of Frost's obsession with the ambiguity of revelatory moments. In this poem, as in others, Frost asks whether meaningful insight into nature and the human condition can be achieved or whether final revelation will disclose only ironic glimpses, ambiguous truths, inconclusive moments. Frost's poetic strategy arises from the obscurity clouding an ostensibly transparent text. Frost's verse plays on the possibility of revelation, hugging it like smoke

curling off a shifting fire, as confusion undercuts comprehension and collapses certainty into anxiety. In "For Once, Then, Something" one locates the
result of vision—"something white, uncertain"—only after an extended discussion of the process of seeing. The poetic deflection is intended, since the
frame is the important thing. The well beside which the speaker meditates
"Always wrong to the light" acts as reflection and analogue of the poetic text.
It marks a site of revelation, a context that darkens as well as clarifies, as light
from the wrong direction does, or as too much light often is. Frost's poems
portend revelation, but revelation becomes catastrophic as text and meaning
go separate ways. And to make matters worse, this is how it is in the nature
of things, "For Once, Then, Something" suggests. Right reading, whether in
poem or life, is a necessary human skill, though reading Nature is sometimes
no revelation at all. That, in itself, is horribly apocalyptic—thus Frost would
answer Emerson.

IV

Like the speaker by the well in "For Once, Then, Something," Frost's people
live always at the ends and the edges of things, whether cycles of nature
("The Onset"); psychical ends ("Home Burial"; "An Old Man's Winter
Night"); or metaphysical dead-ends ("Stars," "Design," "The Draft Horse").
The citizenry of Frost's symbolic landscapes endure ("You couldn't call it
living, for it ain't" [263]) in places created by absence—in broken and breaking marriages, in fear, in loneliness, in death. Like Amy in "Home Burial,"
who mourns over her dead child convinced her husband does not understand
her, and for whom the intimacy of love has uncovered an intimacy of a more
terrible kind, or like the old man in "An Old Man's Winter Night," Frost's
people keep the universe alone, if they keep it at all. What consolation life
affords derives from the narratives they tell and the rituals through which
they acknowledge and tame their anxieties.

Frost feared that he resembled his people too much, and so all the more
strongly denied any link between his life and the poems he wrote. Feeling
life to be a tangle of unrounded conclusions, a chain of incomplete and acci-
dental moments, Frost, however, also relied on the consolations and rituals
of words to summon order "from the vast chaos of all I have lived through"
(Cox and Lathem 20). Poetry brought a sense of ending to life's open-end-
edness. In rhythm and meter Frost "figured" it all out: he designed his way
through life's dilemmas not out of them. Frost would concede, however, that
the poem reaches no great intellectual conclusion or settlement. It merely
offers a "momentary stay," a still-point that briefly but significantly countered
the unstayables of time and change: "The many deaths one must have died /
Before he came to meet his own!" (336).

This is why Frost, who read anxiety well, could make of its telling a thing, however diminished, of simple yet profound beauty. Read, for example, "The Road Not Taken," "Stopping by Woods on a Snowy Evening," "A Servant to Servants," "The Fear," "Once by the Pacific," or "The Wood-Pile"; there are many others. In poems like these Frost shows how the pleasures of telling, the rituals and engagements of narrative, make unlivable situations livable. "Tell me about it if it's something human" Amy's husband pleads with her in "Home Burial" (53), a plea underlying all of Frost's verse. Words render pain symbolic, human, artful. For the poet, to be artful is, finally, to be human. Art closes, finishes, life. No matter that the fictions Frost's people tell are worn and inadequate or that they no longer "say" the truth—even if truth were possible, or, in the face of human tragedy, even desirable. Frost did not blink in the face of failure. Perhaps for this reason Lionel Trilling, while calling him a "terrifying" poet, nonetheless made an interesting distinction between Frost's public reputation and his poetry. Trilling sidestepped the issue of Frost's technical virtuosity, while acknowledging that Frost was well-loved, "chiefly because he made plain to [people] the terrible things of human life." Trilling explained that only a poet who could "make plain the terrible things" of life could "possibly give [people] comfort" (158).

Frost celebrated artistry and design, the figure a poem makes, because such closures represent the figure that a life must, in the end, come to. Frost also understood that a design for living is, necessarily, a design for death: a need to make the most of the least. Life and death consist equally of struggle and violence, though the way we work the violence is telling. The way we design it, tell it, conclude it reveals the extent to which we value form, purpose, design—in a word, it describes the degree to which we value human life. Life imitates the method of art, and sometimes its content, and so one can judge life by the same measures as one evaluates poetry. Life is education by apocalypse, a telling by goals, a revelation by ends, goals, conclusions. Life renders its meanings through *poesis*—action in time—and through *poetry*—time in action.

NOTES

1. "The Lesson for Today," in *The Poetry of Robert Frost*, Edward Connery Lathem, ed. (353). Other citations to Frost's poetry will be to this edition. References to other editions of Frost's poetry will be noted in the text.

2. See Lewis 184–235, Miller 217–39, Bercovitch 50–71, 136–86, Derrida 90.

3. "American apocalypses," Robinson says, "essay both a rejection and a signal exploration of American ideologies of the self, of nature, of God and the supernatural, and of the community" (xi–xii). Considering America's links with apocalypse, one recalls that the expression "New World" itself is apocalyptic. Apocalyptic texts

seem to inscribe the expectations of a political imagination—that is, for temporal and this-worldly solutions. However, the apocalyptic imagination seeks instead an apolitical and timeless world. The expression "New World" is in many respects self-contradictory. Understood geographically, the term "New World" expresses a wish, not for a world that is new, but for one that is *not old*. The "New World" imagines not so much a positive geographic site as a negative condition, an imaginative lack.

4. See Hodder. For more background on Emerson's apocalypticism, Hodder cites, particularly, Packer and Porte, esp. 64–86.

5. This partly explains why Lawrence Thompson, Frost's biographer, so often thought Frost was lying to him. Frost was not lying; but his designs were different from Thompson's, and their senses of closure were different—the difference being that Frost preferred aesthetic integrity to factual accuracy.

6. The apocalyptic speaks, as Lewis suggests, of the elemental need to structure experience in human ways. Most importantly, it renders the patterns of time—its change and decay—manageable, meaningful, even aesthetic. For other studies of American apocalyptic see Altizer, Banta, Ketterer, Lewicki, May, Robinson, and Rovit.

7. Such a rhetorical strategy typifies the wider American discourse which Frost shares with Wigglesworth, Edwards, and others who use the apocalyptic mode—for instance, Melville, Dickinson, Twain, Jeffers, West, Crane, and Robert Lowell. Typically this strain of American romantic writers responds to the demands of time and history by fleeing it. They seek refuge in catastrophe and judgment or nostalgia or utopianism—in Eden or the Secular city Sanctified (a Protestant version of the eschatological City of God). This New World is a land with no history save an expectation of religious hope, one that desires its own consummation. A land without history, it brings history to its final end. Innocent (without pretext, if you will), its presence calls into question the validity of historical discourse. One thinks of James Baldwin's *The Fire Next Time* or the bleak ending of Melville's *The Confidence Man*.

8. In a 1935 letter Frost comments on his earlier reading and notes he "almost learned all of Poe by heart" (Thompson, *Selected* 500). Thompson also cites Frost's abiding interest in Poe, noting that in 1936 Frost acknowledged that Poe's "Tales" was one of his "top ten" favorite texts (Thompson, *Early Years* 549, no. 4). For examples of Frost's Gothicism see his poems "Once by the Pacific" or "Bereft"—these last two poems positioned on opposite pages to heighten the effect. In "Once by the Pacific" God makes his ultimate will known in a most unpacific way: "Someone had better be prepared for rage. / There would be more than ocean-water broken / Before God's last *Put out the Light* was spoken" (250). The image of God, of course, says more about the speaker's need for the *frisson* of melodrama than God's need for vengeance.

9. Likewise, the image of fury that closes "Once by the Pacific" (see n. 8), though it could support a religious, specifically Christian reading, easily suggests other gods and other endings. In addition, *Othello* echoes here, and so does Genesis. The God imagined here parodies the benevolent, light-bearing deity of Genesis. He becomes a Shiva-esque deity who, in the manner of Frost's verse, creates darkness rather than light. The mounting anxiety and the collapse of comfortable certainty that characterizes "Once by the Pacific" interestingly parallels another vision-by-water, "For Once, Then, Something."

10. Revelation is not the source of this image of fiery destruction; that image appears only once in the Christian Scriptures, where it is found in 2 Peter 3.10ff. There the author speaks of the coming "Day of the Lord" on which the earth will be "laid bare" (New English Translation). The typical expression used—"dissolved with fire," "burned up" (RSV)—is not precisely the intent. A note in the New Oxford Annotated RSV Bible explains: " . . . the thought is not the destruction but the renewal and transformation of the universe."

11. To a large extent Frost's poetic method uses anxiety as a controlling poetic *motif*, an anxiety occasioned by the potential for violence and disruption that the poem permits. To control this violence, Frost's private anxieties sometimes led him places poetically that he later denied being—as, for example, in the seeming lethargy of "Stopping by Woods on a Snowy Evening." Richard Poirier notes that the only "assertive sound in the poem" in this sleepily understated poem is by the horse, so passive does the speaker seem (183). Cook quotes Frost commenting on "Stopping by Woods," saying that what the poem "meant" was that he wanted "to get the hell out of there" (33). Be that as it may, the poem—either in incident or form—shows blessedly little haste, which confirms my point that Frost could enjoy a bit of apocalyptic melodrama, even require it, now and then.

12. As in "The Onset," the sinuous grammatical structure of "For Once, Then, Something" highlights its literary quality—its "made-ness." The poem's formal elements insistently draw attention to the craft that keeps it centered and "poetic." Thus, the self-assurance reflected in the speaker's measured diction checks any doubts the reader might feel—rightly or wrongly—about the speaker's conclusions. However, the self-assurance is deceptive and finally misleading. The poem deceives an unwary reader since it ironically deprecates the revelation it seeks, in effect denying the revelation hinted at by the poem's last line: "What was that whiteness? / Truth? A pebble of quartz? For once, then, something" ("For Once, Then, Something," 225). The reader assumes the poem will end in revelation, perhaps offering a clear *question*, if not a clear answer: What is it? Yet here, as elsewhere in Frost's verse, surface appearances, and an observer "Always wrong to the light" (225), fail to reflect with certainty all there is. Even more horribly, of course, the poem implies that it *does* reflect all there is, offering as it does a dismissive and vague "Something." Though seeming to insist upon formal, aesthetic closure, the poem's structure returns only apparent compensation for the thematic and epistemological confusion of its subject—here, meaning perplexed speaker as well as unclear topic.

WORKS CITED

Alter, Robert. "The Apocalyptic Temper," *After the Tradition*. New York: Dutton, 1969.

Altizer, Thomas J. J. "Imagination and Apocalypse." *Soundings* 43 (Winter 1970): 398–412.

Banta, Martha. *Failure and Success in America: A Literary Debate*. Princeton: Princeton UP, 1978.

Bercovitch, Sacvan. *The Puritan Origins of the American Self*. New Haven: Yale UP, 1975.

Cook, Reginald. *The Dimensions of Robert Frost*. New York: Rinehart, 1958.

Cox, Hyde, and Edward Connery Lathem. *Selected Prose of Robert Frost*. New York: Collier, 1968.

Derrida, Jacques. "Of an Apocalyptic Tone Recently Adopted in Philosophy." *Semeia* 23.2 (1982): 90.

Emerson, Ralph W. *Selected Prose and Poetry*. San Francisco: Rinehart, 1969.

Frost, Robert. *Complete Poems, 1949*. New York: Holt, 1949.

Hodder, Alan D. *Emerson's Rhetoric of Revelation: Nature, the Reader, and the Apocalypse Within*. Philadelphia: U of Pennsylvania P, 1989.

Kermode, Frank. *The Sense of an Ending*. New York: Oxford UP, 1966.

Ketterer, David. *New Worlds for Old: The Apocalyptic Imagination*. Garden City, NY: Doubleday, 1974.

Lathem, Edward Connery, ed. *The Poetry of Robert Frost*. New York: Holt, 1969

Lewicki, Zbigniew. *The Bang and the Whimper: Apocalypse and Entropy in American Literature*. Westport, CT: Greenwood, 1984.

Lewis, R. W. B. "Days of Wrath and Laughter." *Trials of the Word: Essays in Literature and the Humanistic Tradition*. New Haven: Yale UP, 1965.

Marks, Herbert. "The Counter-Intelligence of Robert Frost." *Robert Frost: Modern Critical Views*. Ed. Harold Bloom. New York: Chelsea House, 1986.

May, John. *Toward a New Earth: Apocalypse in the American Novel*. South Bend: U of Notre Dame Press, 1972.

Miller, Perry. "The End of the World." *Errand into the Wilderness*. Cambridge: The Belknap Press of Harvard UP, 1956.

Pack, Robert. "Robert Frost's 'Enigmatic Reserve.'" *Robert Frost: Lectures on the Centennial of His Birth*. Washington, DC: Library of Congress, 1975.

Packer, Barbara L. *Emerson's Fall: A New Interpretation of the Major Essays*. New York: Continuum, 1982.

Poirier, Richard. *Robert Frost: The Work of Knowing*. New York: Oxford UP, 1977.

Porte, Joel. *Representative Man: Ralph Waldo Emerson in His Time*. New York: Oxford UP, 1979.

Robinson, Douglas. *American Apocalypses: The Image of the End of the World in American Literature*. Baltimore: Johns Hopkins UP, 1985.

Rovit, Earl. "On the Contemporary Apocalyptic Imagination." *The American Scholar* 37 (Summer 1968): 458–63.

Scott, Nathan. "'New Heav'ns, New Earth'—The Landscape of Contemporary Apocalypse." *Journal of Religion* 53 (1973).

Thompson, Lawrence. *Robert Frost: The Early Years, 1874–1915*. New York: Holt, 1966.

———. *Selected Letters of Robert Frost*. New York: Holt, 1964.

Trilling, Lionel. "A Speech on Robert Frost: A Cultural Episode." *Robert Frost*. Ed. James M. Cox. Englewood Cliffs, NJ: Prentice, 1962.

Wallace, Patricia. "Separateness and Solitude in Frost." *Kenyon Review* 1 (Winter 1984): 1.

GEORGE F. BAGBY

"Assorted Characters"

> On snow and sand and turf, I see
>   Where Love has left a printed trace
> With straining in the world's embrace. (120)

1

A characteristic metaphor in "A Lone Striker" suggests several of Frost's basic assumptions about the natural world and its relationship to the human observer. A rather Thoreauvian mill worker feels the impulse to abandon his industrial chores, wander into the woods, and stand on a cliff "among the tops of trees, / Their upper branches round him wreathing, / Their breathing mingled with his breathing." The last line contains the freshness both of biological accuracy (trees produce oxygen, men carbon dioxide) and of metaphor. Nature, by implication, is not merely physical; like humans, it is inspirited. From this assumption comes, among other things, Frost's recurrent animism. Natural presences may be as friendly as the breeze that turns the page of the poet's book "to look / For a poem there used to be on Spring" (342),[1] or the mist and smoke that serve as "guardian wraiths" of a cabin and its pioneer inhabitants (414). Or they may be as threatening as the snowstorm which, like a "beast," roars "with a sort of stifled bark" (9), or the monstrous ocean of "Once by the Pacific." In either case, natural objects tend for Frost to be presences, not merely objects.[2]

The metaphor of "mingled breathing" also suggests a further possibility: that, in favorable circumstances, nature and human being, tree and wanderer, can "conspire" together. That "conspiracy"—the subject of this study—is designed, as we will see, to enable the human observer to derive meaning from physical objects, scenes, and processes; it functions in a complex but (in its own terms) logical process; and it is rooted, like so many elements of American language and culture, in seventeenth-century England.

The process by which the human observer and nature may conspire to create meaning depends on a number of epistemological assumptions: not only that both partners are inspirited, but that there is an extraordinary, almost mysterious, congruence between certain natural phenomena and certain elements or states of the psyche. A visceral sense of this extraordinary sort of kinship runs deep in American nature writing, of course—not least in two of the nineteenth-century forebears most immediately related to Frost.[3] Emerson, visiting the Jardin des Plantes in July 1833, reacts with the sensibility that will shape the 1836 *Nature*: "Not a form so grotesque, so savage, nor so beautiful," he writes, "but is an expression of some property inherent in man the observer, an occult relation between the very scorpions and man. I feel the centipede in me—cayman, carp, eagle, & fox. I am moved by strange sympathies" (Emerson, *Journals* 4: 199–200). Thoreau, likewise, considering "sun and wind and rain, . . . summer and winter," is struck by the "sympathy . . . with our race" which they demonstrate. "Shall I not have intelligence with the earth?" he asks. "Am I not partly leaves and vegetable mould myself?" (*Walden* 138).

This is exactly the sort of attitude which lies behind the otherwise curious drama of a poem like "A Leaf-Treader." The poet spends an entire day not merely raking but almost ferociously "treading on" leaves, not for any utilitarian purpose but in a clearly manic response: "Perhaps I have put forth too much strength and been too fierce from fear." What he fears, what motivates his manic treading, is a "threat" from the leaves themselves: "All summer long I thought I heard them threatening under their breath. / And when they came it seemed with a will to carry me with them to death." The "invitation to grief" which Frost senses in the fall of leaves results, clearly, from his Emersonian sense of "strange sympathies" or "an occult relation" with the foliage, from being "partly leaves" himself. As he explicitly recognizes, "They spoke to the fugitive in my heart as if it were leaf to leaf."

In "Leaves Compared with Flowers," another characteristic poem that might at first glance seem curious, Frost senses not one but two kinds of "strange sympathies" between people and trees: the blossoms of trees reflect the observer's brighter moods, while their foliage and bark again reflect darker states of mind:

Leaves and bark, leaves and bark,
To lean against and hear in the dark.
Petals I may have once pursued.
Leaves are all my darker mood.

Here Frost appreciates leaves for the same epistemological reason that
Thoreau appreciates owls, whose hooting, he tells us, "is a sound admirably
suited to swamps and twilight woods which no day illustrates, suggesting
a vast and undeveloped nature which men have not recognized. They represent the stark twilight and unsatisfied thoughts which all have" (*Walden*
125).

Like Thoreau's, Frost's sense of "occult relations" between natural phenomena and human moods derives from a venerable intellectual and imaginative tradition. Particularly in view of his youthful exposure, chiefly through
his mother's influence, to Emersonian and Swedenborgian ideas,[4] it is not
surprising to find throughout Frost's poetry echoes of the doctrine of "correspondences." That doctrine is an important feature of Renaissance thought,
especially in the seventeenth-century poets whom Emerson and Thoreau
most admire. Herbert, for instance—in a poem which Emerson quotes near
the end of the 1836 *Nature*—celebrates the limitless "symmetry" and "proportions" that link man as microcosm with created universe as macrocosms.[5]

Emerson, searching for an epistemological mechanism to solve the fundamental dilemma of Cartesian dualism—"souls never touch their objects," as
he puts it in the powerful opening of "Experience" (*Collected Works* 3: 29)[6]—
discovers, by the circuitous route of Sampson Reed and Emanuel Swedenborg, the philosophical doctrine which lies behind a poem like Herbert's.
Though he soon passes beyond the details of Swedenborg's cumbersome version of correspondences, the general idea remains a linchpin of Emerson's
thought. "The fundamental fact in our metaphysic constitution," he regularly assumes, "is the correspondence of man to the world" (*Complete Works*
7: 300–301). And it is a "metaphysic" fact with immediate epistemological
consequences: if indeed the mind can be certain that "nature is its correlative"
(*Collected Works* 2: 21), if there is in fact "perfect parallelism between the laws
of Nature and the laws of thought" (*Complete Works* 8: 8), from such a grand
parallelism may come a cognitive bridge between the soul and its objects, and
hence "the naturalness of knowing" (*Journals* 5: 168).

In its full development by Emerson, the doctrine of correspondences
provides a particularly apt solution to the basic Cartesian dilemma. On the
one hand, it preserves the autonomous status of both spirit and things. Mind
need not be reduced to substance in the obvious impoverishment of mate-
rialism; matter (at least in Emerson's theory, if not his practice) need not be

subsumed to mind in the solipsistic dead end of complete idealism. Mind and matter, subject and object, can coexist without being compressed into a single entity. Yet, at the same time, the theory of correspondences or analogies guarantees that there can be commerce between spirit and substance, since each mirrors the other. Sensory perception, even of the most commonplace objects in nature, can lead to more than sensory truths.

This Emersonian theory provides the unstated philosophical rationale for Thoreau's constant sense of analogies between the natural world and the human perceiver: not just between owls and dark corners of the mind, but between the Concord River and "The current of our reflections" (*Week* 158) or between unmapped continents and unexplored regions of the self (*Walden* 320–21). Wherever he travels, whatever he sees, Thoreau finds that "Our external senses consent with our internal" (*Journals* 6: 353).

So, too, Emerson's doctrine lies behind Frost's continuous visceral sense of correspondences between outer and inner. It is not just leaves that parallel "darker moods"; "A season-ending wind" answers to the "deathward" impulse of the poet's despondency (336); or, in a similar but better-known instance, the "desert places" in a winter landscape are analogous to the poet's own spiritual emptinesses. Not all of the changes of season and weather correspond to such dark moods, of course; natural phenomena provide equally useful correlatives for more positive states, even for love. The same storm wind that frequently images distress still, on other occasions, "seems like the time when, after doubt, / Our love came back amain" (27). In sum, "The weather's alternations, summer and winter," effectively correspond to "love's alternations, joy and grief" (317).[7]

Clearly, one of Frost's favorite metaphors: for the correspondence between external and internal circumstances is the similarity between "outer" and "inner weather," the parallelism which he explores in "Tree at My Window." Here the correspondences are so thorough, the man inside the window and the tree outside balanced so symmetrically, that the two realms virtually mirror each other. (That symmetry is reflected in the verse itself, in the almost Augustan balance between lines—"tree, I have seen you taken and tossed," "You have seen me when I was taken and swept"—and chiasmus within lines—"Tree at my window, window tree"—as well as in the *a-b-b-a* rhyme scheme.) The essential kinship between man and tree is underlined not only by their proximity and symmetry, but also by the constant personification of the tree—a "Vague dream-head" with "light tongues"—and by the unusual intimacy of the poem's central trope, the chatty apostrophe to the tree.

The setting of the poem points to Frost's moderate epistemological assumptions: the tree is unmistakably distinct from the poet, seen through a perceptual window, but Frost insists that such a medium is no impermeable barrier between perceiver and perceived:

> Tree at my window, window tree,
> My sash is lowered when night comes on;
> But let there never be curtain drawn
> Between you and me.

This companionable object is a "window tree" not only because of its location, but also because of its potential utility: the poet may see something through it. Frost jokes that "Not all your light tongues talking aloud / Could be profound," but the implications of the metaphor itself are serious: to see the tree's leaves as tongues and the sound of their rustling as talking is surely to imply a good deal about the potential intelligibility of the natural world to the human mind.[8] Such intelligibility, in orthodox Emersonian fashion, depends on the essential parallelism between tree and poet:

> tree, I have seen you taken and tossed,
> And if you have seen me when I slept,
> You have seen me when I was taken and swept
> And all but lost.

The "if" here is typical of Frost's precision in his claims for the kinship of human and natural: though the poet watches the tree, he is too well versed in country things to yield to the conceit that it watches him with similar concern. But regardless of its solicitude, the tree, "taken and tossed" by the wind, is a precise reflection of the sleeping poet, "taken and swept / And all but lost" in the welter of dream activity.

Of the figurative elements in "Tree at My Window," not the least important is the submerged romantic metaphor that goes back at least as far as Coleridge's "Eolian Harp" (1795): just as the wind moves the tree's leaves, so some kind of mental impulse moves the sleeping poet's mind—the real "dream-head" here—in the nocturnal variety of imagining. If there is any doubt that the poem is about the workings of the imagination, we need only note the introduction in the last stanza of a third force, which is credited with having arranged the symmetry of tree and poet: "Fate" and "her imagination." That fated imagination is both the agency and the ultimate goal of the conspiracy between the natural and the human; imagination sees self and tree as "putting their heads together" and "conspiring" precisely in order to imagine—to make the images that constitute—the world we live in.

2

This deep-seated sense of correspondences helps to explain why for Frost, as for so many other American nature writers, natural phenomena are almost never purely physical or random; they seem to have been "put there" as signs or messages for the human observer. The "frozen-ground-swell" undermining stones and mortar is taken (by one of the characters in "Mending Wall") to be evidence of "Something" in nature "that doesn't love a wall"; it "makes gaps even two can pass abreast," as if hinting broadly that it favors, not artificial barriers between men, but human fellowship. A single flower, spider, and dead moth are assumed (until the last line of the poem) to have been arranged in a grim tableau by another force, which has "brought" the spider and "steered" the moth to the same flower even in the night—all with the apparent design of teaching the observer about the dark side of nature. A stray Dalmatian who wanders in to the poet's house is taken (tongue in cheek, to be sure) to be a messenger from the dog star, "A symbol," "An intimation" of "A meaning I was supposed to seek" (421). The chirping of a thrush in the woods is "Almost like a call to come in / To the dark and lament" (334).

Again it is Emerson who provides the essential philosophical rationale for such an attitude toward sights and sounds: because they correspond to spiritual truths, such phenomena may serve, in Emerson's most characteristic terms, as symbols or emblems of those truths. As he writes in *Nature*, in the central chapter on "Language," "Nature is the symbol of spirit. . . . Every natural fact is a symbol of some spiritual fact" (*Collected Works* 1: 17, 18). It is the poet, of course, who most thoroughly perceives the emblematic meanings of objects and, by using them symbolically, "rides on them as the horses of thought" (*Collected Works* 3: 13). Or, as Thoreau puts it, referring specifically to animals, "They are all beasts of burden, in a sense, made to carry some portion of our thoughts" (*Walden* 225).

In Emerson's theory, natural symbols are often so clear and forceful in their meaning to the human observer that they become at least metaphorically verbal—"a picture-language . . . of beings and duties" (*Collected Works* 4: 66), "a Sanscrit cipher covering the whole religious history of the Universe," "the sublime alphabet" of divine revelation (*Journals* 7: 375; 3: 258), "words of God," "nouns of the intellect, and . . . the grammar of the eternal language" (*Collected Works* 2: 186; *Complete Works* 6: 304).

For Thoreau, such symbols tend to remain only marginally verbal—objects are "runes," "hieroglyphics" (*Week* 251, 159), "unfathomable" "sibylline sentences," "untranslatable aphorisms" (Thoreau, *Journals* 2: 392, 1: 380). "The Maker of this earth but patented a leaf," as he suggests characteristically in *Walden* (308); we still need a Champollion to "decipher this hieroglyphic for us, that we may turn over a new leaf at last."[9]

For Frost in our own century natural symbols, not surprisingly, are seldom as forward in conveying their meaning as Emersonian theory might want to make them. Yet they do, on a number of occasions, at least approach the fully human clarity of words. That clarity is suggested in a rudimentary way, for instance, in an unusually Emersonian poem, "Bond and Free," where Frost stresses the earthliness of "Love" (as opposed to the otherworldliness of "Thought"):

> On snow and sand and turf, I see
> Where Love has left a printed trace
> With straining in the world's embrace.

Here Frost seems to be harking back to a displaced version of the (ultimately Augustinian) notion of *vestigia Dei*, the "footprints" or "traces" of God in the created world.[10] The undisplaced metaphor, like correspondences, is a seventeenth-century commonplace; Milton's newly fallen Adam asks, for instance, in something like the archetypal question of the visionary poet: "In yonder nether World where shall I seek / His bright appearances, or footstep trace?" (*PL* 11: 328–29). Frost's version of the idea is distinctly secular but not unassertive: the "printed trace" of Love is readily available in the earth's surface. When he says "printed," Frost is in one sense playing on a familiar translation of *vestigium*, which can be rendered "footprint" as well as "trace." But he is also suggesting another kind of print, of course: the lettering by which Love leaves its message in the natural world.

Exactly the same play on words occurs in a considerably less serious context in "Closed for Good." Tracks in the snow on an abandoned country road become something more than tracks; the road will soon be so deep in snow that even the speaker will "have ceased / To come as a foot printer," leaving it to a mouse or fox to "print there as my proxy." In another similar figure, the poet sees in "A Patch of Old Snow" "a blow-away paper," "speckled with grime as if / Small print overspread it."

A more important instance of this sort of metaphor occurs in "Design," where Frost calls the flower, spider, and moth "Assorted characters of death and blight." "Characters" is doubly metaphorical: it sees these three things not only as living presences, *dramatis personae*, but also as letters in a message that the poet must decipher. Or again, echoing one of Whitman's favorite wordplays, "leaves" in the sense of foliage are also pages in the vegetable text: fossilized remains, which Frost calls "leaves of stone," are "The picture book of the trilobite" (364), an age-old natural encyclopedia.

In itself no one of these instances would be greatly significant, perhaps; but cumulatively, all of these (and other) plays on and metaphors of "print" and "characters" and "leaves" surely project an implicit view of the created world as a kind of text. The trope becomes explicit on two occasions. "My Brother's Keeper," the bookstore owner in *A Masque of Mercy*, insists that, for all the difficulties facing the seer, "there's no lack of light"—

> A light that falls diffused over my shoulder
> And is reflected from the printed page
> And bed of world-flowers . . .

This source of reflected illumination, this "printed page / And bed of world-flowers,"[11] is none other than the secular half of the twin books of revelation upon which Milton and his contemporaries relied. In the words of Sir Thomas Browne, "There are two bookes from whence I collect my Divinity; besides that written one of God, another of his servant Nature, that universall and publik Manuscript, that lies expans'd unto the eyes of all; those that never saw him in the one, have discovered him in the other" (20–21).[12] Francis Quarles, in another typical formulation, likewise argues that the Bible is not the only text of revelation: "Before the knowledge of letters, GOD was knowne by *Hierogliphicks*; And, indeed, what are the Heavens, the Earth, nay every Creature, but *Hierogliphicks* and *Emblemes* of His Glory?" Milton laments his blindness above all because it extinguishes one source of revealed wisdom, "the Book of knowledge fair" constituted by "Nature's works" (*PL* 3: 47–49).

But again, as in the case of correspondences, the crucial metaphor of nature as a text of revelation is transmitted from the seventeenth century to Frost chiefly through Emerson and Thoreau. Emerson, as usual, formulates the idea more systematically: "Nature is language & every new fact that we learn is a new word; but rightly seen, taken all together it is not merely a language but the language put together into a most significant & universal book. I wish to learn the language not that I may know a new set of nouns & verbs but that I may read the great book which is written in that tongue" (*Journals* 4: 95).

The sources of the metaphor are suggested with unusual clarity in the most explicit version of it in Frost's poetry, in that important sonnet "Time Out." The wanderer, as we have seen, pauses and realizes:

> The mountain he was climbing had the slant
> As of a book held up before his eyes
> (And was a text albeit done in plant).
> Dwarf cornel, goldthread, and *Maianthemum*,
> He followingly fingered as he read . . .

Given the fact that this poem was probably written in 1939 (Thompson and Winnick 390 n.5), the archaism of the crucial parenthetical line— "(And was a text albeit done in plant)"—amounts almost to a bow to the venerable tradition that descends from the seventeenth century. But the last two quoted lines show clearly how that tradition has been filtered through Frost's nineteenth-century American forebears: both the naturalist's attention to the species of plant involved and the hands-on "fingering" of those plants represent Frost at his most Thoreauvian.

3

The assumptions which lie behind the metaphor of "Time Out" help to explain one of the defining traits of Frost's poetic activity, the constant effort to "read" the meaning implicit in objects and scenes encountered in the natural world. Brad McLaughlin, the comic hero of "The Star-Splitter," insists that "'The best thing that we're put here for's to see.'" For Frost, as for Emerson, sight is the most important sense because it always, at least potentially, involves reading and therefore vision.

The effort to "read" natural objects, which, I argue, is central to Frost's nature lyrics, is also dramatized in a number of the narrative poems. The longest and most important section of "West-Running Brook," for instance, consists of the husband's attempt to read in the brook and its wave a kind of "annunciation" (to use his wife's term) of the life current in the human spirit. The young man and woman in "The Generations of Men" are drawn together by their common efforts to get the meaning, first, of the "old cellar hole" that remains from their ancestral home and then of the "purer oracle" delivered by a nearby brook. The heroine of "Maple" spends most of her life trying to decipher the meaning of her name and of the tree that it stands for; she knows only that her mother wanted her to "'be like a maple tree. / *How* like a maple tree's for us to guess.'"

Despite the profoundly Emersonian presuppositions that motivate these constant efforts to "get the meaning of hillsides or flowers, brooks or trees, the enterprise is inevitably more problematic, strenuous, and precarious for Frost than for Emerson or Thoreau. Frost dramatizes that fact (among others) in "For Once, Then, Something," one of the best of his allegories about the reading process. Conning one of those sources of water that recur in such allegories (most notably in "Directive"), the poet finds that it is difficult both to perceive any underlying reality in the phenomenal world and to be sure of its meaning if we do catch a glimpse of it.

> *Once*, when trying with chin against a well-curb,
> I discerned, as I thought, beyond the picture,

> Through the picture, a something white, uncertain,
> Something more of the depths—and then I lost it.

Frost's image for his epistemological uncertainty here is remarkably close to a figure that Wordsworth uses in *The Prelude* (4: 256–70) to describe the complications of memory, which at times "cannot part / The shadow from the substance." Frost, however, is not talking about recollection but about perception itself, and his uncertainty involves not only the operations of the mind but external reality. Here the natural world, in fact, actively discourages the poet's efforts to see:

> Water came to rebuke the too clear water.
> One drop fell from a fern, and lo, a ripple
> Shook whatever it was lay there at bottom,
> Blurred it, blotted it out.

This source of water is far from oracular; because of its willful refusal to let him see the fundamental whiteness that it covers, Frost can only wonder: "What was that whiteness? / Truth? A pebble of quartz? For once, then, something."

The zeugma of the final line strikes some readers as typical of Frost's own willful refusal to clarify; only a skeptic or worse, presumably, would threaten to equate "truth" with "a pebble of quartz." But the near equation works two ways. Not only does it, at first glance, threaten to trivialize "truth." If we keep in mind the inordinate fondness of American poets for the commonplace, and Emerson's faith that "there is no fact in nature which does not carry the whole sense of nature" (*Collected Works* 3: 10), the equation may also, at second glance, imply the potential transcendental significance of a pebble of quartz: perhaps in that seemingly insignificant whiteness does lie an emblem of truth itself. Thus the overall burden of the poem, like its title, is not wholly skeptical, but problematic.

The sources of such post-Emersonian complications in the reading process are numerous; one of them, in fact, is Frost's very animism. Not surprisingly, the sense that the external world is inhabited by spirit—or spirits—is not always reassuring. As a result, the natural world often has a mysterious, even eerie menace in Frost which is found only rarely in his nineteenth-century predecessors. An urban couple, newly arrived in the country, may view the new moon as a kind of guardian spirit—but may also feel the need to keep an uneasy eye on the woods outside their kitchen window, "'Waiting to steal a step on us whenever / We drop our eyes or turn to other things'" (114). An old man alone in an echoing house may sense—in the demonic equivalent of the symmetry described in "Tree at My Window"—that "All out-of-doors looked darkly in at him" (108). In "Directive" the would-be seer must be prepared to undergo "the serial ordeal" of passing by the work of a glacial giant, "Of being watched from forty cellar holes / As if by eye pairs," and of "the woods' excitement over you." Not only the ocean, in "Once by the Pacific," but the land itself, in "Sand Dunes," may monstrously assault the human; the dunes rise up to try to "bury in solid sand / The men" whom the ocean "could not drown."

This side of Frost's animism certainly adds to the difficulties inherent in the reading process. An even more important complication, however—and a distinctly post-Emersonian one—results from the impact of twentieth-century science; indeed, that impact is more substantial on Frost's work than on that of his more obviously modernist contemporaries—Pound, Eliot, Stevens, Yeats, and even Williams.[13]

As both the poems and the biographical evidence demonstrate, Frost is familiar not only with the general directions taken by contemporary science but also with a remarkable number of specific developments. "A Passing Glimpse," for instance, dramatizes one of the cardinal epistemological notions of modern physics. Trying to fathom the meaning of the natural world, Frost suggests, is like trying to distinguish the species of flower glimpsed from a train speeding by:

> I name all the flowers I am sure they weren't:
> Not fireweed loving where woods have burnt—
>
> Not bluebells gracing a tunnel mouth—
> Not lupine living on sand and drouth.
>
> Was something brushed across my mind
> That no one on earth will ever find?

The intensity of the poet's will to apprehend natural truth is indicated by the Thoreauvian concern with species (even of flowers which the poet is certain he hasn't seen) as well as by the particular varieties listed: like the wished-for vision of natural truth, they all blossom brightly in apparently unpromising ground. But the lesson that Frost draws from this speeding half-sight is genuinely skeptical: "Heaven gives its glimpses only to those / Not in position to look too close." That lesson is an exact application to the realm of reading the vegetable text, or of epistemology generally, of Heisenberg's uncertainty principle from quantum mechanics.

But, for the most part, Frost's view of nature is affected relatively little by physics (or by chemistry). The atomistic, mechanistic, and therefore deadened view of the natural world which the findings of these microsciences might suggest is not Frost's view to any great extent. It is instead the macrosciences—geology, archaeology, and above all astronomy—that consistently fascinate Frost (like Emerson before him) and, by the very breadth of their perspectives, lead him to a distinctly less anthropocentric view of the natural world and its accessibility than he might otherwise have.

For Emerson, characteristically, the discoveries of nineteenth-century geology seldom have a dispiriting effect;[14] for the most part, they expand his perspective on the past in such a way as to confirm his faith in the purposiveness of natural process and the supreme role of human beings in natural history. Geology, he reports enthusiastically, demonstrates the "sublime" fact "that Man who stands in the globe so proud and powerful is no upstart in the creation, but has been prophesied in nature for a thousand thousand ages before he appeared; that from times incalculably remote there has been a progressive preparation for him; an effort, (as physiologists say,) to produce him." When we study geology, like other contemporary sciences, "our views are expanded and our sentiments ennobled" (*Early Lectures* 1: 29, 3: 168–69).

For Frost, by contrast, archaeology and geology, in the course of expanding his view, seldom ennoble his sentiments; instead, by demonstrating the eccentric place of humans in the order of nature, these sciences tend to make time and natural process seem impersonal, indifferent, even chilling. "Our Hold on the Planet," with its conclusion that nature is only "a fraction of one percent" more "in favor of man" than opposed to him, is only a marginal exception to the rule; typically, geological time strikes Frost as almost sardonically unconcerned about merely human fates. Methodically rearranging continents, time remains unmoved itself, and the human observer is unlikely to be greatly comforted by its "lack of joy or grief / At such a planetary change of style" (335).

The tone of Frost's quasi-geological poems therefore tends to be that of a grim joke. The poet jokes—defensively, surely—about the insignificance of human life in the face of geological processes like erosion ("In Time of Cloudburst") or mud slides. In "On Taking from the Top to Broaden the Base," the joke is clearly on foolish defiance of natural forces, on a complacently anthropocentric perspective. The poem begins with humans hurling defiance at a mountain which looms over their home, and which they mistakenly judge to be too old to muster another avalanche. But time and the mountain, of course, have the last laugh; "even at the word" of the human taunt, a mud slide comes to bury the people who have so badly underestimated geological forces. It comes, ironically, "in one cold / Unleavened batch"—the kitchen metaphor the final rebuke to the excessively domestic imagination. Having begun by speaking in the voice of the foolish humans, the narrative ends with an inhuman, impersonal, essentially geological perspective—something close to that of the mountain itself "none was left to prate / Of an old mountain's case." The poem thus enacts just the shift of perspective, from comfortably domestic to vast and impassive, which renders the natural world ominous in so many of Frost's geological poems.

An equivalent shift—spatial rather than temporal—has an equivalent chilling effect in most of the poems involving astronomy. The effects of Frost's lifelong fascination with astronomy, in fact, offer a particularly good illustration of the differences between his imaginative circumstances and Emerson's. Just as pre-Darwinian notions of evolution serve chiefly to reinforce Emerson's ameliorism, so the vast perspective of astronomy largely corroborates his spiritual and moral idealism. Emerson is confident that "the atmosphere was made transparent with this design, to give man, in the heavenly bodies, the perpetual presence of the sublime," "a perpetual admonition of God & superior destiny" (*Collected Works* 1: 8; *Journals* 4: 267).

For Frost, again by contrast, the cosmic perspective serves chiefly to reduce the individual human being to insignificance. "Stars," a very early paradigm of that effect, begins, like "On Taking from the Top to Broaden the Base," with an essentially anthropocentric perspective; it speculates that the countless stars "congregate" above the "tumultuous snow" of earthly life "As if with keenness for our fate." But, within a few short lines, the poem purges that anthropocentric view and recognizes that the stars in truth are clustered "with neither love nor hate." "Marble" both in their lack of feeling and in their lack of "the gift of sight"—two of the definitive human faculties—these stars are a far cry from Emerson's perpetual beacons of the sublime. But such impassivity crops up again and again throughout Frost's astronomical verse. Human experience, with all its ups and downs, strikes no responsive chord in extraterrestrial bodies; we must "look elsewhere than to stars and moon and sun / For the shocks and changes we need to keep us sane" (268).

Eventually, the consequence of expanding his spatial perspective to galactic proportions is not merely to make Frost's sky indifferent. As in the case of the geological poems, impassivity can begin to verge on something more sinister. In "A Loose Mountain," the poet finds astronomical evidence not just for a kind of sullen, unfeeling Prime Mover in the distant reaches of space—"The heartless and enormous Outer Black." He also wonders, with his characteristic brand of dark humor, whether the great "star shower known as Leonid" may not be cosmic punishment aimed at man. Frost is too thoroughly modern to be frightened, like Pascal three centuries earlier, by "le silence éternel de ces espaces infinis"; he insists that "They cannot scare me with their empty spaces / Between stars" (296). But his remarkable familiarity with contemporary astronomy, by making the natural world far less "sublime" and far less involved in human "destiny" than it generally is for Emerson, inevitably lessens the ease with which the natural text may be read.

That final—and crucial—effect comes close to dominating the otherwise hortatory "Take Something Like a Star." For more than half of the poem the speaker protests the abstruseness of this stellar emblem. Though he is willing to allow the star "some obscurity of cloud" because of its great "loftiness," he insists that being "wholly taciturn . . . is not allowed"; he demands a clear lesson from the star.

> Say something to us we can learn
> By heart and when alone repeat.
> Say something! And it says, "I burn."
> But say with what degree of heat.
> Talk Fahrenheit, talk Centigrade.
> Use language we can comprehend.

Again, as in "On Taking from the Top to Broaden the Base," one of the things involved here is a kind of joke about the speaker's excessive anthropomorphism—ironically underlined by the very act of apostrophizing a star. Frost himself, well aware of the profound otherness of celestial bodies, is hardly one to admire the sort of queasy, reductive anthropocentrism that wants a star to "Talk Fahrenheit, talk Centigrade." Yet behind the mockery of such an attitude—which may, after all, be a species of self-mockery—lies a genuine if complicated epistemological nostalgia: natural revelation will not be unimpeded when the human observer and the natural phenomenon are no longer perceived as having a common medium of communication; in our century, it is up to the human observer to translate the star's burning into Fahrenheit or Centigrade.

Knowing a good deal of contemporary science, and recognizing the limitations that it entails for the reading process in his time, Frost nonetheless—in a thoroughly characteristic reaction—accepts and even values those limitations. For one thing, he finds them spiritually appropriate. It is true, as the penultimate stanza of "Sitting by a Bush in Broad Sunlight" tells us, that natural revelation in our time will be un-Mosaic in its reticence. But, with something akin to a seventeenth-century theological perspective, Frost views the distance between human beings and the source of revelation as spiritually and epistemologically functional. "The Infinite's being so wide / Is the reason the Powers provide" natural boundaries, he suggests—one's "hide," one's dwelling, one's nation, all are necessary "defenses" "Between too much and me" (348–49).[15] "My Brother's Keeper" in *A Masque of Mercy* comes close to the conventional theological argument that the source of

truth must be "accommodated" to human perception. He suggests, as we
have seen, that "there's no lack of light" in the world—but that it must be
"diffused" and "reflected from the printed page / And bed of world-flowers
so as not to blind me."

> If even the face of man's too bright a light
> To look at long directly (like the sun),
> Then how much more the face of truth must be.
> We were not given eyes or intellect
> For all the light at once the source of light;
> For wisdom that can have no counterwisdom.

The notion of accommodation here, though secular, is stated in terms and
images remarkably close to Milton's (*PL* 3: 374–89): light may be available
to our eyes only as it is "reflected" from the natural text, but that indirection, designed as it is to spare our limited sight, is a necessary instrument of,
rather than a hindrance to, any revelation we may experience.

But Frost, of course, is even more interested in the artistic than in the
spiritual uses of perceptual adversity. He describes the modern situation
almost melodramatically—"The background in hugeness and confusion
shading away from where we stand into black and utter chaos"—in order to
make the point: "against the background any small man-made figure of order
and concentration. What pleasanter than that this should be so? . . . we like
it, we were born to it, born used to it and have practical reasons for wanting it
there. To me any little form I assert upon it is velvet" (*Letters* 419; rpt. *Selected
Prose* 107).

One of the most important of those practical reasons for relishing modern complication is that it presents opportunities for drama—opportunities
which Frost, of course, takes advantage of not only in the narrative poems but
in the lyrics. The drama in the nature poems arises in large measure, as we
will see, from the fact that, for Frost, the process of reading the natural world
regularly involves struggle and uncertainty. Such struggle, and such drama,
are particularly clear by contrast with Emerson's poetic practice. Despite his
systematic theories of correspondences and of the natural world as a text,
Emerson's dominant philosophical idealism generally undermines the dialec-
tics of what we normally call nature poetry. The result has been aptly characterized by Harold Bloom: "The mature Emerson wanted a humanized nature
so badly that he made his poems, or the bulk of them anyway, egregious
short-cuts to that end" (*Ringers* 222).

For Frost, with his unquestionable "proof of being not unbounded"
(331), such shortcuts seldom threaten the lyrics; on the contrary, the drama

of imaginative struggle is a constant poetic resource. Frost assumes with Emerson that there are ties, even analogies, between observer and vegetable text. But, because the exact nature and extent of such correspondences are neither constant nor immediately apparent, because Frost cannot conceive of the external world as "only a realized will,—the double of the man" (*Collected Works* 1: 25), the process of deciphering the text is both necessary and functional. It is in that very process, in the drama of its twists and turns, its unforeseen successes and failures, that the modern maker of emblem poems discovers and forges the underlying ties between himself and the natural text.

NOTES

1. Quotations from Frost's verse are taken from *The Poetry of Robert Frost*, edited by Edward Connery Lathem. Short passages from poems not identified by title are followed by parenthetical page numbers referring to this edition.

2. Norman Holland suggests that the darker side of Frost's animism, at least, involves the projection of the poet's "dangerous wishes and fears within himself out onto the world around him" (32). Projection is presumably the underlying mechanism of any kind of animism. Whatever its psychological benefits, such a process—unless self-consciousness deflates the animism—clearly involves a poetic benefit: it makes the encounter with nature more dramatic than it would otherwise be.

3. The best general discussions of Frost's Emersonian and Thoreauvian heritage are by Alvan S. Ryan, Reuben Brower (56–74), James M. Cox, and George Monteiro (55–143).

4. See Lawrance Thompson's account in *Robert Frost: the Early Years* (xvi, 11–12, 20–21, 36, 70–71, etc.).

5. For an enlightening historical account of the doctrine of correspondences between Herbert's time and Emerson's, see Wasserman.

6. When possible, quotations from Emerson's essays are taken from the currently ongoing Harvard edition of the *Collected Works*; for those essays not yet issued by Harvard, quotations are taken from the Centenary Edition of the *Complete Works*.

7. Of course, there are also moments in which correspondences are considerably less neatly arranged in Frost's practice than they are in Emerson's theory. See, for instance, Yoder's comments (185–86).

8. Frost was apparently concerned lest the playful remark about the tree's "tongues" be taken too seriously. Four years after first publishing the poem, he was still thinking about "deleting the second stanza" for fear that it might "keep the 'head' in the last stanza from ringing as it should" (*Letters to Untermeyer* 208).

9. See Irwin on the impact of Champollion's work in deciphering the Egyptian hieroglyphics on, and metaphorical extensions of the idea of hieroglyphics in, Emerson, Thoreau, Hawthorne, and Melville.

10. For lucid discussions of the historical background of the concept, see Martz (17–18, 54–57, 68–78, 146) and Madsen (113–44).

11. I am reading this passage as commentary simply on the "book of nature"—i.e., taking "printed page" and "bed of world-flowers" to be in apposition. It is certainly possible to take the two phrases as references to two distinct sources of wisdom, which would approximate the seventeenth-century notion of twin books

of revelation—the "printed page" of biblical wisdom and the "bed of world-flowers" of natural revelation.

12. For useful summaries of the "book of nature" topos before Emerson, see Madsen (85–144) and Brantley (139–70).

13. On Frost and science, see (among others) Baym, Hiers, Harris, and Abel.

14. For this side of Emerson's geological perspective, see Whicher (150, 171).

15. In an irony characteristic of Frost's relationship with Emerson, the language of "Triple Bronze"—a deeply un-Emersonian poem—echoes Emerson's "Grace." In his poem, Emerson gives thanks for the "defences" of "Example, custom, fear, occasion slow," which have "me against myself defended," saving him from sins he might otherwise have fallen into (*Complete Works* 9: 359).

LEWIS KLAUSNER

Inscription and the Burden of
Judgment in "Directive"

In *Beyond Formalism* Geoffrey Hartman mentions Frost's "Directive" as
a modern echo of the inscription genre practiced in ancient Greece and
revived by nature poets in eighteenth-century England. Nature inscription
is a kind of mask or prosopopeic ventriloquism, causing the landscape to
speak for the poet. In "Directive" inscription functions simultaneously as
a trope of immediacy and opacity. The topos of inscription, the hint that
the last lines of the poem are actually inscribed at the imaginary site of the
brook beside the house, promotes an illusion that places us at the brook. On
the other hand, the inscription also reminds the reader of being just that,
a reader, in the absence of a live, authorial presence. These two ways of
reading the final inscription epitomize the tension in "Directive" between a
strongly asserted sense of actual fact and place on one hand, and the subli-
mation of fact into elaborate poetic fiction on the other.

The passage of primary facts into poetic afterthought is the theme
of many of Frost's poems. Anyone who has thought about "Hyla Brook"
or "New Hampshire" knows how Frost likes to remind his readers that all
poetry is prosopopeic, and that poetry's basic metaphor is transference of
a (once) living author to printed characters upon the page. Yet "Directive"
has received more anxious and probing attention than any other single
poem of Frost's owing to the power of the poem to make readers feel that

From *Studies in Romanticism* 34, no. 4 (Winter 1995): 569–82. Copyright © 1995 by Boston
University.

interpretation is a question of high moral order.[1] The disclosure at the end of "New Hampshire" ("presently I am living in Vermont") only reminds us that the poet's actual whereabouts, (Vermont or New Hampshire? possibly Maine?) are not guaranteed by statements in the poem. "Hyla Brook" leaves us with a suggestive, but hardly painful, question about what happens to a brook—an originary living presence, and a likely trope for the author—that dries up and leaves paper-like leaves behind it. The disappearance of the brook would seem to warrant that we love the things we love for what they *were*. Yet Frost mischievously writes that we love them for what they *are*. The imaginary brook in the poem or the mental image of the brook in memory seem to displace the original brook as the object of our love. In "Hyla Brook" Frost does not imagine such displacement in response to human tragedy. In "Directive," in contrast, Frost asks us explicitly to weep for its mysteriously missing children, and implicitly to forgive undisclosed sins. Elegy for a brook may end in conundrum and questions of stylistic unity. This elegy for children that the author himself may have sinned against enjoins us, however inadequate we may be as judges, to somehow judge.

It is toward the open question of forgiveness that the following is aimed by investigating the topos of inscription within "Directive." The topos reminds us that as readers we are already removed from an authorial presence; it can also remind us—in the case of a great poet's overt poems of self-elegy and bequest—that the fate of an author's reputation is bequeathed to us in hypostatized forms of literary artifacts. Recognizing this may remind us that the burden of judging and forgiving is foisted upon us by a poem much as wayside markers enjoin the piety and attention of passers-by.

* * *

Poets who want to be remembered in their own words have sometimes left us one final, pithy summarizing statement of themselves by writing their own epitaphs. Yet poets have also been wary of the rigid and sterile limitations of words inscribed upon stones. An Emersonian poet, such as Frost, may be especially distrustful of fixed, monumentalizing traces of living presence. In his essay, "Wordsworth, Inscriptions, and Romantic Nature Poetry," Geoffrey Hartman suggests that the central paradox in all modern poetry is the desire to bequeath a living spirit in fixed poetic texts, what Hartman calls a "monument to spontaneity" in which the poem "coincides with the act and passion of its utterance." One way to instill life into the epitaphic statement is to prosopopoeically carve the statement into the natural landscape, on a tree or by a stream, so that the short moment of grieved utterance is linked to the longer duration of the living tree or the flowing brook. Among Hartman's examples is Wordsworth's "Lines Left upon a Seat in a Yew-tree." When reading Wordsworth's poem we only encounter the engraved place in the long, explanatory title of the poem. For the poet hasn't actually carved the poem into the tree, Hartman reminds us, but has only simulated the act of inscription by writing his poem within the conventions of the inscription genre.[2] The poem, we might say, swallows and represents nature; the topological energy of the poem, love of place, gives way to the tropology of the poem: topos as geographical place merges with topos as poetic figure.

Wordsworth's great innovation upon the archaic inscription, according to Hartman, was to liberate it from its locale and occasion. This is consistent with the larger Wordsworthian and Coleridgean project of liberating the inward eye of reflection from the outward eye of sense perception. (In similar Emersonian terms, the poet's tropes liberate us from fate, "afford us a platform whence we may command a view of our present life, a purchase by which we may move it.") Wordsworth's technique, which differentiates him from contemporary imitators of "inscription" poems, owes, as Hartman puts it, to "incorporating, in addition to a particular scene the very process of inscribing or interpreting it" (222). Rather than stressing the wit or neatness of sententiae fictively engraved upon a rock, Wordsworth tries to imbue the poem with consciousness of the pathos that is inherent in petrified speech, the loss of direct human contact of which remains only the mediation of a written text. Wordsworth's "Lines" ask to be read not as inscribed epigrams, but as language still in the process of thinking. The poem begins by describing the life of the dead youth, and then seems as if in the process of its own thinking to spontaneously discover its moralizing purpose. Suddenly "this seat," which is the dead man's "only moment," becomes inadequate representation of the poet's feelings for the youth "who owned no common soul" (12–13); the seat is "only" a monument. The most adequate medium for an uncommon soul, the poem seems to discover, is another soul upon whom the story of the dead youth can be impressed. Wordsworth identifies this inscriptive medium when he shifts from descriptive to vocative emphasis, when he attempts to inscribe his poem into the reader's heart, an alternative "you-tree":

> If thou be one whose heart the holy forms
> Of young imagination have kept pure,
> Stranger! henceforth be warned; and know that pride,
> Howe'er disguised in its own majesty,
> Is littleness; that he who feels contempt

For any living thing, hath faculties
Which he has never used; that thought with him
Is in its infancy. The man whose eye
Is ever on himself doth look on one,
The least of Nature's works, one who might move
The wise man to that scorn which wisdom holds
Unlawful ever. O be wiser, Thou!
        (48–59)[3]

We are supposed to feel the tension between the anonymity of wayside inscription and the directness of second person address, to feel slightly startled by the abruptly and reproachfully interjected vocative: "stranger!" Wordsworth's approximation of spoken syntax and diction, and his turn from description to direct address, are all meant to exploit a generic epitaphic capacity for pathos and uncanniness, ghostly traces that interact with living readers. This kind of effect has no rigid generic or stylistic bounds. Its availability is endemic to the act of recorded performance, is kin to both the posthumous pressure Portia's father exerts with his casket test, and to the mock spontaneity of an answering machine. Yet deliberate and highlighted deployment of the inscriptive topos, such as Wordsworth's, may underscore the seriousness of the reader's interpretive responsibility. If we choose to read Wordsworth's "Lines" as semiotic play, and dismiss their moral import, we know the risk of scorn at which we place ourselves, for Wordsworth typically anticipates such choices in moralized terms, to heed or dismiss proffered wisdom, "stay" or "pass."

It may also occur to us that the anonymity of inscription is the imprimatur by which Wordsworth's poem can exhort, yet evade that pride against which it cautions its readers. There are only words here, the trope of inscription seems to say, no author, no self-proclaimed "wise man" presumptuous enough to judge or intimidate passers-by. This is an example of how the poet's voice, placed at a remove from its author by fictive inscription, becomes both a gesture of humility and a validation of its own moralizing influence. This is done by directing our attention to ourselves, to our moral and interpretive choices, and away from the poet's personal authority.

Like Wordsworth's "Lines," "Directive" presents itself as instruction, a directive left by one who has lived in the world to ones who have yet to live; and like Wordsworth's "Lines," "Directive" imagines itself attached to a geographical site beyond the confines of its own language. As Richard Poirier remarks, there is a strongly felt sense of place, however negatively defined this place may be,[4]

> a house that is no more a house
> Upon a farm that is no more a farm
> And in a town that is no more a town[.]
>   (5–7)[5]

The incantatorily repeated "is no more" (instead of a simpler "there was") maximizes the pathos of the facts and encourages the grieved brooding that is resisted in "The Need of Being Versed": "the sigh we sigh / From too much dwelling on what has been" (15–16). The roundaboutness of "is no more" also raises ontological ambiguities. For like the performative techniques of Wordsworth's "Lines," the grammar of "Directive" is contrived to situate language ambiguously between the present and the absent. A house or town that "is," but "no more," will suggest spectral presences that are as strongly felt as physical ones. In the repetition of the nouns "house," "farm," and "town" it is almost as if two tenses distinguish between two distinct sets of objects. These lines, like the last lines of "Hyla Brook," point toward a potential conflict between actual, past events and present memory. Memory of the house may threaten to displace the house we remember, and the poem may also threaten to swallow the reality of an actual house by transforming it into a poetic fiction. Anxiety about displacing the actual events of the house might explain why Frost in "Directive" continually bifurcates his formulations of origin and terminus, courts ambiguities of here and not-here, or being and not-being, of play and earnestness, as if in order to accommodate both.

The bifurcating grammar that gives us two farms, two towns, and two houses is developed more explicitly into a division between a house in earnest and a playhouse (which is different from calling them real and imaginary).

> First there's the children's playhouse of make-believe,
> Some shattered dishes underneath a pine,
> The playthings in the playhouse of the children.
> Weep for what little things could make them glad.
> Then there is the house that is no more a house,
> But only a belilaced cellar hole,
> Now slowly closing like a dent in dough.
> This was no playhouse but a house in earnest.
>   (41–48)

We tend to associate the children's playhouse with the fiction making of the poem, and the "house in earnest" with a starker, less refracted view of tragic reality. The temporalized relation of "first" and "then" argues a process of working through fictions toward uncovering a reality as naked and uncheering as the cord of maple in "The Wood-Pile." But the starkness of the funereal object is never the final terminus of a Frost poem, for the mind will always turn at the last to some new invention of comfort. Stark, tragic truth tends to be an intruder in Frost's poetry, while fictions are the truths we live in most of the time. The "slowly closing dent in dough" might describe the mind's absorption of fact into memory and fiction as well as the reality of the disappearing house.

Is the absorption of fact then something less than earnest? Frost's speaker, like Chaucer's Pardoner, impugns his own honesty, calling himself a guide who is a thief ("I stole the goblet" [60]) and a deceiver ("who has at heart your getting lost" [9]). It may disturb us that this deceitfulness may refer to the deceit inherent in any act of mimetic representation, or to some human, biographical guilt that predates the poem. And if we suspect the latter, then we will be still more disturbed that the moral authority of the poem can be strengthened by incorporating elements that show the poem suspecting itself.

Roger Gilbert stresses the necessity of the walk that precedes the final inscriptive lines of "Directive," a journeying toward the place of the inscription that we can think of as a physical equivalent to the mental divigations in Wordsworth's "Lines." The movement that takes us "out of all this now too much for us," through a "serial ordeal" of byways and up to elevated ground, Gilbert would suggest, represents a process of preparation for epiphany and final recovery, a journey upward "toward a height from which the landscape can be viewed in its totality." We might object that this height is attained by the kind of fiction-making and projection that is contrasted with being in earnest. Gilbert adequately overcomes this objection by treating the poem's fantastic figures, such as the personified glacier and elvish eyes peering out of forty firkins, as "overelaborate conceits" that are "meant to put us on our guard." By casting the poem as a quest of poet-guide and reader-pilgrim, Gilbert argues, Frost turns the journey into a lesson in becoming skeptical of poetic fictions, led by a guide who has been writing them for forty years. For Gilbert, the archness and rigor of Frost's figures, Frost's awareness of his own fanciful excesses and the intelligence of his determination to push beyond them to an enlarged and clarified perspective, earn him a height from which he can write a poetry "Too lofty and original to rage." The poem, that is, earns its own validation, and the life that might lie beneath or behind it is not our concern as readers of poetry; for we are ultimately concerned, Gilbert suggests, with "the contemplation of the power of contemplation itself." This formulation pays high tribute to the self-consciousness that can be achieved in writing poetry, but it also points to a sterility and closedness of reading the poem "only *through* such play" of its own figures (Gilbert 68–72).

I want therefore to consider the last lines of "Directive" in comparison with Wordsworth's "Lines," and to ask if inscription upon the landscape asks us to push our reading past the poem's own figurations, onto a more referential, perhaps biographical, landscape. First we have a wayside inscription that tells us where to look for our terminus:

> Your destination and your destiny's
> A brook that was the water of the house,
> Cold as a spring as yet so near its source,
> Too lofty and original to rage.
> (We know the valley streams that when aroused
> Will leave their tatters hung on barb and thorn.)
> I have kept hidden in the instep arch
> Of an old cedar at the waterside
> A broken goblet like the Grail
> Under a spell so the wrong ones can't find it,
> So can't get saved, as Saint Mark says they mustn't.
> (I stole the goblet from the children's playhouse.)
>   (49–60)

Then we have lines that might be inscribed at the brook itself. "Here are your waters and your watering place. / Drink and be whole again beyond confusion" (62–63). If we read "here" as an inscription at the sight of the brook, we might compare this inscription to the one famously etched into the gate of Hell in Book III of the *Inferno*, for these are two passages where the fictitious place of the poem merges with the text of the poem. There is a fiction of immediacy at work here. For if we read the last two lines as inscription we become momentarily joined with the silent addressees in the poem. We see the same text in our book that they would see at the brook.

In Dante's infernal landscape, such a merging suggests to John Freccero damnable sins of misreading. To read by the letter of the law, and not to read through the literal, to its figurations and prefigurations, constitutes a textual idolatry. Commenting on the gate of Hell, Freccero writes: "In terms of C. S. Pierce's theory of signs, we might say that the words on the page cease to be symbols and have become icons, signs that resemble their own significance."[6] The interpretive danger for Dante's or Frost's reader is any fetishization of the signifier that would separate it from its deepest significance. Dante's reader encounters the danger of taking the physically imagined place of Hell too literally, and forgetting that Hell is a state of spirit.[7] Frost's reader faces a danger of forgetting that in poetry identity is masked by metaphor.

It is well-established that the ending of "Directive" confronts us with the opacity of parables; we have Frost's overt reference to Mark 4:11–12, "That seeing they may not see and not perceive; and hearing they may hear, and not understand; lest any of them should be converted, and their sins should be forgiven them." I am suggesting here that the physicality of the inscription is another trope of opacity, and of literary dangers for the writer and the reader. For the poet the topos of inscription bespeaks a fear of hypostatized identity within the textual artifact. For the reader inscription presents the dangers of that fetishization, or literal-mindedness, that would mistake "Directive" for Frost's autobiography.

The hidden allusion to Dante's inscription, if there is so direct a link as allusion, might be (as is frequently the case with Frost) metrical, for the last five lines of "Directive," like Dante's inscription in the *Inferno*, are hendeca-syllabics. Admittedly, the topos of inscription in Frost and Dante, regard-less of the metrical similarity, may be taken as purely generic. But pursuing this generic similarity into thematic ground will enhance our sense of the reader's drama of choice in "Directive," and of the hypostatization of guilt at the site of the house. Recalling Mark 4:11–12 tells us that the crux of this poem is forgiveness. Similarly, recalling Dante's gate will remind us that this Frostian tour by poet-guide and reader-pilgrim is a return to the place of former sins. (Why else need we recall a parable of forgiveness?) Hell, in the *Inferno*, is the place where sinners not only confront, but are permanently embodied as their sins. Francesca tells Dante that "There is no greater sorrow / than thinking back upon a happy time / in misery."[8] The kind of regret that insists upon a physical return to the geographical place of the house, and reinforces this sense of place by suggesting that the poem is inscribed on that location, has a Dantesque physicality, at once graphic and metaphorical. Dante's physical description of Hell, and Frost's return to an actual house might simply remind us that form, however metaphorical, can imprison.

It is of the nature of life on earth, Frost tells us, that we commit ourselves to finite forms. "The bard has said in effect, Unto these forms I commend the spirit."[9] While fears of hypostatization may occur at any time to a writer, toward the end of a life and a career, one may look upon these commitments with a greater sense of their finality, and consequently a greater fear. (Frost was seventy years old when he published "Directive.") About five years earlier Frost had played more casually with the idea of writing his own epitaph, in "The Lesson for Today":

And were an epitaph to be my story
I'd have a short one ready for my own.

I would have written of me on my stone:
I had a lover's quarrel with the world.
   (158–61)

Certainly there must be days in the poet's life when he is glad to have committed himself to the forms he chose, when, like Stevens in "The Planet On
the Table" he looks upon his oeuvre with satisfaction: "Ariel was glad he
had written his poems." Other days, the poet may find himself, to borrow
another Stevensian phrase, an "inquisitor of forms," and, if he takes forms
to be the containers of his soul, an inquisitor of the spirit as well. The guide
who revisits the ruined playhouse may be described as a vengeful inquisitor,
not institutionalized like Torquemada, but embedded in the mind like the
super-ego.

*   *   *

How are we, as readers, to get beyond confusion, especially when "Directive" seems so skeptical of its own inventions? Frost's inscription is more
suspicious of its own fictitiousness than Wordsworth's "Lines Left upon a
Seat," and less willing to bypass the confusion of whether poems are spoken
in earnest or in play, whether they are moral or merely aesthetic acts. The
inscriptive fiction in "Lines Left upon a Seat"—self-consciously archaic
though it may have been—enables Wordsworth to affirm more than he
could in his own person. It leads Frost, however, to say much more (as a
poet) than he can affirm (as a human being). Wordsworth's "Lines" may
be conscious of their own stiltedness—the overly long title, the overly long
inscription—but not ironic about their message, "be wiser thou." Thus
Wordsworth's inscription achieves this affirmative purpose: it leaves us
with a lesson of humility that we will accept more readily from Wordsworth
the poet than from Wordsworth the man. "Lines Left upon a Seat" moves
beyond the confusion of a reproachable life. Frost's poem, in contrast, sails
close to the shoals of autobiographical confession, and keeps the problem of
the author's life before us throughout. (Roger Gilbert reminds us that at the
time he wrote "Directive" Frost had buried his wife and two of his children,
that his own "house" had literally returned to earth [72].)
   Is it *good*, as Charles Berger asks, to get beyond confusion?[10] Can Frost
do this the way Wordsworth does, by subsuming the flaws of personality
in the inscription's anonymity? Frost's tortuous riddling, the untrustable
guide, the stageyness, puns and shibboleths of the last fourteen lines ('hole'
in "whole," the parodic use of Christian symbols, the smug tone of election
in quoting *Mark*, the theft of the goblet, the oppositions between destiny

and destination, or brook and stream, etc.) all suggest that we can't and aren't supposed to get beyond moral or interpretive confusion. Herbert Marks takes this problem to its logical conclusion when he reads the poem as a parable of insufficiency, a ritualized return to the sacramental *temenos* which reminds us that the poem is only an icon or an artifact, not a redemption of life. "Frost's sovereign principle of metaphor is, on the contrary, a machine of displacement, and every attained meaning must redeem a correspondent loss" (146). What do poems displace, and can they do more than just point to displaced things, and actually "redeem" them?

Frost's insistent location of his inscriptive lines at the site of the house's brook, his return to a place of remembrance, regret, and self-reproach seems to bring the poem to a rift between man and poet that inscription in "Lines Left upon a Seat" had largely elided. One might even say that Frost's bringing us to the site of the house is a confessional gesture to be compared with the apparently inexplicable and self-lacerating compulsion that led Frost to demolish his own reputation by revealing monstrous confessions about himself to Lawrance Thompson. The "height of country" argues an elevated vantage point from which Frost would survey his life and work. Frost ascends this summit with uncharacteristically Yeatsian feelings and diction, a state "Too lofty and original to rage" (52). (Robert Lowell, interestingly, copied this phrase when he was creating *his* confessional mode about another, very autobiographical, and unhappy house at "91 Revere Street.")[11] Frost is asking the kind of question Yeats asks in "A Dialogue of Self and Soul":

> The unfinished man and his pain
> Brought face to face with his own clumsiness . . .
> How in the name of Heaven can he escape
> That defiling and disfigured shape . . . ?
>   (II, 7–8, 10–11)

Unlike Yeats, for whom poetry is a dialogue with one's self, Frost is not content to measure the lot, forgive himself the lot. He brings us along with him, like moral witnesses, placing *us* before the springs of forgiveness. For whose sake would we drink, our own, or the speaker's? Does our acceptance of this invitation imply granting the speaker forgiveness on behalf of the children?

When Frost writes "too lofty and original to rage" he seems to be asking whether Yeatsian grandiloquence can work for him as it does for Yeats: can the theatricality of poetic voice so transfigure life into art that one becomes the mask of one's own substitutive persona? This is a pitch of theatricality, however, outside Frost's usual range, one in which even Yeats was not always safe. Should inscriptive marking remind us of Yeats's epitaph, "Cast a cold eye / On life, on death / Horseman pass by," it may remind us too of Auden's remark that the horse may seem too much like a stage prop. The passer-by is more likely to be a motorist.[12]

I am speculating that "Directive," like Frost's confessions to Thompson, could be read as Frost baffling himself with the question whether he as a man was qualified to teach as a poet. Herbert Marks says the goblet in the cedar tree resembles the broken drinking bowl in *The Excursion*, both being sad fragments of ruined homes. For the Frostian narrator who may be personally responsible for some aspect of demise in this house, the toy goblet may also remind us of the hermit's "stone table" and "mouldered cave" in Book II.60–72 of *The Prelude*, that lie "beneath the oak's umbrageous covert." These are objects which "tame the pride / Of intellect and virtue's self-esteem"; they "temper" "the vain-glory of superior skill" by reminding us of values beyond competitive exertions, and of the futility of demonstrating one's skills.

Despite Frost's assertions—as notably to Poirier in the *Paris Review* interview[13]—that poets ought to be judged like athletic performers, for feats of skill, his best poems, such as "Home Burial" and "Directive" remain haunted by griefs that will not be mended by performing ingenious poetic feats. The height of feeling in "Home Burial" (the mother's grief) remains as inaccessible to Frost the poetic performer (there, at the height of his poetic ability) as to his clumsier male persona within the poem. Amy's complaint that grief is an unbridgeable solitude ("The nearest friends can go / With anyone to death, comes so far short / They might as well not try to go at all" [97–99]) is never effectively gainsaid by that or any other poem by Frost. "Directive," with its (quasi- or mock-) ritualistic pilgrimage, incantatory opulences, cheering inventions, and mazy figurations reminds us throughout of fictive mediations between grief and poetry. If the poem does not apologize for these mediations, it seems to shrug its shoulders at the ideal of overcoming them absolutely. If "Directive" is a confessional poem, however, the poet-husband-father might be fretted by a more painful self-reproach: did the presumption of wisdom that accrues to the role of poet-guide contribute to the destruction of the house? Were the relations between husband and wife, or father and child, destructively mediated by the persona of the poet?

Looking for a biographical reading of "Directive" risks admitting that one has not understood the metaphorical nature of poetry where meaning is the mask, or vice versa. On the other hand, the tropology of "Directive" seems to warn us that we have to try to step beyond the hermeneutic circuit of reading and writing. How else can poetry become, not a playhouse, but a house in earnest? One answer might be that poetry is most in earnest when the persona and the human being are most nearly identical. Yet here one feels on the contrary that while the speaker presents himself as the sufferer ("I stole the goblet"), the classicism of Romance-Latinate language in the poem, noted by Marie Borroff, establishes "the intellectual overview appropriate to the traditional bard of poetic narrative."[14] Herbert Marks similarly complains that elitist posturing in "Directive," the rift between the guide and the quester, can exasperate us, and make the poem seem to be imposing rather than discovering its purposes (142). Didactic posturing is especially troubling in a poem that makes brazen emotional demands on its readers. Should we call this imperious command or an extortion of pity: "Weep for what little things could make them glad"? It is risky to use a family's tragedies as a rhetorical device, and to exploit tragic sentiment as a force for moral enlightenment. Even granting the ways Frost acknowledges the inadequacy of poetry as a redemptive device, the poem is at risk of moral blunder.

The great esteem allotted this poem by critics (Poirier calls it "misplaced adulation") owes much to "modern" (i.e., since Wordsworth) adoration of poetic self-consciousness, the metaphor-making mind contemplating its own inventiveness. Moreover, "Directive" raises the question of legitimate fictions to a pitch of personal, moral blame rarely experienced in poems of epistemological poetic self-examination. (No one ever thought Stevens should be hanged for the persona of the "he" in "Esthetique du Mal.") Poirier doesn't underestimate, but deliberately resists the urging of this poem to couple the speaker's guilt with our sorrow, to weep for the little things of the children while still winking complicitously at the artifice of poetry, stealing the toy goblet from the playhouse to perform poetic make-believe. He rejects in particular the ritualistic aspects of the conclusion. One might accept the ritualistic aspects of the poem, and still wince at the conspiratorial approach of the speaker when he says "(*We know* the valley streams that when aroused / Will leave their tatters hung on barb and thorn)" (53–54; my emphasis). Can we balk at Frost's invitation precisely because it may be part of a personal confession? Such refusal can demean us, reduce us to the literal-mindedness and suspecting inquisitiveness of Wordsworth's narrator in "The Thorn." Yet I read "Directive" asking myself if I am being asked to condone or forgive those fits of anger Frost confessed to Thompson, the pistol brandished in the kitchen in the dead of night.[15] The inclusive "we know" may feel like Montresor's ice cold paw wrapped around one's shoulder.

I end where others end reading this poem, wondering how far the saving joy of imagination can take us in redeeming lost houses. What I hope to have added is emphasis that the poem demands of us more than approbation of a stylistic whole. It asks, as few poems dare, for us to pity the innocent children, and to grant ourselves and the speaker the right to feel whole again after their loss, even if we may have been partly responsible for it. Like the proverbial horse, we are led to the waters of forgiveness, but can't be made to drink. The inscriptive topos reminds us that we are interpreters with choices. Can we afford to be too chaste, to withhold forgiveness from ourselves or from others? The poem as aesthetic object cannot answer these questions. Its insufficiency reminds us that the poem is a parable that only fulfills its use when we look through it to other, supplementary frames of reference.

We, the readers of the poem, are guarantors of the author's posthumous presence, but more than this, we are required to occupy the central role in the drama of guilt and forgiveness. The topos of inscription offers a textuality deliberately unauthorized, one that asks us to reproduce, anew, the activities of reflection and judgment. A localized elision of consciousness, hint of the artifactual status of the text, is strategically appended to the poem to make room for the new subject, the reader, who is invited to share and contemplate the drama of lostness and salvation.

Seeking a self in the poems, Frost tells us in "Iota Subscript," we seek not him, but ourselves:

> Seek not in me the big I capital,
> Nor yet the little dotted in me seek.
> If I have in me any I at all,
>
> 'Tis the iota subscript of the Greek.
> So small am I as an attention beggar.
> The letter you will find me subscript to
> Is neither alpha, eta, nor omega,
> But upsilon which is the Greek for you.

"Iota Subscript" reminds us that all poems are prosopopeic, written characters standing in for human character. But for Frost the human character is not lost in the textuality that conveys it. It is transferred from me to you.

Notes

1. The readings of "Directive" I have in mind, and those to which I am most indebted are to be found in Charles Berger, "Echoing Eden: Frost and Origins," in *Robert Frost: Modern Critical Views*, ed. Harold Bloom (New York: Chelsea House, 1986) 161–65; Herbert Marks, "The Counter Intelligence of Robert Frost," *Yale Review* 71.4 (July 1982), reprinted in *Robert Frost: Modern Critical Views* 125–46, and Roger Gilbert, *Walks in the World* (Princeton: Princeton UP, 1990) 67–74. Each of these stresses the self-consciousness of poetic fiction in "Directive," and the elusiveness of redemption within the confines of poetic artifice. See also Frank Lentricchia, *Robert Frost: Modern Poetics and the Landscapes of Self* (Durham: Duke UP, 1975) 112–19, and Sidney Lea, "From Sublime to Rigamarole," *SiR* 19.1 (Spring 1980), reprinted in *Robert Frost: Modern Critical Views* 85–110.

2. Geoffrey Hartman, *Beyond Formalism: Literary Essays 1958–1970* (New Haven: Yale UP, 1970) 206–30.

3. David Perkins ed. *English Romantic Writers* (New York: Harcourt, Brace & World, 1967). Subsequent references to Wordsworth's poetry are from this edition.

4. Richard Poirier, *Robert Frost: The Work of Knowing* (New York: Oxford UP, 1977) 100.

5. *The Poetry of Robert Frost*, ed. Edward Connery Lathem (New York: Henry Holt, 1969). Subsequent references to Frost's poetry are from this edition.

6. John Freccero, *Dante: The Poetics of Conversion*, ed. Rachel Jacoff (Cambridge, MA: Harvard UP, 1986) 96–99.

7. For Freccero the pilgrim's encounter with the inscription is a paradigmatic trial of interpretation wherein salvation and damnation hang in the balance. He likens the momentary bewilderment of Dante the pilgrim (in contrast to the redeemed knowingness of Dante the author) to that of the disciples at the last supper when they cannot understand Christ's eucharistic offer: "Durus est hic sermo" [This is a hard saying].

8. "Nessun maggior dolore / che ricordarsi del tempo felice / ne la miseria" (*Inferno* V.121–23), trans. Allen Mandelbaum (New York: Bantam, 1980).

9. *Selected Prose of Robert Frost*, eds. Hyde Cox and Edward Connery Lathem (New York: Holt, Rinehart and Winston, 1966) 24.

10. See Berger 164 and Poirier 100.

11. Lowell's Great Aunt Sarah Stark Winslow was "a beauty too lofty and original ever to marry" (*Life Studies* and *For the Union Dead* [New York: Noonday P, 1956] 33). It is tempting to imagine that Lowell read "Directive" as a pointer in the direction of the confessional, autobiographical mode of *Life Studies*. The sense of place Frost achieved by situating inscription at the site of the house and brook suggests a stay of factuality against the distortions of unreliable memory, and might be compared in that regard with a painting of Lowell's Great Grandfather Mordecai Myer. The portrait was "mislaid past finding, but out of my memories I often come on it in the setting of our Revere Street house, a setting now fixed in the mind, where it survives all the distortions of fantasy, all the blank befogging of forgetfulness" (*Life Studies* 12–13).

12. W. H. Auden, *The Dyer's Hand and Other Essays* (New York: Random House, 1962) 353.

13. The interview originally appeared in *The Paris Review* 24 (Summer–Fall 1960). It is quoted in *Interviews with Robert Frost*, ed. Edward Connery Lathem (New York: Holt, Rinehart and Winston, 1966) 229–36.

14. Marie Borroff, *Language and the Poet: Verbal Artistry in Frost, in Stevens, and Moore* (Chicago: U of Chicago P, 1979) 39.

15. "About age six at the time, she [Frost's daughter Lesley] was awakened one winter night by her father and led downstairs where her mother lay weeping at the kitchen table, hands over her face. The child then noticed that the father was brandishing a revolver, pointing it first at Elinor then at himself, while announcing that Lesley was to take her choice since before morning one of her parents would be dead" (William H. Pritchard, *Frost: A Literary Life Reconsidered* [New York: Oxford UP, 1984] 54). Pritchard illustrates, dubiously but not naively, the dangers of aestheticizing Frost's life when he asks if this episode could, for all its hurtfulness, not be also called "a very bad piece of theatricality" or "playing at a bad game." Frost narrated this event to Lawrance Thompson; see *Robert Frost: The Early Years* (New York: Holt, Rinehart, and Winston, 1966) 308.

JOHN HOLLANDER

Robert Frost's Oven Bird

Mythologizing a construction of nature's—an animal, plant, geological formation, moment of process—could be seen as both a desecration and a celebration of pragmatically considered fact. When this goes on in poetry— what Frost called "the renewal of words for ever and ever"—it is accompanied and invigorated by a reciprocal mythologizing, as it were, of the very words used in the poetic process. Literature is full of purely mythological, mostly composite, creatures—phoenix, unicorn, basilisk, chimera, hydra, centaur—as nature is even more full of creatures totally innocent of interpretation—woodchuck, anteater, turbot, Shetland pony, jellyfish, quail.

But then there are the fallen creatures—lion, eagle, ant, grasshopper, barracuda, fox, hyena—that have been infected with signification from Aesop on. It is one of the tasks of poetry to keep renewing the taxonomic class of such creatures, by luring them, unwittingly, into a cage of trope (which of course they are not aware of inhabiting). Such new reconstructions of animals are almost a post-Romantic cottage industry, even as the rehearsal again and again of the traditional ones characterized pre-Romantic emblematic poetry. Significant emblematic readings of previously unread creatures can do the work of reinventing them—I think of Oliver Wendell Holmes's chambered nautilus, for example, as well as animals of Baudelaire and Rilke. I want to

From *Sewanee Writers on Writing*, edited by Wyatt Prunty, pp. 80–91. Copyright © 2000 by Louisiana State University Press.

reconsider in these pages a well-known instance of such reconstruction in the case of Frost's oven bird.

North American poetry has no living nightingales or skylarks upon which to descant, meditate, rhapsodize, or preach. Our literature inherited a museum of textual ones, from Ovid's Philomela through Milton's almost personally emblematic nightingale, through the more naturalized bird of Coleridge's conversation poem, "The Nightingale," and on to Keats's. John Crowe Ransom's account is more mythic than ornithological:

> Not to these shores she came! this other Thrace,
> Environ barbarous to the royal Attic;
> How could her delicate dirge run democratic,
> Delivered in a cloudless, boundless public place
> To an inordinate race?

A glance at the etiology of the poetic bird would certainly take in the old, blind Milton's later nightingale (not his youthful question-raiser, of whom more later on), who "sings darkling" at the beginning of *Paradise Lost*, Book III. It is answered by Keats ("darkling, I listen") in his nightingale poem. Shelley's skylark, Blake's lark, George Meredith's wonderful "The Lark Ascending" are all daylight's reciprocal poetical birds and poetical surrogates. Even Yeats's aggressively unnatural clockwork golden bird in "Sailing to Byzantium" partakes of the lark-nightingale tradition. But in the transatlantic New World, skylarkless and unnightingaled, another mythologized bird replaced them. There is a sequence of poems—from Richard Lewis's remarkable poem of the 1740s through those of Joseph Rodman Drake, Sidney Lanier, and Walt Whitman—which retrope the skylark-nightingale for American poetry as the mockingbird.

Lewis's "A Journey from Patapsko to Annapolis," telling in Augustan couplets, but from a Thomsonian perspective, of a trip along the eastern shore of Maryland in the 1730s, describes an encounter with a mockingbird. It so allegorizes the creature as the voice of the new-old American imagination that, regardless of the poem itself's remaining largely in oblivion until this century, never again would mockingbirds' song be the same:

> O sweet Musician, thou dost far excell
> The soothing Song of pleasing *Philomel*
> Sweet is her Song, but in few Notes confin'd
> But thine, thou *Mimic* of the feath'ry Kind,
> Runs through all Notes!—Thou only knowst them All,
> At once the *Copy*,—and th' *Original*.

It is only the anticipation both of Thoreau's echo that is "to some extent, an original sound" and of Frost's "counter-love, original response" in "The Most of It" that is slightly uncanny here. It is almost as if a transcendence of limitation in genres, modes, conventions, styles—the belated not as incapacitated but inspired by its knowledge of what preceded it—were being embodied in an attendant of the Muse of the New.

Lewis's poem prepares the ground for what will be a subsequent tradition. Joseph Rodman Drake's claim in "The Mocking-Bird" (published 1812) for the bird as poet is a bit more plonkingly expository. The interesting southern poet Richard Henry Wilde (1789–1847) refigures the mockingbird in a sonnet. But by and large, the mockingbird of subsequent southern tradition partakes of the sentimental souvenir in the refrain of Stephen Foster's song ("listen to the mock-ing-bird, listen to the mock-ing-bird"). But Sidney Lanier's "The Mocking Bird" ends with a pseudoriddle; the bird having gobbled up a grasshopper, the sonnet weakly inquires, "How may the death of that dull insect be / The life of yon trim Shakspere on the tree?" While Shakespeare can be considered legitimately adduced (given that the bird can say what was both done and dreamed), the fairly empty question embraces what isn't much of a paradox after all.

The greatest and most poetically powerful mockingbird, the male of the pair of "feather'd guests from Alabama," is Whitman's "singer solitary . . . projecting me," the bird singing of its loss to the "outsetting bard," to the "undertone" of the sea, "the savage old mother incessantly crying." The transumption, in "Out of the Cradle Endlessly Rocking" of Keatsian and Shelleyan nightingale and skylark and of earlier poetic mockingbird alike, is a far more profound matter than the mere Americanization of English poetic tradition. The bird is shaken loose from even contingent personification, and extended another, a new, kind of personhood.

It was to the received avian agenda in general that modern poetry felt unable to subscribe. Richard Wilbur spoke for all his twentieth-century precursors in the early 1950s, I believe, saying in "All These Birds" that

> Hawk or heavenly lark or heard-of nightingale,
> Perform upon the kitestrings of our sight
> In a false distance . . . the day and night
> Are full of wingèd words
>   gone rather stale,
>   That nothing is so worn
>   As Philomel's bosom-thorn. . . .

But Wilbur's late-modernist plea for a powerful ornithology to replace empty mythological clichés goes beyond its own strong demands for a

demythologizing of what are, imaginatively speaking, stuffed owls. It pleads
for tropes of birdhood and avian particularity by showing both the limits
and the consequent utility of a biological reductionism:

> Let us, with glass or gun,
> Watch (from our clever blinds) the monsters of the sky
> Dwindle to habit, habitat, and song,
> And tell the imagination it is wrong
> Till, lest it be undone,
>   it spin a lie
> So fresh, so pure, so rare
> As to possess the air.

But perhaps the essential modern rejection of a trope of birdsong is Wallace
Stevens' in "Autumn Refrain," his near-sonnet of 1931—ten years earlier
than "Come In." In this poem (about not being able to write anything for
two years), grackles lately blathering recall to him the whole avian tradition
and its perhaps empty literariness:

> The yellow moon of words about the nightingale
> In measureless measures, not a bird for me
> But the name of a bird and the name of a nameless air
> I have never—shall never hear. . . .

And he opts out of all of it: the typically bivalent phrase "the evasions of the
nightingale" refers both to evading the poetic nightingale issue and to what
said nightingale issue itself evades. The poem ultimately finds, as Harold
Bloom suggests, some difficult but important "residuum" in the desolate
sound of the grackles. There is a great deal to be said of the Stevensian
distrust of birdsong, but it is now time to turn to my central text, Frost's
powerful and problematic contribution to poetic ornithology, the—in this
case, accepted—thrush of "The Oven Bird." The poem invoking it negoti-
ates a remarkable course between a rhetoric of certainty about what a bird
is singing/saying/doing and a strong inner sense of its "evasions." And it
maintains a very un-Stevensian, albeit parabolic, awareness of natural fact.

   First, though, the unpoetic ornithology: *Seiurus aurocapillus*, a ground-
walking warbler, is common in deciduous woods; it builds a domed nest
on the ground and sings from an exposed perch on the understory. That an
American poem addressing—or addressing itself to—this thrushlike bird
might consider its ground-built, oven-shaped nest, would seem obvious, with
interpretations of some sort of pragmatical sublime—being well-grounded

instead of lofty—immediately offering themselves. But the poem we are to consider does not.

THE OVEN BIRD

There is a singer everyone has heard.
Loud, a mid-summer and a mid-wood bird,
Who makes the solid tree trunks sound again.
He says that leaves are old, and that for flowers
Mid-summer is to spring as one to ten.
He says the early petal-fall is past,
When pear and cherry bloom went down in showers
On sunny days a moment overcast;
And comes that other fall we name the fall.
He says the highway dust is over all.
The bird would cease and be as other birds
But that he knows in singing not to sing.
The question that he frames in all but words
Is what to make of a diminished thing.

Robert Frost's sonnet was started in New Hampshire around 1906 but probably finished in England around 1914, far from the shared habitat of bird and poet. Its ending leaves us with a kind of riddle. The opening puzzles us also, slightly, but in a different way: sonnets don't start out with couplets unless they intend to continue—and as they rarely do—with six more of them. But both octave and sestet of this one are initiated by couplets, and in the latter instance, somewhat strangely for other reasons as well. From the outset, too, we notice at once how casual and how problematic its rhetoric is. "A singer everyone has heard"?—come now, people in London who have no more heard that singer than a New Englander could hear a nightingale? No: this is the conventional palaver of nature-writing, of a newspaper feuilleton of the sort that you might still find in a rural newspaper in England (or, more likely, being sent up in a Monty Python routine). But the low-literary, prosaic tone is modulated with a jolt, as the second line declares its ulterior agenda, with a "*Loud*, a mid-*summer* and *mid-wood bird*": because of the contrastive stress marking the new coinage "mid-wood," the spatial reciprocal of the ordinary, temporal "mid-summer," the line ends with three stresses (you might call it two overlapping spondees), confirming the opening, intrusive, almost self-descriptive, "Loud."

The bird "makes the solid tree trunks sound again," but at a first reading this always itself sounds strange. It is not just the densely alliterative pattern, first pointed out by Reuben Brower. "Sound again"—have they been unsound? No, not Germanic "sound" (Modern German *gesund*) but French and Latin sonorous "sound"; still, why do we pause momentarily? Do we mistake this bird for a kind of woodpecker, hitting the trunks directly, and thus making them less gesund as they make them resound? But it is this purely English and non-Latin way of putting "resound" that then allows the matter of an echo of a prior sounding—that of the earlier—and perhaps for this poem, ordinary and, despite literary cliché, unpoetic—spring birds, since silent.

Then comes the first of the three reiterated assertions of his asserting: "He says ..."; it will be apparent later why it is not the seventeenth-eighteenth-century locution, the transitive "he sings," or its version in the nineteenth century and later, "he sings of [whatever it is]." What "He says" first is hardly celebratory, but pragmatically observational, quite this side of sounding dirge-like.

The next thing he says is more interpretive, at first reminding us of the dropping of spring blossoms and of how we tend to read these as nothing more dire than the end of a particularly gorgeous overture or prelude, but then letting the resonance of the term "petal-fall" linger on—as if to make us think, *yes, they do fall, don't they*? We half notice, too, the phonological patterning here, in which one dactylic foot embracing a hyphenated compound is echoed by another on another (unhyphenated) one: " ... early [*petal*-fall] is past / When pear and [*cherry* bloom]. . . ." But woven across this is an alliterative pattern, in which *petal*, *past*, and *pear* enact a different kind of connection, followed by the analogous but more potently expressive assonance of "went *down* in *show*ers." Yet this line is not end-stopped here but flows into the phonologically plain "On sunny days a moment overcast." But there is another mode of resonance at work, one of word rather than of word-sound. There is a subtle aroma of nuance here: the leaves are cast under, in—and for—a moment, even as the sky is momentarily overcast; the point isn't loudly made or brandished triumphantly but allowed wonderfully to happen.

But then things become problematic again. *Who* says "And comes that other fall we name the fall"? This line is all the more complex and problematic here because it initiates the sestet, and we want the full stop at the end to be a comma, as if to say, "When fall—that other fall—comes, he says [with respect to that] that the highway dust is covering everything." The normal grammar would be that of "come the fall" ("come Sunday," etc.); the present third-person singular verb form here suggests a counterthrusting inversion ("And [then] comes that other fall"). But the first reading would also reaffirm syntactically a linkage that the couplet rhyme (again, in an anomalous place for a sonnet) is implying. Yet the couplet is broken. And we are reminded by the disjunction that the covering of highway dust—the stasis in between

petal-fall, which initiates fullness of leaf, and leaf-fall, which initiates bare-
ness of branch—is midsummer stuff, and we can't have the syntax the way
we'd like to. As for the coming of the *real* fall (the "early petal-fall" is the
"other"), we'd needed the oven bird to point out to us that it was a version of
the primary one, a shadowy type of the truth of autumn (and, by Miltonic
extension, the autumnal "fall" as type of the Fall from Paradise, the original
one we name the Fall, which brought about the remodeling of Paradise into
Nature, fracturing spring from fall, promise from conditional fulfillment).

Relations between literal and figurative falling are made even more
interesting by the fact that in the Romance part of English, "cause" and "case"
are based ultimately on *cadere*, as in the Germanic part we still have residues
of the earlier usage "it fell" for "it happened." There are all those other falls,
too. (I'm not sure whether the poem's relative reticence on this question keeps
them at a safe distance or not—or is there any safe distance from the Fall?)
Richard Poirier remarks of this moment in the poem that "any falling—of
leaves, of snow, of man . . . can be redeemed by loving, and the sign of this
redemption is, for Frost, the sound of the voice working within the sounds
of poetry." Certainly, the cadential full stop at the end of this line makes us
momentarily more aware of the working of the poet's voice. But in any case,
the peculiar one-line sentence, which makes us keep wanting to open it out
into a dependent clause and a full couplet with a comma, gives us meditative
pause. Perhaps it works as something of a springboard *pour mieux sauter* into a
final quatrain, which—in sonnet form—can seem itself to initiate a moment
of (at least structural) renewal.

Some of that quatrain's complexity emerges in a straightforward paradox: what does it mean not to sing in singing? Well, if the "singing" birds do
herald and celebrate spring and the morning—or, as with swallows, fill the
sky with skitterish evening hymns—then the oven bird's repeated disyllabic
utterance is not that. "He says," "he says," "he says," "he knows," "he frames"
(and here, another kind of figurativeness in the trope of material construction); we call the sounds birds make singing, but this bird demands that we
suspend the overtones of the word "sing." His are not songs, but propositions:
the very subtle rhythm of the line makes this clear, for, in order for the rhyming syllables to be sufficiently stressed, it must go not as "in singing not to
sing," as the intoning of the paradox seems to demand, but rather "in singing
not to sing"—not to be claimed by allegorizing human attention as music, but
instead as speculative discourse.

By this point in the poem, the casual older fiction of birdsong—like that
of wind in the trees sighing and brooks babbling—cannot be acknowledged.
So it is that he frames a question "in all but words," a formulation that is
rhetorically quite reticent (birds don't *really* talk, of course, but . . .). The very

grammar of the phrase "knows in singing" is unusually resonant: (1) as has been suggested, the bird knows—while singing—not to "*sing*," but rather discursively to raise questions; (2) the bird knows not to sing (literally) in-and-by singing (figuratively); (3) is it as if knowing-in-singing were like Sidney's "loving in truth," a kind of knowing in singing, or as if singing were itself a kind of mental process here? In any event, this song is a matter of knowledge, not of charm, of sense making a claim on *tra-la-la*: I think here—regarding the issue, always crucial for Frost, of the sound of making sense—of how great jazz musicians would often play their purely instrumental solos *to the words*, singing the text (with a complex system of rhythm all its own) internally, in order properly to inform the inventions of the melody alone. In the oven bird's case, perhaps, we implicitly reject "frames in all but music"—birdsong being only figuratively that—and leap over any literal musical agenda even as a poet's *cano* means "I write."

It could also be observed that this sonnet itself, like so many of the other poems in *Mountain Interval*, "knows in singing not to sing." This is not in the way of Yeats's "Words for Music Perhaps" (a phrase which in its way defines all lyric poetry in English from Wyatt and Surrey on); this is more of an implicit revisionary construction of the lyrical of high modernism and may in some ways anticipate the rejection of the thrush's musical pseudoinvitation in Frost's poem "Come In."

Be that as may be, we come to the oven bird's question itself, which may indeed be two questions. Our colloquial phrase "to make [something] of X" can mean to reshape it, use it as material for some new Y, etc. But to ask, "What do you make of X?" means "How do you explain, analyze, interpret X?"—"What's with X?" These strangely paired meanings are those of *to construct* and *to construe*. They both come from the same Latin verb (and are indeed, with unfortunate consequences about fifteen years ago, both designated by the same French word, *construire*). The first of the bird's implied questions, then, is that of what to do with something residual—in this case, summer, but by implication life itself we are *nel mezzo del cammin* here—something diminished by half. How shall we live the rest of our summer?

The oven bird does not celebrate spring, whether cheerfully, or even problematically, like the cuckoo of *Love's Labors Lost*; it does not pierce the night, in cheerful lieu of illumination, like the winter owl paired with it at the end of that same play. It is neither skylark, singing invisibly at the height of the day, nor the alternatively invisible nightingale. It talks neither of beginnings nor endings, but of a time that is both, in a Janus-like July, looking back and forward at once to an original and a final fall. Midpoints are strange, and they tend not to generate the ceremonies that beginnings and endings do. Midsummer in England tends to mean the solstice, June 21 or thereabouts. But that is not what he celebrates. We tend to think of our northeastern American "midsummer" as somewhere around July 30 or so, and this is the oven bird's time, a somewhat indiscernible *middle* (rather than a clearly marked *center*).

And thus the bird's other possible question points toward and away from this matter: "What to make of"—how to construe, understand, interpret—the residual? Is the bottle of summer half full or half empty? The invitation to consider the question is not that of the ordinary, crackpot realist cynical put-down of epistemology. I think that the invited discourse on the question, and what it would mean about you and summer to answer it either way, would lie along a line of pragmatic approaches to questioning somewhere between William James and later Wittgenstein. Poirier looks at the question from the point of view of the imaginative energies it generates, referring to "the creative tension between a persistent rising and a natural falling—a poise of creativity in the face of threatened diminishments."

Another way of putting this suggests that one of these diminishments might be thought of as that of the prior tradition itself—Richard Wilbur's "wingèd words / gone rather stale"; and in that kind of subsequent allegorizing that strong poems tend to exude, one thing to make of *that* diminished thing is, by means of newly animated words, "The Oven Bird" itself. And then, as is the case with very powerful and deep poetic ambiguities, the invitation extends to considering the relation between the two kinds of *making of,* between construing and constructing, in which representation is creation, and understandings are imagined: this relation is poetry's realm (as it may not be philosophy's, despite the woodpecker hammering at such a suggestion of the kind of institutional construing recently called deconstruction). And finally, we observe how the line itself ("what to make of a diminished thing") sings its way into the reader's attention with its assonantal *dimini*shed th*ing* that itself diminishes the accentual and thereby the rhetorical weight thrust upon the word "thing" by being put in terminal rhyming position (not "di*mini*shed thing" but "di*mini*shed *thing*").

The way in which the oven bird—"as other birds," too—got to speak, learned what we might call not his sing-song but his say-song—and his way of framing questions "in all but words"—are also part of Frost's concern. Virgil invents what Ruskin would call the pathetic fallacy in his very first eclogue, in which the shepherd Tityrus, *lentus in umbra*—at ease in the shade—*formosam resonare doces Amaryllida silvas*—teaches the woods to resound with the name of his girlfriend Amaryllis and thereby teaches nature to talk poetically to us for the first time.

Another one of Frost's great sonnets, "Never Again Would Birds' Song Be the Same," tells its own etiological story of how birds got to talk, and it is worth considering here for a moment in its relation to the oven bird poem. (A much weaker earlier poem, "The Aim Was Song," propounds another version of such an etiology.) That story involves the imprinting of a human "tone of meaning, but without the words" onto birdsong, an added "oversound" (perhaps as Frost's revision of the ambiguous post-Spenserian word "undersong"). The "he" of the opening line ("He would declare and could himself believe") frames the fiction that Eve's voice, "When call or laughter carried it aloft," added to previously unmeaning birdsong "Her tone of meaning but without the words." That "he" seems to be both Adam and a poet (writing, and then possibly even "believing," his myth). The oven bird's question obviously comes along fairly late in the development of avian discourse. A linkage perhaps more than trivial with the earlier sonnet can also be found in the much more dramatic use of the broken—here, final—couplet. The poem looks at first to conclude with a "bottom line," as it were, the consequential reiteration of the title: "Never again would birds' song be the same." But then, after the full stop, comes the carefully intoned afterthought: "And to do that to birds was why she came" (leaving the implicit question, "To do exactly *what* to birds, by the way? to teach them? infect them? trope them? what?" resonating after this second ending).

I should like to return to one comment from the *Field Guide to North American Birds* that I omitted when quoting from it earlier in this discussion. The oven bird's song is characterized as "a loud and clear *teacher* repeated about 10 times, louder and louder." (It has been argued that, since the oven bird, like many others, also produces a different, high-flying song for a time in spring, the poem is either suppressing discussion of this with a rhetorical strategy of its own, or repressing it. I believe that neither of these is the case and that the lesser-known fact is not, in this instance, to be considered as being deployed in the poem—either for the fact of early, youthful spring-song versus sober, didactic middle-age or, more complicatedly, for the fact of its being very little known.) Like many good teachers of certain kinds, his lesson goes far beyond what "he says," into parable and into questions about questioning. As a poetic fiction of a teaching bird, he seems to be a very guarded, transumptive revision of a particular earlier one, Wordsworth's throstle in "The Tables Turned":

> He, too, is no mean preacher;
> Come forth into the light of things,
> Let nature be your teacher.

The last of these lines is rather awkward in its sound: the near-rhyming, echoic relation of *nature/teacher* is so out of character for the language of poems from *Lyrical Ballads* like "We Are Seven," "Expostulation and Reply," and this one that it feels inadvertent and out of control. This awkwardness casts modern doubt on the authenticity of the quoted expostulation. Thus all birds—even pulpited ones—are not true teachers, and I must note in closing how Frost's bird again recalls a subtradition—but a less diminished one—of poems that consider not merely eloquent but questioning birds. The young Milton's first sonnet was on the nightingale, and what to make of it: for the young, poetically ambitious, virginal poet, was the bird's song a call to attend to a muse or a lover? Was it about sex or poetry? The poem ends with this question, the bird in question in this case involving Milton's nightingale knowing in singing not to say.

W. H. Auden, in a poem of 1950 called "Their Lonely Betters," not only denies the possibility of figurative discourse in birdsong, but in the final stanza invokes Frost, with perhaps the ulterior implication that he is the sort of poet who continues to ascribe words to birds, at least:

> Let them leave language to their lonely betters
> Who count some days and long for certain letters;
> We, too, make noises when we laugh or weep:
> Words are for those with promises to keep.

But within the natural history of poetry, birds seem to have learned to put questions—at any rhetorical level—fairly late in poetic history. Frost's oven bird, is not a universal, but a local singer, framing a question of which you can make a number of things. He is not, like Minerva's owl, an emblem of wisdom but rather an instance of acquiring wisdom—"doing philosophy" in the parlance of Anglo-American analytic philosophers rather than standing for it. As a poetic bird, he is an American poet-teacher. And the teacher-poet who makes a poem out of him is fully able to acknowledge that. There are all sorts of complex attitudes—let alone whatever it had come to make of Eve's "call or laughter"—that must be gleaned from modern birdsong. And yet it sometimes sounds as if the song of the threshold—the qualifications, retractions, considerations, economies of the powerfully unsystematic—can only be philosophy.

DAVID HAMILTON

The Echo of Frost's Woods

Everyone knows "Stopping by Woods on a Snowy Evening," and when remembering it, nearly everyone remembers right off, I should think, its repeated last line. Here is a unique moment in Robert Frost's poetry, and so a unique effect. Nor can I think of a close parallel in anything I have ever read. It is deeply satisfying, and strange, yet somehow, for all its strangeness, familiar. Hence it has monopolized our commentary, which to my knowledge has never gone far enough, for we are in the territory of Echo who is always a mystery and a provocation.

Who has not felt the return of Echo to have enlarged his or her voice? Echo is more demanding than rhyme and is, paradoxically, both quintessentially poetic and antipoetic. Exact repetition often seems a blunder, a want of grace, the way Homer nods, even though it is also one of the more profound markers of the Homeric poems. We go back and back to "wine-dark sea" and "clean-limbed Hera," and the more we repeat those words the more their suggestions expand.

For just as exact repetition can seem a defect, it can deepen the mystery so that poetry might be defined as, precisely, that which bears repetition. If so, the more repetition borne, the more poem. Consequently little seems more certainly a poem than a villanelle, a pantoum, a sestina, or a blues song, with all their demanding repetitions—so long as we are not bored. If we are

From *Roads Not Taken: Rereading Robert Frost*, edited by Earl J. Wilcox and Jonathan N. Barron, pp. 123–31. Copyright © 2000 by the Curators of the University of Missouri.

bored, the work fails, for it has not borne repetition well. But when we read with deepening attraction—admittedly our less frequent situation—we have found a "maiden" all but "makeles," as another old poem that bore its repetitions well knew to put it.

For these reasons, it seems to me that the single best commentary on Frost's last lines is the anticipatory insight of Christopher Smart: "ECHO is the soul of the voice exerting itself in hollow places."[1] "Not the voice of the soul," Rebecca Clouse remarked as she brought that line to my attention. The voice of the soul, that shopworn figure, now hardly gives us pause. But Echo, the soul of the voice, she who repeats exactly—with that figure, Smart prefigures Frost, who by holding to the letter of the line, for whatever reason—as if reason would explain it—makes a blues song of his lyric and breathes such spirit into it as has yet to exhaust itself.

*   *   *

The blues repeat a line and advance, their movement incremental. In that, they overlap with the formalities of terza rima which repeats sounds, rather than lines, while inserting a new note by which to extend itself—aba bcb and so on. Dante apparently felt such a system required rounding off, so he added a line after the final stanza of each canto: . . . xyx yzy z. That last "z" sound finds its rhyme, which allows for closure. I mention this because Frost's quatrains employ the same principle of incremental extension: aaba bbcb. . . . The lonely "b" sound, "here," in the first stanza, becomes the dominant rhyme of the next: "queer," "near," "year" and so on. This is a top-heavy or off-balance terza rima. Moreover, Frost's concluding repetition of "And miles to go before I sleep" would seem a parallel way of bringing his "canto" to closure. His solution alludes, we might say, to Dante's underlying principle of incremental advance with no potential rhyme left dangling. We hear an echo of Dante in the formal matter of Frost's poem, and our reading seems very much a matter of attending to Echo.

My own awareness of this particular reverberation was sparked by a lecture in Spain, when Professor Viorica Patea suggested that the "owner" of those woods might have a providential aspect and that Frost's lingering by them was passing strange. Mediterranean language was in my ear, and Dante's "selva oscura" leapt to mind. It probably helped that Patea was from the University of Salamanca, from which Fray Luis de Leon had been taken to prison during the Inquisition for translating the Song of Songs, and where after five years, according to legend, he returned to his lecture hall, with its crude wooden benches, and greeted his students that first morning back with, "Dicebamus hesterna die . . ." ["Decíamos ayer"; "We were saying yesterday. . . ."]

It was as if his last day in class had been echoing in him all those years to come through finally, and then ring over and over again as the tale has been repeated.

Not that I had stumbled onto anything new by catching Dante from Patea's remarks. John Pollock's note of 1979 reminds us that "Frost . . . knew Dante thoroughly."

> Thus when the speaker of "Stopping By Woods" states that he has paused in his journey "Between the woods and frozen lake" . . . it is difficult not to think of Dante's experience in the first book of *The Divine Comedy* . . . which begins in a dark wood and progresses to a frozen lake at the center of hell.

George Monteiro also draws Dante into a discussion of this passage, though he discusses only the "woods," not the lake, and hurries on to a comparison with "The Draft Horse" and its "pitch-dark limitless grove."[2]

*   *   *

Wherever we find Dante, we may find Eliot, and that is the echo that I would draw out further. *The Waste Land* appeared only one year before "Stopping by Woods," and I suspect in the latter an oblique reply. Responses to *The Waste Land*, after all, are not in short supply. In his provocative anthology, *Top 500 Poems*, William Harmon singles out "Directive" and "Spring and All" as poems that replied to Eliot.[3] As Harmon notes, the word *waste* appears in "Spring and All," and "Directive" includes lilacs, a rock–water contrast, and reference to the Holy Grail, to which I may add that Williams's poem begins as a long series of "sentence fragments" that we could say are "shored against" the mid-poem arrival of spring. We wait that long for a complete sentence which, by offering grammatical shape, puts winter "waste" to order. "Spring and All" also appeared in 1923. Harmon suggests that Eliot challenged poets to portray their own ideas of "the good place," just as "The Deserted Village" had helped evoke *The Waste Land*. In that case, "New Hampshire" may be yet another reply to Eliot, a half-ironic tribute to a good place, it being "restful," Frost observes, "just to think about New Hampshire," even though, as he no doubt enjoyed adding, he was "living in Vermont."

Eliot drew on Dante repeatedly, for the epigraph for "Prufrock," for "*il miglior fabbro*," *The Waste Land*'s dedication to Pound, and in "Tradition and the Individual Talent," to mention several instances. In "Tradition," he describes artistry as a "pressure" that transmutes the materials of memory and

emotion. "It is not the 'greatness', the intensity of the emotions, the compo-
nents, but the intensity of the artistic process, the pressure, so to speak, under
which the fusion takes place, that counts," is the way Eliot put it in 1919, and
his examples are from Dante.[4] Allusions to Dante became a kind of signature,
and several passages in *The Waste Land* become such pastiches of the *Com-
media* that "After Dante" could have served as their title.

It seems to me that Frost turns on all this and works his own will on
remembrances of Dante but in a style that makes any sense of pressure, as
such, only lightly felt. His is a poem with a light touch even if its implications
are weighty. "Stopping by Woods" has been much loved as a Christmas card
scene, though being alone in woods filling up with snow could prove unlucky.
Indeed quite a bit of dread adds up quietly but quickly. The lack of a farm-
house could suggest something to the horse, and to us, that the speaker mini-
mizes. The darkest evening may not specify the coldest or the most forlorn,
but it implies as much. No skating party and bonfire glitter on that frozen
lake. As Thompson's biography makes evident, Frost had enough experience
of death, silence, and suicidal thinking to make his famous last line anything
but restful, and "death wish"—as Ciardi suggested, and suffered for suggesting—seems not at all far-fetched.[5] How can we define "lovely" as "dark and
deep" without entertaining its equation to heart-stopping desire? Our general
rejection of Lathem's ameliorating emendation ("lovely, dark, and deep") has
been, perhaps, one more way of leaning toward Ciardi's reading.

For all these reasons, we may say that Frost writes a North American
wasteland in sixteen lines. He alters and extends the terza rima stanza, pro-
viding a short string of them rounded off as a canto, not precisely as Dante
does it, but with an allusion to Dante's method of closure. Whose woods
these are we can guess. The darkest evening of the year suggests cosmic matters. The frozen lake is where the woods lead, and where the downward journey ends. As in Dante, there is no rest; the speaker must keep on and on. Even
the "easy wind," one of the more Currier and Ives touches, is in keeping with
how easily one slides into the *Inferno* by way of Paolo and Francesca, whose
restless, erotic play sets them whirling on a ceaseless wind.

*   *   *

Once I heard Frost read this poem. Actually he "said" it. He would "say" his
poems, he told us, differentiating himself from those who did not wholly
know theirs. So he said "Stopping by Woods" all the way through and then
raised the question of the repeated last line. His tone was bantering, mocking commentators who would give it "meaning," readers like Ciardi and
perhaps Ciardi in particular. He said nothing about solving the problem

of bringing his off-balance terza rima to closure. He insisted on an "easier" explanation, more in the nature of Ockham's razor. He wanted to go to bed; that was all—that was all?—and repeating the last line was his quickest way of getting there. At the time, I took his explanation as an invitation to share in a small joke, but it is a joke that bears repetition.

There are, of course, other explanations of this lyric, and among them we might privilege two credited to Frost himself. One comes from an anecdote told by N. Arthur Bleau. Bleau recounts having attended a Frost reading at Bowdoin in 1947 and of having asked, from the audience, what was his favorite poem. At first Frost ignored the question, saying they were all his favorites and ended the session. Then he invited Bleau to the podium and spoke with him privately. "Stopping by Woods" was his favorite poem because it arose from a particularly bleak Christmas and the "darkest evening of the year" just before it. Having no money, Frost loaded a wagon with farm produce and went to town, but he found no buyers and returned empty-handed, without even small gifts for the children. He felt he had failed his family, and rounding a bend in the road, by woods, and quite near his house, the horse, who seemed to understand his mood, and who had already been given the reins, slowed and stopped, letting Frost have a good cry. "I just sat there and bawled like a baby," Bleau reports Frost as having said.[6] In a following note, Frost's daughter, Lesley, confirms the story, saying her father gave her that same explanation "sometime in the forties," that she assumed he had told no one else except her mother, and that Bleau's telling was particularly persuasive for his use of the word *bawl*. "Oh, come now, quit bawling," her father would say. She adds another few words of her father's that she remembers: "A man has as much right as a woman to a good cry now and again. The snow gave me shelter; the horse understood and gave me the time." She even remembers the name of the horse, Eunice.

This is a remarkable anecdote. For one thing, it shows Frost as readier to let poetry arise from his emotions than Eliot would seem to be. Not "the intensity of the emotions," Eliot had said, "but the intensity [and pressure] of the artistic process." For Frost, the emotions had to be strong, and he applied his pressure, but it is the pressure of astonishing restraint, a pressure that hardly shows. No "bawling" enters the poem. The surprising phrase by which the woods "fill up with snow" could be read as a correlative for it, the abundance of snow being imaginatively commensurate with an abundance of tears. Had we had tears, no one would have seen this as a winter wonderland scene. That such a reading remains possible, however, is further tribute to Frost's restraint, for the "little horse," "harness bells," "easy wind," and "downy flake" are all details that a speaker, wishing to emphasize his sorrow, would be likely to suppress. Without them we would be more directed to the evocation of a personal wasteland. With them, Frost maintains a balance, or a "suspension" as Jarrell suggested, between despairing and regenerative tones.[7]

To put it differently, those phrases suggest an apparent ease, rather than pressure working upon the materials of memory and emotion, which no doubt has had much to do with the poem's staying power. The real pressure Frost felt appears to have been to deflect the feeling that was there, from the speaker to his horse, to the woods themselves, and to the snow. Lesley Frost remarks that her father withheld this story because he did not want "pity" from the reader; "pity, he said, was the *last* thing he wanted or needed." Once the reader is relieved of investing in the speaker's need, other aspects of the poem surge forward, and these tend to obscure the darker reading that I, too, favor.

Bleau's anecdote was apparently unknown to Thompson, who died five years before its printing, and who only records Lesley Frost's comment that a woodside pond near their Derry, New Hampshire, farm was the "frozen lake" in question. The Frosts lived there between 1900 and 1909, when the family was at its poorest. That was the period, too, when they had a horse named Eunice. The story about the poem that Thompson records is a summer story set several years later.

Thompson reminds us that Frost was something of a mythmaker about himself, one favorite being his writing poems of miraculous inspiration. "Stopping by Woods" was an example, which was, in turn, a reason for his favoring it. In June 1922, after Frost's first year at Michigan, when he was no longer quite so plagued by poverty, he was working on "New Hampshire." After working all one June night, he was surprised and pleased by dawn. Standing at the window, stretching, looking at the sun, he was overtaken by a thought and returned to a fresh page and quickly, "without too much trouble" drafted the complete poem.[8]

Ciardi took this story at face value, without knowing what poem Frost had spent the night working on and with the confident assertion that were it known, "it would be found to contain the germinal stuff of 'Stopping by Woods'" (Ciardi, 156–57). Thompson took offense at Ciardi's certainty. "There is no connection between either the themes or the subject matter of 'New Hampshire' and 'Stopping by Woods,'" he asserted (I, 597). That Frost finished it at one sitting seems a bit of a stretch since drafts exist that indicate his revisions. For example the key Dantean line was "Between a forest and a lake" before Frost found his more fortunate second thought.[9] When informed of all this, Ciardi tempered his view and thanked his former teacher John Holmes for the information and for "his understanding from Mr. Frost that the long poem in question is 'New Hampshire.'" Then he added that if all that be so, his guess about its containing the "germinal stuff" of the new poem "becomes questionable" (Ciardi, 158).

So Frost had two good stories to tell about his poem. We know that it was first published on March 7, 1923, in the *New Republic* (on the same page as "Moon Rider" by William Rose Benét and under the common title, "Two Winter Poems"), then in *New Hampshire* later that year, making likely its composition the summer before. His Christmas story need not rule out its composition early one June morning. Frost did not say what more than early sun had inspired him. Judith Oster finds a connection between the two poems in that both balance notions of responsibility and wildness.[10] And I suspect that Eliot, along with the prior night's work, played a part.

Thompson believes that the composition of "New Hampshire" was influenced by an intellectual current of the early twenties with which Frost, characteristically, was at odds. The *Nation* ran a series of articles, state by state, about capitalistic corruption in the United States with Edmund Wilson, among others, contributing. Wilson wrote of New Jersey. Having sold "The Pauper Witch of Grafton" to the *Nation*, Frost was asked to add to the series. So he composed "New Hampshire." Amy Lowell and Emerson were targets, because of their dismissive attitudes toward upper New England (Thompson, II, 233). Even unnamed, Eliot could be in the background of all this, for the common denominator seems to be fashionable denigration from which Frost stood apart.

One could, in fact, consider "Stopping by Woods" a radical revision of "New Hampshire," the long work of the night before, which is what Ciardi seems to have imagined. He speaks of "what was a-simmer . . . all night without finding its proper form" (Ciardi, 157). Sometimes the best revision comes not from tinkering but from starting over, making a new cut through the material from an entirely different point of view. We can only conjecture, but suppose on that early morning, standing in the sun, after one of the shortest nights of the year, Frost remembered its opposite. Derry became his starting point and that moment "between a forest and a lake" on a night still poignant to him. His lengthy, detailed, often tongue-in-cheek discussion of New Hampshire gives way to a moment that could stand as the emblem for it all. Such a background would add to the reasons why Frost once remarked "that 'Stopping by Woods on a Snowy Evening' was the kind of poem he'd like to print on one page, to be followed with 'forty pages of footnotes.'"[11] And that, with a touch of irony, brings us around again to Eliot.

* * *

If recent criticism has taught us anything, it is that no writer's explanation is to be trusted, and readers have their own claims in these matters. But in that respect, too, Frost anticipated us. Frost never closes off our own restless

and doomed way of seeking meanings in what he wrote. That night in May
1961 when he invited the audience I was part of to share his joke about his
final line, he teased but did not repudiate our will to make a riddle of it.
"I'll take credit for anything you find," he said while walking off the stage.

It is an admonition I have long heard echoing. In a way it is silly to
think of Frost devising this poem as an "answer" to Eliot. Eliot publishes *The
Waste Land* the year before. Frost reads it, frets, and devises a reply. Our better
poems don't usually get written and published quite that quickly or with such
singular motives. But whether or not Frost had Eliot in mind, his lines evoke
a pattern of thinking from which we can construct such a reading. Writing
much more quietly than Eliot, with exquisite subtlety, and with numerous
echoes, Frost offers a most ambiguous poem. Is this a Christmas card or a
more serious scene of threat? Is his speaker only a short distance from the
barn, or must he endure longer, colder travel? Could "Stopping by Woods" be
a negative Twenty-third Psalm? Ideas such as these may not be necessary to
our reading, but as they come to us, they are not easily displaced. And I for
one would like to think they lean toward an interpretation for which Frost
would have been pleased "to take credit."

Notes

1. Christopher Smart, *Selected Poems*, ed. Karina Williamson and Marcus
Walsh (London: Penguin Books, 1990), 76.

2. Pollock, "Dante and Frost's 'Stopping by Woods,'" *Notes on Contemporary
Literature* 9 (March 1979): 5; Monteiro, *Robert Frost and the New England Renaissance* (Lexington: University Press of Kentucky, 1988), 50–52.

3. *The Top 500 Poems*, ed. William Harmon (New York: Columbia University
Press, 1992) in headnotes to the respective poems.

4. *Selected Essays* (New York: Harcourt, Brace and World, 1964), 3–11.

5. "Robert Frost: The Way to the Poem" in *Dialogue with an Audience*, ed.
John Ciardi (New York: J. B. Lippincott Company, 1963), 147–68.

6. "Robert Frost's Favorite Poem" in *Tharpe III*, 174–76; Lesley Frost's
"Note," 177.

7. "Two Essays on Robert Frost," *Poetry and the Age* (New York: Vintage
Books, 1955), 39.

8. *Early Years* and *Triumph*. See *Triumph*, 236–37 and the extended notes,
Early Years, 595ff. and *Triumph*, 596ff.

9. Charles W. Cooper and John Holmes, *Prefaces to Poetry* (New York: Harcourt, Brace, 1943), 604.

10. Oster, 151–52.

11. Reginald L. Cook, "Frost's Asides in His Poetry," in *On Frost: The Best
from American Literature*, ed. Edwin H. Cady and Louis J. Budd (Durham: Duke
University Press, 1991), 34.

RICHARD J. CALHOUN

"By Pretending They Are Not Sonnets": The Sonnets of Robert Frost at the Millennium

Robert Frost would have been pleased to know that he would be discussed in retrospect at the millennium. He let his audience know that he liked to envision himself taking part in such momentous occasions. I have a strong memory of Frost playing cryptically with the idea of witnessing the millennium. He was speaking at Chapel Hill in 1957, and after reading "It Is Almost the Year Two Thousand," he said, "You know some of us are looking forward to it." Some members of the audience laughed, and he responded, "You don't laugh. I thought you had laughed at me for saying that." Then he added softly, "I was about to weep."[1]

At the century's end I also remember all too well Robert Frost's unsettled reputation with critics back at midcentury. I was at the Kenyon School of English in the summer of 1949, learning how to read modernist poetry in the light of the formalism of the New Criticism. The status of Robert Frost came up at a breakfast discussion being dominated by one of his "enemies," Yvor Winters, known for categorizing Frost just the year before as an Emersonian "spiritual drifter."[2] On Winters's neohumanist ethical scale, this placed Frost about as low as one could register. Frost's friend among these critics, John Crowe Ransom, was not present. I was the only one foolish enough to risk defending Frost by suggesting that a formalist reading would disclose complexities masked by apparent simplicity. To the New Critic sophisticates, I

From *Roads Not Taken: Rereading Robert Frost*, edited by Earl J. Wilcox and Jonathan N. Barron, pp. 217–35. Copyright © 2000 by the Curators of the University of Missouri.

might as well have been advocating Carl Sandburg, with whom Frost was equated, but I remained convinced of the applicability of New Critical techniques to Frost's poetry. I was only vaguely aware in 1949 that Frost wrote sonnets, and so I was unable to use this achievement to give him status. The only consolation I had then was the consensus recognition that Frost was better than Edgar Guest.

Any witness to what Robert Lowell, in his sonnet on Frost, called the "great act" of "saying" his poems might have suspected that his difficulty with the modernist establishment did not come only from his uncommon popularity as a stringently American poet. Frost could not resist dispensing to audiences occasional witty verbal barbs in what was almost a public quarrel with T. S. Eliot. There were reasonable suspicions that the sonnet "The Broken Drought" was aimed at Eliot in response to a lecture by the chief modernist before fourteen thousand people in Minneapolis. Eliot had, in his own quintessential style, expressed his opinion of Frost publicly as early as 1922: "His verse, it is regretfully said, is uninteresting, and what is uninteresting is unreadable, and what is unreadable is not read. There, that is done."[3] Fortunately, it was not done, and the relationship between the two poets improved. But Frost appeared to be Eliot's direct opposite—American and traditional, a poet whose poetry was personal, not impersonal. Honors came, even Pulitzer Prizes, but Frost remained sensitive to a reputational discrepancy between popular adulation and a critical cold shoulder from much of the establishment intelligentsia. Frost at Harvard came to know his enemy simply as the "Pound, Eliot, Richards gang."[4]

Half a century later, I am confident Robert Frost would be pleased with his standing among critics at the millennium. Frost criticism has come far in promoting what has been designated the "rehabilitation" of Robert Frost. The traditional term would be "apologizing," a cause obligatory for all the faithful in the prolonged aftermath of Lawrance Thompson's biography. My regard in this process is for an appreciation of what has yet to be sufficiently appreciated: Frost's sonnets. Frost rightfully belongs in the company of poets who have managed to write highly acclaimed poems in this deceptively demanding form. I am also concerned with a minor puzzle. Frost is known as a traditionalist in poetry who sought form and could not abide free verse, and yet he wrote some perplexingly irregular sonnets.

An assessment of Frost's approaches to the sonnet that confirms his technical expertise may be the most tangible contribution left for any further appraisal. William Pritchard, Stanley Burnshaw, Jay Parini, and even Jeffrey Meyers have apparently managed to exorcise the "monster of egoism" that Lawrance Thompson's demythologizing of the myth of Frost as a New England shaman farmer had fabricated.[5] The discrepancy between Frost's positive popular reputation and his negative reception by establishment critics has been narrowed. By the end of the 1980s Jay Parini could announce the good news in a new literary history that "book-length studies" had "permanently settled the question of whether or not Frost was a major poet in the sense that we apply the term to say Eliot, or W. B. Yeats."[6] All owed a debt to their predecessor Randall Jarrell, who appreciated Frost from the perspective of a poet as well as that of a critic. Surprisingly, Jarrell did not, in his assessment of the "other Frost," include Frost's accomplishments with the sonnet. Nor did Parini.

Even overdue recognition as a major poet did not necessarily mean that Frost would also be by the millennium universally acknowledged as either a serious thinker or a poet of exceptional skill and creativity. Mark Twain faced much the same ordeal in finding respect for his thought and his craft. Popular writers with sometimes unpopular politics, either too liberal or too conservative, are among the usual suspects for lack of depth. At the 1997 Winthrop University International Frost Conference, a position paper for a panel on biography professed that substantiating Frost's intellectual and artistic powers was the next responsibility for Frost scholars. Some understanding of Frost's craftsmanship has come out of work by Rueben Brower, Richard Poirier, and William Pritchard, and later by Frank Lentricchia, Judith Oster, and Mark Richardson. Homage was paid by three Nobel Prize winners—Seamus Heaney, Joseph Brodsky, and Derek Walcott—to one of the most conspicuous nonwinners.[7] Still Frost at the millennium is probably better recognized as a thinker, which he prudently never claimed to be, than he is as craftsman, which he always proclaimed himself to be. Mark Richardson's significant study *The Ordeal of Robert Frost* convincingly describes a Frost who was much more aware of significant issues for the poet in his time than had been suspected.[8] My caveat is that we must be careful, as Richardson is, to know Frost, first of all, as a poet dedicated to understanding his craft. A careful reading of what Frost thought on and did with the sonnet should suggest a substantial knowledge of that form and a serious interest in poetics that contributed to a remarkable craftsmanship.

There is interest in Frost's poetics, but there are few formal essays, no philosophical treatises, and we never got the book of prose that he joked about writing. We know that he rejected the late Victorian view that music was the essential element in poetry and turned instead to the realism evoked by the spoken voice. Equally well known are his definition of a poem, "it begins in delight and ends in wisdom," and his contention that the wisdom might provide temporary stability—"a momentary stay against confusion." "The background in hugeness and confusion shading away from where we stand into black and utter chaos; and against the background any small man-made figure of order and concentration. What pleasanter than that this should be so?"[9] Frost valued any amount, however small, of control that form and structure could bring to a poem, or to a life for that matter. He was fond of saying about form, "it'll have to do for now" and then, "you'll have to get another one." Form was as necessary for the poet to write as the net was for the tennis player to play his game. I heard Frost use what he called "another analogy": the game of hop, skip, and jump. The "hop" and "skip" provided the form that was necessary for the ultimate value, the creative "jump." It is not surprising that the prescribed forms and conciseness of the sonnet were a challenge to conform and to resist. The sonnet is also, as Helen Vendler has demonstrated in her splendid new study of Shakespeare's sonnets, the most "voiceable" of poetic forms.[10] Poetic voice was a specialty in which Frost excelled.

Frost's prose commentary, especially that taken from tapes of his readings, has only recently been read as useful observation on his own and other poetry. We are becoming more aware, as the inclusion of prose in the Library of America edition evidences, that many of these comments contribute to an understanding of his own ideas about poetry. "The Constant Symbol" is one of Frost's best-known published comments. But it has not been read for its insights into the difficulties a poet may have with the sonnet form, especially in fitting what he wants to say into the anticipated fourteen lines. In Frost's view the sonneteer is never entirely a free agent; on the contrary, he may even be deprived of the "say of how long his piece will be, whether he will outlast or last out the fourteen lines." He can even "appear to finish in 12 lines and not know what to do with the last two." The sonnet raises a matter of concern about irregularities, just how much control a poet has over the writing of his poem once he has begun.

What is most pertinent to the sometimes irregular structure of Frost's sonnets is the tension between a need for form and the corresponding need for a freedom from form. Mark Richardson sees as central in Frost's "poetry, poetics, and vocation" the need to balance "the tendency towards conformity on the one hand and towards extravagance and difference on the other." In "The Figure a Poem Makes" there is a cryptic discussion of the "wildness" that Frost, no doubt influenced by William James, found in himself and realized the need for in his poetry. He believed that wildness was necessary to balance form, just as he knew the irregular rhythm of the spoken word had to break across the regular beat of the meter. For emphasis, perhaps because readers had failed to see it, Frost even exaggerates the importance of wildness: "If it is a wild tune, it is a poem."[11] No poetic form was more adaptable to this kind of tension or dualistic balance than the sonnet. It is long enough for meditation, too short for much narrative, and a challenge through its concise prescribed forms to the poet's formal skills. It has tradition behind it.

It also permitted Frost a choice of two time-tested versions, Petrarchan, or Italian, and Shakespearean, or English. Each of these has variant forms and offers an opportunity to contest with some of the greatest poets in Western civilization. Frost preferred the Shakespearean sonnet but risked writing the Petrarchan, which most critics regard as the more difficult form. When Frost needed form to balance wildness, he provided it often by the insertion of rhyme to make a couplet. When he needed even more wildness, he could, as he liked to say, "cut loose," especially from the expected rhyme scheme or by moving toward a freer "speech sound" similar to the blank verse he used so effectively in longer narrative. On occasion this was simply a matter of going with the syntax of things—on to the end of the sentence.

As for influence, Frost admired Wordsworth's sonnets and surely shared with him the views in "Scorn Not the Sonnet."

> Scorn not the Sonnet; Critic, you have frowned,
> Mindless of its just honors; with this key
> Shakespeare unlocked his heart. . . .

Wordsworth's sonnets are sometimes regarded as "loose sonnets," an indication that Wordsworth had his own "wildness." The traditional sonnet did provide a structural skeleton and served as a formalizing device. But Wordsworth, like other major poets, did not adhere strictly to all the prescriptions of the Italian sonnet. Most obvious, his diction was less formal, and his major breaks may occur within lines.

The standing of Frost's sonnets at near millennium echoes the question raised by Wordsworth of "just honors." Unjustly, no major critic has persuasively verified that Robert Frost wrote a significant number of the best sonnets in English in the twentieth century. He is rarely mentioned in accounts of the twentieth-century sonnet, unlike his contemporary Edwin Arlington Robinson. In fact, Frost's sonnets are his least-known success, as attested to by how few of them have been explicated in any detail. Critical articles have been infrequent and not comprehensive enough to do justice to either the quantity or the quality of Frost's sonnets. The only book-length study, H. A. Maxson's *On the Sonnets of Robert Frost: A Critical Examination*, is more valuable for the explication of individual poems than it is as a definitive study of Frost's theory and practice of sonnet making.[12] Maxson does recognize that the troubling factor in assessing Frost as a sonneteer has been that he created irregular variants. Consequently, his sonnets have been undervalued as near sonnets and even judged as "failed" sonnets. Instead of perfecting a trademark sonnet of his own, Frost seems to have regarded writing sonnets as an opportunity to experiment with familiar prescribed forms. He recognized that the sonnet structures, as their history discloses, could either provide the structural pattern *within* which the poet might write or present a framework *against* which the poet could work. Frost could write within the pattern, but he also was attracted to writing against the pattern. The quotation most apropos surfaces in a letter to Louis Untermeyer: "The sonnet is the strictest form I have behaved in, and that mainly by pretending it wasn't a sonnet."[13]

Prior to Maxson's book the most valuable study was Oliver H. Evans's article "'Deeds that Count': Robert Frost's Sonnets."[14] Evans understood that the irregular sonnets are products of Frost's serious play with restrictive, prescribed forms. The deeds that count are the "liberties taken with the conventions." Critics have tended to judge Frost's sonnets rather strictly in comparison with the best of conventional sonnets. Even Frost enthusiasts have, on occasion, doubted Frost for not conforming to certain expected modes and not competing directly with the best work in regular sonnet forms. What was overlooked was what Frost seemed well aware of—the flexibility of the sonnet form as evidenced by the practice of the great sonnet-makers in producing numerous variants of the original Petrarchan form. Evans makes the valid and important claim for a grand occasion like the millennium: "Frost wrote some of the greatest sonnets in American poetry." An appropriate reply to Eliot and other doubters would be: "There, it has been done."

Critics have long noticed Frost's obsession with form to counter chaos. Frost never made a more germane statement about his life in art than in "To the *Amherst Student*": "When in doubt there is always form to go on with."[15] And one might add: the greater the doubt, the more intense the fear, the greater the need for more form. The maximum seven rhymes in "Once by the Pacific" would be appropriate for a poem Frost always made clear was based on terrifying experiences of his youth. An essay by Karen Rood on Frost's Italian sonnets deserves attention because she focuses on his need both for form and variants like his characteristic three to seven rhymes, rather than the usual four or five.[16] She prefers the norm, neither too much nor too little form, but she admits that some of Frost's most powerful poems are those in which the "confusion" is so strong as to require maximum form to maintain "a momentary stay." She notes that where regularity is expected Frost often introduces a new rhyme, makes a couplet, or (her major interest) allows sentence sounds and syntax to intrude on regular meter. She also links Frost's variations to his dualistic belief in an opposition between form that renders meaning and the wildness that mirrors the confusion of his world. Her study is the kind we need to explain the irregularities but limited too much to the effect of sentence sounds.

Aware of his reputation as a poet who scorned free verse and most tenets of modernism, Frost, on occasion, felt challenged to declare his own identity, unorthodoxy, even audacity, as a serious modern poet. Early in his career he wrote to his friend John Bartlett of his discovery of the "sound of sense": "I am one of the great craftsmen of my time."[17] The importance of "the sound of sense" crashing across regular meter to Frost's poetry is now pretty well understood. But the intricacies of the struggle with both form and wildness have not been adequately explored, even by the few critics who have discussed his sonnets. Elaine Barry's succinct account of the sonnet tells only half the story: Frost's search for form rather than his need for both form and wildness.[18] We know that Frost never intended a sonnet sequence, but he did a better thing. He produced, as one of the great craftsmen of his time, a body of sonnets remarkably diverse in subject and complex in form—not modernist but certainly modern.

Helen Vendler reminds us that the usual conception of the sonnet is simpler than the diversity a history of all its variations reveals. Actual practice specifies that a sonnet is a poem "usually" in iambic pentameter and "most often" fourteen lines long. The reality is even that there have been sixteen-line sonnets (George Meredith wrote them), seventeen-line sonnets (especially in Renaissance France), and sonnets in tetrameter. Of the two principal kinds of sonnets, Frost preferred the Shakespearean but risked the more difficult Petrarchan. He also liked to use elements of both in the same poem. The Italian is normally a two-part poem, usually with an eight-six division, rhyming originally abba abba cde cde; and the English sonnet, a four-part poem, with three quatrains and a couplet, rhyming abab cdcd efef gg. Variants were quickly developed, beginning with cdc, dcd for the Italian. Frost's favorite variant was to insert a couplet or two. The Italian sonnet usually poses a question or problem in the octave and provides an answer or resolution in the sestet. Frost may ask a question that has no satisfactory answer or suggest a problem but supply no resolution. The English sonnet may follow this pattern or utilize either repetitions or variations of the question and answer form. The Italian sonnet usually has a rhetorical turn in thought in line nine, at the beginning of the sestet. The Shakespearean sonnet usually has its turn at line thirteen, the beginning of the couplet. But there is sometimes a turn at line nine, following the Italian version. Frost also varies his turn based on whether he wants balance or imbalance between the parts. Vendler adds as structural elements the key word and the "couplet tie," which is simply the key word reappearing in the final couplet. The repetition of the word "water" in "Once by the Pacific" would be a striking example by Frost, as would the recurrence of some form of "whisper" in "Mowing." If the Petrarchan sonnet features a problem-and-solution schematic, it may also be put out of balance with a twelve-two division characteristic of the Shakespearean sonnet. Another variation, often overlooked, is in what some critics call the Spenserian sonnet, which links each quatrain to the next by a continuing rhyme: abab bcbc cdcd ee. Frost's skillful "Putting in the Seed" has this sestet form. What is important to record is that Frost employs most of these variations and adds some of his own, including letting natural speech alter meter.

The number of sonnets Frost wrote is sufficiently impressive to command attention if we accept Maxson's count of thirty-seven and add, as I would, "Mowing" and "Hyla Brook." Frost's practice was to write several sonnets, take leave from the form for a few years, and then return with three or more additional sonnets. Since there are questions as to which poems are actually sonnets, I shall list my thirty-nine. Frost began with four in *A Boy's Will* (1913), "Into My Own," "A Dream Pang," "The Vantage Point" and the "virtual" sonnet "Mowing"; five in *Mountain Interval* (1916), "Meeting and Passing," "The Oven Bird," "Putting in the Seed," "Range-Finding," "Hyla Brook"; six in *West-Running Brook* (1928), "Acceptance," "Once by the Pacific," "The Flood," "Acquainted with the Night," "A Soldier," "The Investment"; four in *A Further Range* (1936), "The Master Speed," "Design," "On A Bird Singing in its Sleep," "Unharvested"; three in *A Witness Tree* (1942), "The Silken Tent," "Never Again Would Birds' Song Be the Same," "Time Out"; seven in *Steeple Bush* (1947), "Etherealizing," "Why Wait for Science," "Any Size We Please," "The Planners," "No Holy Wars for Them," "Bursting Rapture," "The Broken Drought"; nine in the Library of America edition (1995), "Despair," "When the Speed Comes," "The Mill City," "Pursuit of the Word," "The Rain Bath," "On Talk of Peace at This Time," "The Pans," "Trouble Rhyming," "A Bed in the Barn." These sonnets were previously uncollected and unpublished prior to the Library of America Edition. I find only "The Mill City" interesting. There were no sonnets in *North of Boston* (1914) and only one, "On a Tree Fallen across the Road," in *New Hampshire* (1926). Frost's sojourn in England did not promote the writing of sonnets. The Georgians there did not share the Victorian taste for Italian sonnets as a part of their interest in things Italian. *Palgrave's Golden Treasury* was a better resource for Frost.

The diversity of these sonnets, their range in subject and theme, has never received the notice merited. There are several conventional lyric sonnets, including the traditional compliments to a woman, beautifully formulated in "The Silken Tent" and "Never Again Would Birds' Song Be the Same." I find in the latter sonnet a line that, taken in the context of the poem, is one of his most graceful: "And to do that to birds was why she came." At the other extreme, Frost used the sonnet form for humorous and satirical play on the concept of progress, as in "Why Wait for Science" and "Etherealizing," both crowd-pleasers at his readings and marvelously suited to his voice. Then there are traditional nature sonnets, like the extraordinary "The Oven Bird";

Emersonian poems, like "Hyla Brook," with man on the natural scene, finding there truth, even if only modest or ambiguous truth; and celebrations of work performed in nature, in poems like "Mowing." Significantly, there are also Frost's great dark sonnets: "Once by the Pacific," "Acquainted with the Night," and "Design," which Lionel Trilling, in a consequential half-truth, called one of Frost's "terrifying" poems.

There is diversity in type of sonnet. Karen Rood finds twelve Italian sonnets among the collected poems. These include the most often explicated, "Design"; the most orthodox, "Why Wait for Science," and two of the most underrated, "The Vantage Point" and "Range-Finding." Others are "The Flood," "A Soldier," "The Investment," "A Dream Pang," "Meeting and Passing," "Any Size We Please," "The Broken Drought," and "Bursting Rapture." Three could be added from the uncollected poems, "Pursuit of the Word," "The Rain Bath," and "Trouble Rhyming." I find seventeen to be basically Shakespearean. Among these are his first sonnet, "Into My Own," "Putting in the Seed," "On a Tree Fallen across the Road," "Acceptance," "Once by the Pacific," "Acquainted with the Night," "The Master Speed," "On a Bird Singing in Its Sleep," "The Silken Tent," "Never Again Would Birds' Song Be the Same," "Time Out," "Etherealizing," "Any Size We Please," "No Holy Wars for Them," "On Talk of Peace at This Time." Among those formerly uncollected are "The Mill City," and "Pursuit of the Word." There is striking variety. Three of Frost's Shakespearean sonnets are formed from seven rhymed couplets, while one, "The Planners," actually employs four rhymed triplets, followed by a couplet in only near rhyme. There are borderline cases of poems with elements of both the Italian and the Shakespearean sonnet forms; these could be classified, following Evans, as "compromise sonnets."

In passing judgment on the quality of Frost's sonnets, I would borrow a metaphor (as Frost would urge) of Randall Jarrell's that suggests judging the greatness of a poet by the number of times he was "struck by lightning" in the creative process.[19] In my judgment, lightning energized the poet at least seven times and came close three or four more. My choices for the best of the group would include "Mowing," "The Oven Bird," "Once by the Pacific," "Acquainted with the Night," "Design," "The Silken Tent," and "Never Again Would Birds' Song Be the Same." I would list as near strikes the sonnets "The Vantage Point," "Range-Finding," and the much underrated "Putting in the Seed" and "A Soldier." Jarrell required a dozen or more poems for poetic greatness. I believe Frost nearly attains that status on the merits of his sonnets alone. These best sonnets are mostly poems that critics have admired but explicated as dramatic lyrics rather than as sonnets. Space limits my own comments on reading them as sonnets.

Frost's first sonnet, "Into My Own," was, according to him, written in 1901 though not published until May 1909 in the *New England Magazine* and republished in *A Boy's Will* as the initial poem. It was displaced in the *Collected Poems* by "The Pasture," which would introduce Frost's New England version of pastoral verse. The earlier poem, however, is important because it provides an introduction to the Frostian voice. It is also mildly experimental, as Maxson notes, the first of "experiments calculated to discover just how far the poet could stray, and the form could flex to accommodate." As Frost strays from the norm in the sonnet form, there is a parallel desire for the speaker to stray from civilization. He would wish that "those dark trees . . . stretched away unto the edge of doom" in case he should one day actually venture into that unknown. He would not expect to return but would rather invite those "who would miss me here" to follow and join him, finding him altered only by an increase in self-confidence.

The experiment is, as most often in Frost, with the rhyme scheme. The basic structure is the three quatrains and a final couplet of the Shakespearean sonnet, but this is also a Shakespearean sonnet written entirely in couplets, a form also used in three of his finest sonnets, "Once by the Pacific," "The Oven Bird," (irregularly) and "On a Bird Singing in Its Sleep." Through the use of couplets Frost retains the seven rhymes of the Shakespearean sonnet but arranges them in quatrains according to his own scheme, often determined by the thought pattern or a speech rhythm. Frost also does something else distinctive by employing "sentence sounds" against the prescribed iambic pentameter of the sonnet form. The opening line of "Into My Own" is couched in such natural speech rhythms: "One of my wishes is that those dark trees. . . ." In the Shakespearean sonnet the rhetorical turn is expected at line thirteen, initiating the final couplet, which in this poem is

> They would not find me changed from him they knew—
> Only more sure of all I thought was true.

The turn in this reading is from the speaker's wish to his certainty that he would be found "not changed" except to have become "more sure." But the turn might also occur in line nine ("I do not see why I should e'er turn back") as the speaker suggests that those he left behind follow his tracks. If the turn is at line nine, I do not see the poem as specifically declaring either his future success as a poet or his reassurance to himself and to Elinor that, should he run away in youthful despair to the Dismal Swamp again, he would emerge the better for it. The borrowing of the phrase "edge of doom" from Shakespeare's great Sonnet 116 would support this view. His bold assertion of confidence is made in a poem that requires the restraining form of a sonnet of seven couplets and possibly an ambiguity as to the rhetorical turn. While retaining the quatrain and final couplet pattern and preserving the maximum rhymes of the Shakespearean sonnet, "Into My Own," if the turn is at line nine, may have also adopted the octave-sestet structure of the Italian sonnet to compose what Evans calls a "compromise" sonnet.

Another early sonnet, "Once by the Pacific," serves as a reminder that the "momentary stay against confusion" a poem might provide was not just for the reader but also for the poet. Anyone who witnessed Frost's reading of this poem might testify that it was based on his great traumatic fear of facing an ocean storm alone, which he did as a child when he felt abandoned at the Cliff House beach. He also had a recurring fear of losing his father to the ocean on one of his long swims from this beach. "Once by the Pacific" was, consequently, one of his sonnets requiring maximum form for a fourteen-line poem, a sonnet in seven couplets. Frost increases the effect of the terror by personifying the natural forces ("The clouds were low and hairy in the skies") that threaten. Frost depersonalizes his fears by universalizing the storm's effect into a danger for everything water can threaten, even the shore itself. Frost liked to recall that the poem has been regarded as "prophetic" but actually was based on an event that happened long before the two world wars. It was most likely written during 1906 or 1907 at Derry Farm, and it is more immediately a vision of ultimate destruction than a prophecy.

In this sonnet, too, the place of rhetorical turn is ambiguous. It could occur at line twelve ("Someone had better be prepared for rage") as the poet's tone becomes admonishing, stressing the human need for preparation just as nature has provided a cliff for the ocean, which may not be sufficient. But he also restates in lines thirteen and fourteen the extent of the danger, in a final couplet that stands out from the rest of the sonnet because it alone has feminine end rhymes. The same God who said "Let there be Light" will give the command to "Put out the Light."

> There would be more than ocean water-broken
> Before God's last *Put out the Light* was spoken.

Frost does leave the rhetorical structure open to interpretation. The turn could even be in the run-on of line eight into line nine, when the speaker turns from the threatening scene to compare, in grammatically parallel clauses, the need for preparation by human kind as well as in nature.

> It looked as if a night of dark intent
> Was coming, and not only a night, an age.

A reading of an earlier poem, "The Oven Bird" (1916), reveals that the sonnet can be an effective medium through which to express major themes of Frost's poetry, in this case his acceptance of the diminished view that science (Freud, behaviorism, etc.) has left for the imagination. The oven bird, a midsummer bird, comes late to song, and it sings not from the darkest, deepest woods but from midway into the woods. Its location in time enables it both to remember the fresher spring and to sing of decline into autumn, voicing in "all but words" a major Frost theme, "what to make of a diminished thing." The story of Frost's unhappy response to Sidney Cox's assumption that the oven bird was Frost as poet is well-known vintage Frost. Frost preferred to see the poem as about endurance.

Only Maxson has analyzed the poem as a sonnet, noting its "hidden intricate rhyme" and "technical brilliance." According to him, the first two "He says" lines introduce irregularities into the poem by changing the rhyme scheme. An attempt to approximate speech toward the colloquial leads to irregularities in rhyming. I would point out that Frost's rhyme scheme in this sonnet—aa bcb dcd ee fgfg—resembles neither Shakespearean nor Petrarchan practice, except that it has the seven rhymes of the former. Playing against the structure of "He says" statements, the poet opens with a couplet and then inserts another couplet as lines nine and ten:

And comes that other fall we name the fall.
He says the highway dust is over all.

Maxson considers these to be key lines, interpreting "the fall" as the failure of technology ("highway dust"). But, since the "petal fall" of spring is mentioned earlier in the poem, the "other fall" logically would be autumn, with possible overtones of that Fall in Eden that brought death to humankind. The sonnet's rhetorical turn is also irregular, appearing between the key internal couplet and the closing quatrain, between line ten and line eleven. Closure comes, atypically, in a quatrain (fgfg) as we are told the meaning of the oven bird's song. He knows "not to sing" about midsummer but rather to ponder "what to make of a diminished thing."

Another poem that lends itself to structural analysis is "The Vantage Point." The first eight lines of this irregular Petrarchan, perhaps Wordsworthian, sonnet are emotionally detached from the scene of men's homes and their cemetery; the last six are committed, as the speaker turns around to experience sensually the natural elements surrounding him. Frost manages the transition through meter, as regularity of meter in line nine is followed in the next line by one lone trochee in the midst of iambic regularity.

And if by noon I have too much of these,
I have but to turn on my arm, and lo,
The sun-burned hillside sets my face aglow. . . .

It is as if the reader is forced to participate through an almost physical bodily turn.

If a fifteen-line sonnet can be justified by theory and logic, "Hyla Brook," in spite of Maxson's rejection, has to be a sonnet. The final two lines have both the force and terminal punctuation of joint closure. The last line is a summation of what has been said, a necessary addition for emphasis in order to make explicit what is implicit. The point that is being made in the fourteen lines of the sonnet proper is that this is not the conventional brook celebrated in poetry. To be explicit, to justify his concern, Frost adds the fifteenth line: "We love the things we love for what they are." In the additional line he justifies for himself why he has remembered this unremarkable brook. Such things may not be sufficient, traditionally, for celebration in song, but they are, as this brook is, adequately interesting to be recorded for memory.

The rhyme scheme of this poem is, on the surface, too irregular to be taken as a sonnet. It seems to begin with a Petrarchan quatrain but develops into the pattern abb acc add, coming to closure at a full stop. The middle triplet, describing the vanished "Hyla breed," is enclosed in parentheses. Then follows the couplet ee, which brings to a climax the description of the brook in summer. The couplet stands out in the poem both by the strength of its metaphor and by the slowing of pace through meter in its second line.

Its bed is left a faded paper sheet
Of dead leaves stuck together by the heat—. . . .

The final quatrain (12–15) rhymes fgfg, as the speaker sums up the value of his brook to those "who remember long." The form is complex but, arguably, functional. Maxson has trouble with placing the turn in line twelve. I see this turn leading into the explicit statement in the additional lines required for satisfactory closure. The poem is concerned with why we like ordinary things.

"Acquainted with the Night" is one of Frost's more daring and best-known experiments with sonnet form—a sonnet in terza rima. Its pessimism is highly unusual for Frost, and the form is unique. The setting is atypical, a city at night, perhaps based on Frost's residence in Ann Arbor. This poem conveys a sense of loneliness more characteristic of Edwin Arlington Robinson, a master of the sonnet in his own right, than of Frost but still within his range. Both Elaine Barry and William Pritchard devote some time to reading this poem as a sonnet in terza rima. For the standard Shakespearean three quatrains and a couplet Frost skillfully substitutes four tercets and a couplet aba bcb cdc dad aa. The internal line of the last tercet returns with "height" to the "a" rhyme of the first, creating a circular pattern but also enabling the couplet to employ an "a" rhyme in the couplet so that it can close the sonnet with a repetition of its first line, "I have been one acquainted with the night." There is metrical repetition also, as five of the seven lines beginning "I have" continue with two stressed words—"walked out," "outwalked," "looked down," "passed by," and "stood still"—before returning to iambic meter. Since line twelve runs swiftly on into the couplet, a possible turn might take place with the image of the "One luminary clock" on its "unearthly height," which appears at line eleven.

In "The Silken Tent" Frost definitively demonstrated that he could write a conventional sonnet on a traditional subject, a compliment to a lady. It may have been a compliment to two women, perhaps begun as a tribute to Elinor and, upon her death, redirected to pay homage to his private secretary, Kathleen Morrison. I would agree with Elaine Barry's judgment that the poem is worthy of comparison with the great Elizabethan love sonnets in its sheer tonal beauty. The woman is admired for her poise in the context of the speaker's stormy life. She is the tent's "supporting central cedar pole," only loosely bound by its silken guy ropes. The poem is a tribute to this woman's ability to remain responsive to others' needs while, at the same time, experiencing only "the slightest bondage" when one tie goes "slightly taut." The sonnet's form is appropriately Shakespearean in its rhyme scheme, but the final couplet is a run-on from line twelve, thus avoiding any possibility of a rhetorical turn at this point. Frost does this in a half dozen of his Shakespearean sonnets. It is also unusual that the entire poem is one sentence, the verb for its second clause, whose subject occurs in line five, not appearing until the last line.

On the other hand, in Frost's other great poetic compliment, "Never Again Would Birds' Song Be the Same," the turn at the couplet seems obvious in its definitive restatement of the sonnet's title. Maxson finds ambiguity in two possible readings, dependent on whether we find an octave and sestet, as in the Petrarchan structure, or three quatrains and a couplet, as in the Shakespearean. Whether or not the man and woman of this poem refer to someone in particular, it is "the daylong voice of Eve" that has added a "tone of meaning" to birdsong. Woman has significantly enhanced the Garden. We have, in this perfectly regular Shakespearean sonnet, Frost's lyric voice at its best.

"Design" is Frost's most explicated sonnet, more often read as a dramatic lyric than as a sonnet. It is one of those dark sonnets singled out by Lionel Trilling and a model of how Frost's apparent simplicity may be deceptive.

Many readers have remarked upon how the poem begins with nursery-rhyme simplicity and moves upward to Miltonic questioning of responsibility for evil. The tone of the poem changes in line three with the first hint of death in the word *rigid*, suggesting rigor mortis. There is then a gradual build up within the octave from "death and blight," to "witches' broth" and "dead wings." The scene of spider, heal-all, and moth now set up, three questions are posed about the meaning of this coincidence of whiteness. "Steered" becomes a key word here, suggesting a directive from some outside force. There are two conclusions. The first is terrifying: "What but design of darkness to appall?" But the second is deconstructive of the entire argument: "If design govern in a thing so small." We have within the explicit form of a sonnet an implied epic theological debate.

Only three different end rhymes—the minimum—are utilized in this sonnet. There are two Petrarchan quatrains in the octave and a variant rhyme pattern in the sestet: abba abba ac aa cc. The return to an "a" rhyme in line nine, with "white" echoing the end of line one, while "heal-all" at the end of line ten anticipates "appall" and "small" in the concluding couplet. The question and response of the remaining four lines in the sestet are composed as two couplets, allowing a secondary rhetorical turn at the beginning of the final couplet, when the third question implies its own answer. The three dashes in the poem require pauses that possibly add suspense. Although "Design" has the eight-six division of the Italian sonnet, it is with a marked difference. Questioning comes not in the octave but in the sestet, coinciding with the rhetorical turn.

"Putting in the Seed," considered by Maxson to be a masterpiece, is a sonnet in which the boundaries between narrative and the lyric are obscured. This poem is solidly Frostian, an activity poem spoken by a husband to his wife. The speaker wonders whether he can quit work when his wife calls him for supper and then seems to invite her to share his "springtime passion for the earth." A dramatic shift develops through the course of the sonnet. Beginning in natural speech rhythms, with two contractions and the colloquial "fetch me" and "leave off," the lines slow metrically to describe the work of planting seeds that are intermixed with petals of fallen apple blossoms.

> (Soft petals, yes, but not so barren quite,
> Mingled with these, smooth bean and wrinkled pea). . . .

Then, cued by language in line nine, specifically, "Slave" and "passion," the concluding sentence surges both emotionally and metrically from "How Love burns" to the birth of a seedling, whose "arched body comes / Shouldering its way and shedding the earth crumbs." The poet inserts sexual

overtones into his work as a seed planter by personifying the emerging
sprout. The rhyme scheme is, basically, Shakespearean (abab abab cdcd ee),
made with five instead of seven rhymes because the second quatrain repeats
the rhymes of the first. As for a rhetorical turn, although it seems to occur
at line nine as in the Petrarchan sonnet, syntactically that line belongs with
the preceding quatrain.

Finally, there is the question of "Mowing." Maxson rejects the poem as
a sonnet, not only because it is irregular in rhyme scheme and meter, but also
because he cannot discern a pattern or find an acceptable rhetorical turn. I
cannot regard this poem as having failed in any way. I prefer to retain it as a
sonnet in as much as many readers have accepted it as such and because it is
one of Frost's finest lyrics. It is a product of the Derry Farm days, when Frost
was writing his first sonnets. It is also helpful to know that Frost regarded
"Mowing" as a talk song, his first. This perhaps helps explain its irregularities.
There are more three-syllable feet than usual, functionally interrupting the
traditional iambic flow. Moreover, the poem certainly possesses a key word,
one of Helen Vendler's signs of the sonnet form. "My long scythe whispered"
in line fourteen echoes "My long scythe whispering" in line two, while "whispered" reappears in lines three and six.

Perhaps a pattern can be extracted from the poem's rhyme scheme (abc
abd ec dfeg fg) by coordinating it with its rhetorical and syntactical structure.
The first three lines, ending in a semicolon, set up the question of what the
scythe may be whispering. The next three lines, beginning "Perhaps it was
something about the heat of the sun" and ending with a full stop, suggest a
possible answer. The next two lines (rhymes "e" and "c") tell what the scythe
does not suggest, a dream of leisure or hoard of fairy gold. Then, at what must
be regarded as a rhetorical turn, at line nine as in the Petrarchan sonnet, we
are told, in an unrhymed quatrain that

> Anything more than the truth would have seemed too weak
> To the earnest love that laid the swale in rows. . . .

Resolution appears in line thirteen in an unrhymed couplet closure, in what
Frost once claimed could be a definition of poetry: "The fact is the sweetest
dream that labor knows." Some ambiguity remains as to whether the fact
is work itself or the hay left "to make" is the product of the mower's work.

It should not be overlooked that Frost could write humorous or satirical
sonnets. I mentioned "Etherealizing" and "Why Wait for Science" as good
specimens that allowed Frost full use of his voice for emphasis and for a bit of
wildness. Both poems ridicule abstracting, theorizing, faith-in-progress in an
age of technology. Frost's idea is similar to Eliot's stress on a Cartesian split

between thought and feeling; his ridicule is of the idea that we could become all mind in "Etherealizing," or of the idea that we need to wait for science when we already have common sense as a guide.

As I try to comprehend Frost at the millennium my thoughts go back to 1959. It was a time when there was excitement about Robert Lowell, a long-time admirer of Frost, and his book *Life Studies*, the beginnings of confessional poetry. As Robert Frost was thumbing through his poems for one more selection, he looked up from his text at the audience and said in the most confidential of tones, "There's all sorts of things in here." I would say the same of his sonnets. There is more than one can cover short of a book. It is evident that, not being fully happy in harness with all the prescribed forms, Frost wrote both within and against the required patterns. Perhaps he liked the conciseness, even being forced to be concise himself, and took special delight in the ambiguities that the brevity helped create. Some demands, especially in the rhyme scheme, he did not meet but departed from, with a special delight in adding couplets. He stayed pretty close to the prescribed fourteen lines, but "Hyla Brook" shows that in a good poem an extra line may be added to finish a thought, a sentence, or a rhyme. This is even more justifiable if the extra line accomplishes all three purposes. Evans finds a few sixteen-line sonnets. I do not. The theory would be that the thought outlasts the poem, requiring a quatrain instead of a final couplet. Frost's sonnets, successful with their variances, provide ample evidence that in Frost we had one of the greatest craftsmen of his time. With that done no further apology is needed, perhaps only a reminder of the importance of play to Frost. There is one role that American writers, Emily Dickinson and Mark Twain among them, played in going against convention. When he got to certain poems Frost couldn't resist playing it, especially when reading to mostly student audiences. Perhaps there is also a slightly devilish play in pretending the sonnets were not sonnets while knowing that his audience would not know anyway.[20] Framing his remarks in a political context that could correspond to his literary role, Frost warned,

> See you're going to use some analogy that leads up to something. Someone says, "You aren't much of a New Dealer, are you?" Well, I'm a Democrat. . . . I am not New Deal. I'm *auld diel*. You don't know what that means, do you? *D I E L*. [So spelled by Frost and then so softly said it was not transcribed] *old devil*.

NOTES

1. Richard J. Calhoun, ed., "Frost in the Carolinas," *South Carolina Review* 7 (November 1974): 10–11. This is the transcript of a talk I recorded in 1957 and published with permission of the Frost estate.

2. Yvor Winters, "Robert Frost, or the Spiritual Drifter as Poet," *Sewanee Review* 56 (1948): 64–96.

3. T. S. Eliot, "London Letter," *Dial* 72 (May 1922): 513.

4. There is a good discussion in Pritchard, 201–2.

5. Stanley Burnshaw, *Robert Frost Himself* (New York: George Braziller, 1986) is personal testimony; there is Jay Parini's biography *Robert Frost: A Life* (New York: Holt, 1999); Meyers is factual but controversial among Frost scholars.

6. "Robert Frost," *Columbia Literary History of the United States* (New York: Columbia University Press, 1988), 937–46.

7. Reuben Brower, *The Poetry of Robert Frost: Constellations of Intention* (New York: Oxford University Press, 1963); and Poirier remain two of the best overall studies with good readings of poems. *Homage* provides a fascinating shock of recognition of the craft of Frost by three of his peers.

8. Richardson.

9. "Letter to *The Amherst Student*," in *Prose*, 107.

10. Helen Vendler, *The Art of Shakespeare's Sonnets* (New York: Belknap Press of Harvard University Press, 1997), 17–21.

11. *Prose*, 18.

12. H. A. Maxson, *The Sonnets of Robert Frost: A Critical Examination* (Jefferson, N.C.: McFarland, 1998).

13. Untermeyer, 381.

14. Oliver H. Evans, "'Deeds That Count': Robert Frost's Sonnets," *Texas Studies in Literature and Language* 23 (spring 1981): 123–37.

15. *Prose*, 106.

16. Karen Rood, "Wildness Opposing 'Sentence Sounds': Robert Frost's Sonnets," *Tharpe II*, 196–210.

17. *Letters*, 79.

18. Elaine Barry, *Robert Frost* (New York: Ungar Publishing Co., 1973).

19. Randall Jarrell, *Poetry and the Age* (New York: Vintage Books, Inc., 1959), 134.

20. "Frost in the Carolinas," 11.

JOHN H. TIMMERMAN

Rationalist Ethics

While Santayana may have furnished Frost something of a modernist matrix that shaped his early poetic beliefs, the challenges Santayana held forth implicitly called into question ethical issues of the previous century. The two enthroned guides of Rationalism and Romanticism seemed to have collapsed in moral authority and normative values. It may be argued, although it requires the support of his later writings, that Santayana's aesthetics signaled an effort to extricate the artist from the crumbling debris of those twin towers and to harbor the artist once again in the security of classicism. To a large degree also, Robert Frost shared that longing.

By the turn of the century Rationalism had annealed into a rigid codification of ethical proprieties. Once valuing social well-being in its multiple ethical expressions, rationalist ethics at the end of the nineteenth century seemed to many little more than a book of etiquette that carried no liberating power for society. Romanticism, on the other hand, had expired on its own bed of ashes, consumed by its inward fires of the imagination. Once valuing the intuited initiative of the individual to rise above the strictures of any social contract and to make wise and just actions based upon individual experience, Romanticism vaporized into a fleecy world of incongruent emotions.

If the longing of both Santayana and Frost was for discovery of ethical values through the power of art, it was also for an extrication from worn

From *Robert Frost: The Ethics of Ambiguity*, pp. 62–92, 178–80. Published by Bucknell University Press. Copyright © 2002 by Rosemont Publishing and Printing.

111

ethical guides and for the formulation of new ones. Necessarily, however, the process of extrication had to come first. Part of that process for Frost may be seen in his own positioning in the American and European literary and philosophical traditions at the close of the nineteenth century.

Rationalist Ethics in Historical Context

Although seventeenth-century American literature consisted largely of letters, diaries, and journals intended for the Old World, it was during the eighteenth century, as the young nation fought to free itself from the old, that its literature fell most heavily under the sway of European Enlightenment. That is not surprising. A government had to be founded, a constitution written, people persuaded to a just cause, a war had to be fought. Consequently, the orators and literary spokespersons of the time dredged their heritage of European Enlightenment for all they could.

While those Enlightenment thinkers, and their American counterparts such as Paine and Franklin, assumed certain apodictic values, these values were held in trust by the thinkers themselves. The select few, not unlike Huxley's world leaders in *Brave New World*, had the task of imparting to the common classes which values were ethically acceptable. Not that they expected the commoners to follow necessarily, but they erected their own pedestal of perfectibility anyway and spoke to the masses from it. Since the time of Aristotle, that has been the general task of the rationalist ethics. The philosophical elite analyzes what is truly beautiful and just, discriminating according to logical analysis, and then modeling and positing their conclusions for society to live by. Thereby, reason supersedes any emotional or fanciful qualities of the mind, a point made clear by Samuel Johnson in a letter to Boswell dated approximately 15 March 1774: "Fancy is always to act in subordination to Reason. We may take fancy as a companion, but must follow reason as our guide. We may allow fancy to suggest certain ideas in certain places; but Reason must always be heard, when she tells us, that those ideas and those places have no natural or necessary relation."[1]

The American Enlightenment, although often riddled with egocentric excess, shared the same fervid reliance upon reason to lead one aright. We might be amused today reading in Franklin's *Autobiography* (1771) these words, "It was about this time I conceived the bold and arduous project of arriving at moral perfection. I wished to live without committing any fault at any time. . . . As I knew, or thought I knew, what was right and wrong, I did not see why I might not always do the one and avoid the other."[2] We look askance at such an ethics as an eccentric wishfulness, until we realize that Franklin meant every word he said. The Man of Reason was the hero of the age.

The difficulty perceived by Frost and other young modernists at the turn of the century was that under the aegis of pure reason, meaning in life had been reduced to schemata, a program. The successors to the Enlightenment not only had to create new forms of meaning, but also radically new approaches to discover that meaning. They had witnessed the most devastating effects of rationalist schemata, a mechanized universe which threatened to enslave humanity as one more category in an iron-clad system. A radical reorientation was necessary. Even if humanity proved ultimately to be an irrational being, this fact had to be discovered by unique, personal methods to convince the individual mind. The universal law of reason was no longer the way, but became a barrier that prevented meaning.

The primary sources of difficulty that Frost and the young modernists were to face with the rationalist ethics, then, were the nearly exclusive reliance upon formal, logical analysis over intuition, reason over imagination, the hierarchical and didactic nature of the logically derived ethics, and the imprisoning order of right actions into a system of codified rules. In consort with the idealization of human thinking, moreover, rationalists obliterated any sense of the mysterious presence of the divine, an issue that some modernists, Frost and Eliot and Robinson among them, struggled with powerfully. Perhaps the key Enlightenment thinker on this issue, and surely one of the most influential internationally, was David Hume. Several times in his life Hume met with Franklin (and, for a time, believed that Franklin was going to publish an American edition of the *Philosophical Essays*). Hume's place in philosophy actually wasn't confirmed until shortly after his death, when Immanuel Kant recognized and advocated his genius. Hume's ideas on the divine, however, were seminal on both shores of the Atlantic for many years after his death.

To the point of our comparison of the rationalist ethics and Frost's positioning toward that, consider briefly several of Hume's points in what is perhaps the most challenging chapter of *Human Understanding*, his essay on miracles. The essay might be read as a near proof text for Paine's *Age of Reason* and Emerson's "Divinity School Address." Hume attempts more than a modern-day remythologization of miracles—the explanation of all purportedly supernatural events by natural law. Instead he attempts to discredit the validity of miracles altogether by a lack of primary evidence and objective accounting. That is to say, he finds no rational accountability for miracles. As a man of reason, then, Hume finds himself compelled to provide an argument that will "be an everlasting check to all kinds of superstitious delusions."[3] The argument itself is familiar to anyone in the twentieth century; that is, the arguments to evidence versus testimony, to proof versus probability, to the laws of nature versus violation of laws, to reason versus emotion. Each of these, explicitly or implicitly, seems to impugn the person who might believe in the miraculous, or even the supernatural. Here too we witness the intellectual elitism of the rationalist. Hume puts it thus: "The knavery and folly of men are such common phenomenon that I should rather believe the most extraordinary events to occur from their concurrence [i.e., the folly of men] than admit of so signal a violation of the laws of nature."[4]

Having denied proof for miracles on the basis of natural law, Hume and his fellow rationalists find little need for a divine power to work within natural law. The traditionally received notions of a God who was omniscient and omnipresent were erased to a vaporous Deism. Again, Hume writes on what would become a central dogma of rationalist thought: "It is impossible for us to know the attributes or actions of such a Being otherwise than from the experience which we have of his productions in the usual course of nature."[5] Having denied any special revelation (Scripture or miracles), and limiting the divine to signs of order in natural law, the rationalist effectively drew a veil over God. At the same moment, Rationalism effectively placed the entire groundwork for ethical decision making in the human mind.

The influence of rationalist thinking upon twentieth-century ethical thought arises from the lack of internal order in what seems at first glance to be a tight system. Rationalist ethics may indeed appear orderly and reasonable, but its order was inherently exclusionary. For example, as suggested in the discussion above, it may be observed that for the rationalists, the natural world is assumed to be orderly. Frost is the polar opposite of Hume here, for while natural order often sings with a sweet beauty in his poems, it also raises that Pacific storm that is metaphor for his chaotic spirit, or that New England blizzard that reminds him of desert places, or that Midwestern rain on sad streets—but the streets are only streets; the sadness lies in him. For Frost a vital current links humanity and nature.

At the same time, however, Frost searches nature for signs of the divine. One would be mistaken to call Frost a Pantheist. Rather, it may be said, . . . that nature provides signals to the alert and heedful mind. Nature leads one outside of oneself, enabling the probing of divine possibilities that do not occur in the closed formality of the rationalist.

In his exhaustive study *Robert Frost and the Challenge of Darwin*, Robert Faggen demonstrates the transitions from Emerson, Thoreau, and James, authors generally considered influential upon Frost, and Frost's own conception of nature. The unity assumed between humanity and nature became fractured by Frost's greater skepticism. Frost's poetry seduces one by the appearance of order, both in form and setting, only to jar one into awareness of disorder. Faggen argues that, "Frost is often diabolical, seducing his readers into a world that promises clarity, order, and beauty only to show increasing complexity, irony, and dysteleology. And the style reflects the irony of his view

of nature; it appears lovely but, as Darwin himself envisioned, hides competi-
tion and destruction."[6] Faggen adds that "Frost's poetry aims at those who
claim human superiority to nature as well as those of romantic sentiment
who regarded nature's beauty as an example of its moral purity and fail to
recognize the more subtle examples of the way other creatures suffer and
compete."[7] Frost portrays the dialectic; seldom does he attempt resolution.
All too often, the presumption of order wrenched by apparent disorder closes
a Frostian work in tense ambiguity.

Probably most significant to the case here is Frost's early and lasting
interests in astronomy coupled with Darwinian thought. One of his lifelong favorite books, by his own accounting, was Richard Proctor's *Our Place
Among Infinities*. In his *Paris Review* interview, collected in *Interviews with
Robert Frost*, Frost recalled that "One of the earliest books I hovered over,
hung around, was called *Our Place Among the Infinities* [sic], by an astrono-
mer in England named Proctor. . . . I mention that in one of the poems:
I use that expression 'our place among the infinities' from that book that
I must have read as soon as I read any book, thirteen or fourteen" (*Inter-
views* 231). The poem Frost refers to here is "The Star-Splitter," where Brad
McLaughlin buys a telescope to probe the mysteries of "our place among
the infinities."

Proctor's book, however, is not a mere guide to astronomy or a chart to
the heavens. Appearing as it does in the full bloom of the debate over evolution, Proctor's aim was nothing less than an effort to trace the origins of solar
bodies. Equipped only with the rudimentary astrophysical tools of the late
nineteenth century, Proctor's effort was severely handicapped, relying more
upon speculation than science. Nonetheless, he held adamantly to the evolu-
tionary infinitude of the universe. Robert Faggen points out the conclusions
of such thinking: "He justified his own claims of the infinite evolution of
the solar system and the infinitude of space and time, in part, on the ground
that they do not comfort those who want to see a purposeful God's design in
everything."[8] As with Darwinism at the turn of the century, it is not the case
with Proctor that there is no design, but rather that design is indeterminate
from the evidence given. The proposition, while directly threatening Rationalism, was a common sensibility of early modernism.

Furthermore, Frost is keenly aware of the surprises nature holds. Perhaps nature itself is the miracle, for often in Frost's poems nature adopts
the metaphorical voice speaking both to narrator and also to reader. Nature
constantly discloses, and most often what it discloses is something of what
we ourselves are. Frost himself is ever alert for "what just might be"—the
miracle of a sudden insight that can either change the contours of a poem or
the course of one's life.

Frost also departs significantly from the rationalist ethic by paying close heed to a common people's voice, both their intense secrets and their superstitions. He brings them a degree of credibility by featuring them as characters in his works. Moreover, the narrative tone held toward such people, through Frost's use of sound-sense whereby he enters their lives through the currents of their speech, either dignifies the struggles of such people to find the right actions in their settings, or, at the very least, withholds denigration by the objectivity of a closely listening ear.

With this transition from rational dogmatism to a greater focus on individual experience and searching, it is not inaccurate to describe modernist literature as romantic. In fact, Nathan Scott has done exactly that in *The Broken Center* by claiming that, "It is precisely the extreme self-reliance in the quest for first principles that I have been positing as the inescapable necessity facing the modernist writer—it is precisely this that makes evident his descendance from the great Romantics of the nineteenth century and also makes evident the fact that the literature of the age of Joyce and Kafka is essentially a late development of the Romantic movement."[9] Scott points out that to compensate for the disintegration of traditional guides, of those primordial images that objectify a people's beliefs, the romantic tendency seeks a mythos, a corporate story that also holds true individually. Myth, not objective data, incarnates our mystery. Frost's poetry may well be understood as such—stories embodying the mysteries of humankind.

Robert Langbaum makes a claim similar to Scott's in *The Poetry of Experience* by arguing that the "change of direction" in Romanticism begins when the artist "discovers his own feelings and his own will as a source of value in an otherwise meaningless universe."[10] Langbaum argues that it is the matter of choosing value in the absence of traditional guides to value that marks the romantic tendency, and which marks the modern age as romantic, for we are still caught in the quest for personal value and meaning. This quest must be validated by experience, by acting on individual choice rather than rational justification, hence his title "The Poetry of Experience."

Rationalist ethics celebrated the analytic powers of the individual human to discern matters of truth and right action and set them forth in a form congruent to the ideas themselves. While the prose format suited many rationalist thinkers, poetry too was governed by rigidity of formal patterns to achieve the decorous balance between form and thought. For the modernist, rationalist ethics was altogether too hierarchical. Since ethics for them was indeterminate, the form of the work similarly became more indeterminate. While cautious of the romantic celebration of ethical individualism and sprawling poetic forms, nonetheless many of them participated in what Langbaum called the Poetry of Experience.

Frost in the Context of Rationalist Ethics

While he turned against the romantic excess in poetic form under the influence of Santayana, Frost nonetheless retained the unsettled, questing spirit of the romantic legacy. On a quest for personal value, or a validation of self, his poetic characters must choose and act to make that validation. The choices held open for the character, and the ambiguities of choices that prevent clear and decisive actions, are also those that confront the reader. One of Frost's best-known examples of this ambiguity appears in "The Road Not Taken."

> Two roads diverged in a yellow wood,
> And sorry I could not travel both
> And be one traveler, long I stood
> And looked down one as far as I could
> To where it bent in the undergrowth;
>
> Then took the other, as just as fair
> And having perhaps the better claim,
> Because it was grassy and wanted wear;
> Though as for that the passing there
> Had worn them really about the same,
> And both that morning equally lay
> In leaves no step had trodden black.
> Oh, I kept the first for another day!
> Yet knowing how way leads on to way,
> I doubted if I should ever come back.
>
> I shall be telling this with a sigh
> Somewhere ages and ages hence:
> Two roads diverged in a wood, and I—
> I took the one less traveled by,
> And that has made all the difference.

The poem may seem to many to be the great pastoral symphony of his works; upon closer probing, however, one uncovers discordant notes and tense ambiguities. To fully appreciate the achievement, the poem should be situated in several different contexts, each of which provides differing angles of vision on the work.

After selling his farm in Derry, New Hampshire, Frost moved in 1912 with Elinor and their children to England. There two of the most important events of his life occurred: the publication of his first volume of poetry, *A*

Boy's Will (1913), and his deep friendship with the English poet Edward Thomas. The friendship would be all too brief. Thomas died in 1917 in World War I, but the friendship left a profound and lasting impact upon Frost.

According to Lawrance Thompson's *Robert Frost* (vol. 2, 88–89, 544–48), "The Road Not Taken" was originally written in a piece of correspondence to Thomas, and, Thompson speculates, it was intended to satirize the indecisive Thomas. Indeed, it isn't difficult to detect a tone of jesting, but friendly, conversation in the poem. Regardless of the difficulty of Thompson's reading the author's intentions into the work, the poem itself nicely captures the frequent walks of Frost and Thomas across the English countryside.[11]

Substantial evidence, however, suggests that the idea of the poem antedates Frost's acquaintance with Thomas. In a 1912 letter to Susan Hayes Ward, Frost writes of "two lonely cross-roads" that he walked frequently during the winter. After a snowfall, he would observe the road lying trackless for days, showing that "neither is much traveled." Frost goes on to describe how one evening he was surprised to see a figure in the distance walking toward him. Oddly, he felt he was approaching his own image in "a slanted mirror," or as if two images were about to "float together." In the end, Frost writes, "I stood still in wonderment and let him pass by" (*Selected Letters* 45). That experience sheds substantial light upon the ambiguities that have perplexed readers of the poem, for certainly "The Road Not Taken" dramatizes the narrator's encounter with his own self.

The poem was first published in *The Atlantic Monthly* (August 1915), and was collected as the opening poem in Frost's third volume, *Mountain Interval* (1916). As he had done in his previous volume, *North of Boston*, Frost set the opening poem and the concluding poem, "The Sound of Trees," in italic, rather than roman type. A comparison of the two poems brings forth many striking similarities beyond the function of introducing and concluding the volume. Both poems pose the narrator in a moment of ambiguity, where a choice may be made but no certain responses to that choice appear. While "The Road Not Taken" locates the narrator "in a yellow wood," "The Sound of Trees" locates the narrator in his lodging listening to the sound of trees. In fact, as the trees sway and bend, so too his whole body sways and bends to their pull. To what end, however? As in "The Road Not Taken," the narrator of "The Sound of Trees" is not certain. He announces that "I shall set forth for somewhere / I shall make the reckless choice." But not now. Now he feels the tug of action, but leaves it in the tense ambiguity of "someday." Whereas in "The Road Not Taken" the narrator actually does step out on a "leap of faith," the action of the narrator of "The Sound of Trees" is indeterminate.

Thus, the two poems frame conflicting actions when forced with ambiguous choices and ends.

As seen previously in his essay "The Constant Symbol," Frost declared that the "mind is a baby giant," hurling its toys ahead of itself. So too it is with the poet, flinging out words, prosody, and other playthings of the craft ahead of him. But they land in zigzag paths; thus, the "straight crookedness" of the poem. We should not misunderstand so careful a poet as Frost as abdicating method and design, but rather as using them seductively to bring the reader into the poem and thereby to unveil shades of meaning to the reader. Such is one fundamental trait of his poetic ethics. Rather than shouting the truth, as his poem "Mowing" has it, the poet would prefer to whisper along the zigzag path that is the poem.

The point is important to "The Road Not Taken" for it is indeed one of his superb pastoral poems, perfectly capturing as if by camera one momentary scene in nature. The autumn setting, nearly always a nostalgic and sometimes melancholy season in Frost's poetry, evokes a tone of sweet wistfulness here. Nature's life is passing; if "Nature's first green is gold," its last green is yellow. But nature in this poem also acts upon the narrator, further than a mere evocation of wistfulness. As Johannes Kjorven has argued in *Robert Frost's Emergent Design*, the poem's focus centers primarily upon the choice/action of the narrator. In this case, nature, at one unexpected point, presents him with two leaf-fallen paths—divergent, branching off into the unseen distance. So it is in nature; one reaches such a point, one makes a decision, one travels on. But it is not that way for the narrator, and herein the poem itself branches off into complexities as we observe the narrator's reaction to the choice that nature presents him.

While the pastoral scene may seem simple, the form of the poem itself propels the zigzag paths. In fact, the form belies the pastoral quality for, unlike "Mowing," it is far more intense, suggesting uncertainty and vacillation against the compelling need to make a decision. The stanzaic rhyme scheme appears in perfect regularity: ABAAB CDCCD EFEEF GHGGH. The rhymes are all masculine, with a curious twist in lines five and twenty where the penultimate syllable rhymes, pairing the "undergrowth" and the "difference." Within this tightly clad system, however, rhythm and word patterns shift and strain, reflecting the narrator's own mind. With his reliance upon sound-sense, as many scholars have pointed out, Frost should not—perhaps cannot—be placed tightly within a regular line prosody. Even his sweetly flowing "Mowing" is broken by irregular accents since he speaks as a laborer, not as a poet writing about a laborer. So too in "The Road Not Taken" accents shift spontaneously, trochees mixing freely with iambs. Frost captures the mind of the woods-walker in such a way, eliciting discovery, uncertainty, and sadness by the varied structures.

The linguistic deployment of the poem abets this fluctuation. The first thing one notices is a shift in the wood itself. Line 1 discovers two roads in a "yellow wood." The opening trochee manifests the surprise of the walker stumbling across those roads. His relationship with and decision according to those roads constitute the bulk of the "telling" of the poem until the last stanza where the decision is made. In line 18, however, the reader finds an echo of line 1. Something is missing. It reads simply, "Two roads diverged in a wood." The "yellow" wood, with its beauty and surprise, has been suspended, held in thrall by a decision between two roads that has to be made. It is possible, in fact, that if one follows this transition one could read the poem as expressing a wholly negative attitude toward decision making. The beauty of the world around us slips away under the weight of the need for pragmatic decisions. Whether read this way or not, the formal techniques of the poem nicely evidence the baby giant using its toys to set a zigzag course. In this case, it most powerfully lures the reader into that course for deeper probing. What further evidence in the poem's setting can be determined to guide that course?

After the objective description in stanza 1—what in fact lay before him—the narrator engages the why of his choice. The evidence in stanzas 2 and 3 is inconclusive. Yet, in the third stanza the imposition of the context of time on the poem again subtly shifts the meaning. At the present moment, the yellow leaves have not been "trodden black." Something of the narrator's passage will indelibly change that, but so too he will be changed. Although he claims to keep the first path for another day, he knows full well that with one step it disappears forever into the past. The "sigh" of the fourth stanza is anticipated in the third as the narrator makes his choice, "Oh, I kept the first for another day!" But there will be no other day, no other precise moment such as this.

Even as he stands in the present, then, at this seemingly harmless juncture in the woods, the poet feels the dramatic moment of the future. The fourth stanza shifts to the future, which, of course, he can't know. All he has is the present moment. The indecision of the narrator here contrasts sharply with the fierce energy of the narrator of "A Leaf Treader," something of a parallel poem. There the narrator, by his own admission, has trod the leaves to stamp out fear. Not so with the narrator here. He steps out at last on the path that he chooses to call less traveled, but it is only his choosing to call it that that makes all the difference for his sense of the future. In his essay, "Whistling in the Dark: Robert Frost's Modernist Quest for Meaning," William Doxey emphasizes that the choice/act determines meaning since "each choice excludes its alternative." Doxey adds, "What is done cannot be undone, so the meaning here seems to be that one must live as though his judgment were correct, regardless."[12] In this context also, it is not difficult to see the implications for Frost's personal commitment to be a poet. His choice during the England years was fretted by unusually heavy financial concerns, a lack of a reading public, and a commitment to a poetic form unlike that practiced in the modernist trend. The risk of the future weighs like a sigh in the poem.

"The Road Not Taken" does indeed, then, follow several zigzag contours. It may be an ironic jest with his friend Thomas. It is indeed a pastoral scene. Its formal qualities expertly snare and lead the reader. It reveals nature working upon the narrator by offering the complexity of seemingly identical choices. Finally, it holds forth the tension—unresolved in spite of the last line—between the present moment and the unknown future, and the need to shape some ethical stance toward present and future through human action rather than received tradition. In these ways it also manifests what Langbaum calls "The Poetry of Experience." The choice to be made is not grounded in some rationalist scheme; rather, it is an existential product of the immediate moment.

Rationalist Ethics: Behind the Masque

Frost insisted that *A Masque of Reason* and *A Masque of Mercy* be placed at the end of his *Complete Poems*, a fact that has in itself raised considerable speculation among scholars. Mordecai Marcus, for example, is of the opinion that by Frost's placing them at the end he was "surely viewing them as summary comment on his life and work."[13] Similarly, Reuben A. Brower, who reads the poems as "the final experiment in his search for a 'form of outrage' in which he could push to the limit the stress of opposites," believes they are Frost's "culminating" poems.[14] Here, Brower argues, the poet "refashions forms he had used earlier and . . . sums up concerns persistent throughout his poetry."[15] Also, working from evidence in Frost's unpublished *Notebooks*, Dorothy Judd Hall asserts that "Frost regarded [the Masques] as the culmination of his poetic achievement."[16]

It may also well be that Frost set the poems apart from other works because of the generic distinction. He had written many works with dramatic qualities, including several attempts at plays, but none with the starkness of a masque. Moreover, if these poems are seen as "culminations," one has to ask culminations of what? In language, tone, and setting they are different from anything written before. Furthermore, they differ in subject, for while certain poems foreshadow the Masques, none of them treats the subject matter of the encounter with suffering with quite the same stark, confrontational drama. In other poems, the subject is muted by images and settings; here it is shouted.

Finally, one may account for the placement by the fact of the altogether different publishing avenues of the two poems. *A Masque of Reason* was published
in 1945 (during the irrational carnage of WWII) in a limited edition of only
800 copies signed by the author. *A Masque of Mercy*, although first published
in *The Atlantic Monthly* (November 1947), was also published in a signed
edition of 751 numbered copies. The limited and distinctly more private (by
this time Frost was one of the best-selling poets in the world) distribution
of the poems suggests that Frost might have wanted them individualized in
the collection not necessarily because they were any sort of culmination—he
did, after all, publish many more poems after 1947—but simply because they
constituted a different sort of writing and thinking than his other works. That
point may seem trivial. If we isolate this sense of artistic and thematic indi-
viduality in the Masques, however, we are also in a better position to understand the full range of Frost's effort in them, from the wit to the wondering,
from reason to outrage, from mockery to meaningfulness.

The dramatic form of the masque developed particularly during the
Renaissance with its appetite for courtly processionals and elevated speech
and song. The speakers wore masks, thus becoming more allegorical types in
the drama than actors. The "idea" was the thing of importance. Since it was
a courtly production for celebration and entertainment, however, even the
allegorical idea was subservient to the sheer spectacle of the procession and
songs. Perhaps the most famous masque is Milton's *Comus*, presented at Lud-
low Castle on 29 September 1634, to celebrate the inauguration of the Earl
of Bridgewater as Lord President of Wales. Milton accepted the assignment
as an interlude from his private studies at home, but he practically reinvented
the whole genre from those masques with which Ben Jonson had been lining
his pockets. Milton followed standard conventions—spectacle, song, dancing;
he even included the grotesque of the "antimask" to conflict with the order
of the whole. However, the breadth of intellectual seriousness set the play
apart from others of its time. Influenced by Homer's story of Odysseus and
Circe, Milton made Comus the son of Circe and took the story from there
into a probing examination of the conflict between good and evil. Comus,
appearing as the perfect gentleman of reasonable and cultivated order, is
revealed as a corrupted vessel of moral disorder. Thus he contains in himself
the conflicting good and evil, the appearance and the reality, the reasonable
and irrational, the ethical and the corrupt. In "Robert Frost's Masques and
the Classic American Tradition," Peter J. Stanlis accurately points out that,
"Frost's two plays depend more on poetry than on spectacle, and like Milton
his main purpose is to state a serious theological and moral principle about
an important religious or philosophical problem."[17] If there is a model for

Frost's masques, it does not lie in the sunnier works of Jonson, Thomas Campion, Thomas Carew, and James Shirley. Clearly it lies in the at once more agonizing and difficult, and therefore altogether at once more human, *Comus*.

Some of the ambiguity and conflict that Frost struggles with in the two masques appear in earlier works. Although the forms may vary, the sense of searching for some clear sign is an oft-repeated theme. "Neither Out Far Nor In Deep," first published in *The Yale Review* (spring 1934), exemplifies this perfectly. In the first of four quatrains, Frost depicts people standing on a beach. They have all turned their backs on the land to stare at the sea. The land behind them is the familiar, what is known; the sea before them the unfamiliar and unknown. What is it that so fascinates them as to stand watching all the day?

The second stanza seems to supply an answer—a ship passes by. Nearby a gull stands upon the wet shoreline. Both of these, however, are simply demarcations between the people and the sea itself, as if they were some signs in a foreign tongue of the secrets the sea might hold. Thus in the third stanza, Frost thrusts the reader into the world of ambiguity with the line, "Wherever the truth may be." Where is it? In the familiar landscapes of our lives, or in the unfamiliar sea, so unyielding of its mysteries.

The closing stanza is a fascinating one, quite unlike many of Frost's deliberately ambiguous poems that he leaves in final suspension. Here he recognizes the limitations upon the human condition to search out such mysteries: "They cannot look out far / They cannot look in deep." Rarely does he make so overt a comment on the human condition. In "Frost's 'Neither Out Far Nor In Deep,'" Peter Poland understands this commentary as explicitly negative. The people stand like gulls, "Symbolically turning their backs on their domain, the land, to stare incessantly seaward." Thus, they are "unnatural," and "Their efforts are life-denying in the extreme."[18] It seems possible, and perhaps more likely, however, to see the people straining at their limitations, seeking to know what is presently unknowable. The final two lines, although posed in the form of a question, celebrate the human tendency to try to look far and deep. Human limitations are never a final bar "To any watch they keep."

The two Masques, however, are more than an effort to probe the mysteries of God; in fact, one goes seriously astray by limiting the poems to such. The poems are also very much about the mysteries of humanity in two areas especially: the nature of epistemology and the problem of human suffering. Philosophically the two issues always intertwine.[19] Poetically, the issue for Frost was a lifelong wrestling with the problem of suffering. One finds it starkly present already in "Trial by Existence" from A Boy's Will:

'Tis of the essence of life here,
    Though we choose greatly, still to lack
The lasting memory at all clear,
    That life has for us on the wrack
Nothing but what we somehow choose;
    Thus are we wholly stripped of pride
In the pain that has but one close,
    Bearing it crushed and mystified.

Not only is that a tightly packed final stanza in and of itself (are we only victims of our own pride? Are we able to transcend pride and thus suffering?), it could well serve as an epigraph to the two Masques.

    The ideas of these "Neither Out Far Nor In Deep" and "Trial by Existence" tie neatly into the two Masques, for in each the characters look far and deep into the nature of God and his actions, but also into the nature of the human condition. The human characters are thoroughly human, but they are also watchkeepers, searching for some sign of revelation while they stand at their dry little shorelines.

The Experience of Unreason

In *A Masque of Reason*, the searching of Job and Thyatira[20] in many ways represents someone looking out far and in deep. Indeed, Robert Faggen sees a significant trace of all Frost's poetry embodied in the poem: "Frost's *Masque of Reason* encompasses a tension that runs throughout his poetry, a tension between a human desire for ultimate causes and designs and a natural world that always refuses to satisfy that desire."[21] Such appears to be the case as we enter the poem. In this instance, instead of an ocean shore, Job and Thyatira rest under a palm tree at an oasis in the midst of a desert. Entangled in a tree that they alternately call the Burning Bush or the Christmas Tree, a figure of light attempts to extricate itself. The Burning Bush refers to the Theophany to Moses at Mount Horeb, recorded in Exodus 3. There God identifies himself to Moses as "I Am That I Am," the one who is all being and who does not need to be identified by any referent beyond himself. For the Old Testamental Job, this is the God Yahweh that figures prominently in the story. But Frost takes license with time. The fact that this "forty-third" chapter of Job is set approximately a thousand years after biblical events is irrelevant, for the second tree, "The Christmas Tree," evokes not the authoritative Father but the sacrificial Son. Ironically, however, Job and Thyatira recognize the figure from neither of these references, but from Blake's masterful painting of God. It's a subtle point, not to be missed. The recognition comes by means of human perception rather than divine revelation. Indeed, this will be the essential issue of the poem. Do we contain God by our reason, as rationalist thought would have it, or do we accept that God has reasons for events that we can't possibly understand?

Such, of course, is the issue also of the biblical Book of Job, but with some important differences that serve as backdrop to this "forty-third" chapter. The first two chapters of Job, recounting the wager in heaven and the awful affliction upon Job, serve as a brief preface to the larger issues of the book. The second chapter closes with his wife's imprecation to "curse God and die"—an appeal to blank nihilism—and the arrival of Job's three friends—Eliphaz, Bildad, and Zophar. The dramatic quality of the book, then, is whether any of the three can argue a position more tenable than nihilism.

Each of the three captures some facet of Deuteronomic tradition. Eliphaz praises Job for his good deeds and piety, but is quite certain (through a vision he had) that Job has committed some unknown or secret sin. Therefore, his advice is to appeal to God. Frost's *Masque* affords that opportunity. Eliphaz, however, simply relies upon his own variation of Deuteronomy 8:5, "Blessed is the man whom God corrects." The difficulty with Eliphaz's advice is that it is cast entirely in human inability. He isolates portions of Deuteronomic tradition to depict humanity as the subject of impulsive errancy and God as a master of divine caprice:

> As I have observed, those who plow evil
> and those who sow trouble reap it.
> At the breath of God they are destroyed;
> at the blast of his anger they perish.
> (Job 4:8–9, NIV)

Recall "Neither Out Far Nor In Deep." There the watchers at least had the sea itself to search out. The biblical Job's response to Eliphaz touches on that same point, "If only my anguish could be weighed and all my misery be placed on the scales" (6:2). Job wants to understand his suffering in concrete, practical terms rather than in abstractions. Few of Frost's poems have elicited so widely varied and often contradictory views as this one, but John Doyle penetrates to the heart of it in his observation that "Because Frost's approach to life has always been essentially empirical and nonconformist and his poems based upon observation and experience, Job was the perfect character for his poem on Reason, for Job was an empiricist and the great nonconformist of the Old Testament."[22] Unlike Eliphaz, Job seeks experiential evidence.

Nor does the situation change much as Zophar and Bildad enter with their admonitions and advice. Zophar essentially urges Job to be a kind of

mindless statue, face turned toward God but expecting nothing really. To
their words, Job responds, first, that he would have answers from God rather
than from mortals; second, that his friends should comfort him rather than
try to convince him by their sophistries; and third, that he adamantly believes
there is a God who can deliver him. Those assertions lead Job to his famous
proclamation that inspired Handel's *Messiah* and has inspired countless others: "I know that my Redeemer lives, and that in the end he will stand upon
the earth. And after my skin has been destroyed, yet in my flesh I will see
God" (19:25–26). This is a choice of the human spirit, not at all the consequence of rational pursuit.

With Job's final insistence that he will speak only with God, his three
philosopher-friends fall silent. But standing in the wings is a young man
named Elihu, who thus far has deferred to his elders. He now wants a chance
to show that all four of them are wrong. His aim, as he announces it, is that
God does speak to humanity in many different ways. Although Elihu treats
Job as a person rather than a subject of theological discourse, one of these
ways of God's speaking, he argues, is through human suffering. His message is that God has supplied a lesson for Job. Now Job has to figure it out.
According to Elihu, God speaks in such various ways as natural revelation,
metaphor, human mediators, and personal experience. This is necessarily so
because "The Almighty is beyond our reach and exalted in power" (37:23).
Thus any revelation of God is veiled and indirect. Ironically, precisely at that
moment God himself speaks.

The pattern of the divine discourses in Job is fascinating. God does not
say a word directly about Job's suffering or divine judgment—the subjects
of *A Masque of Reason*. But neither does God condemn nor chastise Job, a
fact that disclaims the earthly philosophies of Job's accusers. The implication
instead is that Job is vindicated. In some of the most memorable poetry in the
Bible, God discloses the ways in which he has revealed himself to humanity,
and they are all evidentiary rather than rational proofs. Having heard God,
Job now repents of his presumption to "accuse" God (42:4–6). Accepting the
repentance, God restores Job's fortunes multiple times, and grants him, once
at the point of death, an additional 140 years to enjoy his blessing.

As Frost introduces us to his Job, however, the man is not "old and full
of years." Rather he is of some indeterminate age in some limbo-like region
where time seems suspended. Yet the subject matter is much the same as the
biblical Job. When human reason simply cannot account for the actions of
God, what possible *reasons* can God have for acting the way he does? The
issue bore paramount importance for Frost himself, who in the face of certain sufferings in his own life found reason itself vain and reasons for events
absent. In April, 1934, as his daughter Marjorie lay dying, Frost wrote to

his son Carol, "But I try not to give way to either hope or fear. I am simply determined in my soul, my bones, or somewhere, that our side shall win. Reason is no help" (*Family Letters* 164). Again, after Elinor died, Frost wrote his daughter Lesley that "No matter how humorous I am[,] I am sad. I am a jester about sorrow" (*Family Letters* 210).

Something of both of those letters echo in *A Masque of Reason*. Reason is abandoned, but what do we have left in its place? If there are only reasons that God hides from us, then we have the inscrutable, unknowable God of whom Elihu spoke. But both the biblical Job and Frost's Job are situated in God's presence, bringing their grievance before him. Similarly both characters are trying to account for the suffering in their lives, with the notable exception that Frost uses, as was his custom, his slicing wit to be a "jester about sorrow."

In Frost's *Masque*, God's effort to disentangle himself from the Burning Bush/Christmas Tree may be understood two ways. If from the Bush, then God extricates himself from the years of Hebraic commentary and tradition that evolved from his first stunning theophany to Moses. The option is fascinating because in the book *Job* the three friends/accusers address Job solidly from within that tradition, appealing repeatedly to Deuteronomic law and custom. Job, however, longs for an unveiled God. In effect, he would like to be like Moses, standing at the burning bush.[23] The Christmas Tree, on the other hand, represents the modern mythology of godhood from which the actual God disentangles himself. Lines 11–16 detail a tree chock-full of Yeatsian artifice, its very self a kind of gaudy present.

After extricating himself, God pitches his plywood porta-throne, so flimsy a contraption that he has to hold it upright rather than the other way around. Again, Frost may be exercising some sly wit here in his love for contrarieties. The rickety, prefab throne God totes around with him, like divinity in a briefcase, may suggest that God himself is as empty of significance as the battered plywood. Or, it may suggest precisely the converse—that God has no need of real thrones or props, that the person inhabiting the prop is king whether the throne is made of plywood or gold, and that Job is now getting to see the unveiled God precisely as he wishes.

Job starts the discussion with his questioning (37–45), but God quickly turns the tables on him, thanking Job for his help in establishing the principle "There's no connection man can reason out / Between his just deserts and what he gets" (49–50). There is no reasonable congruence between action and results, virtue and rewards. Is life then all whimsy, relative to God's caprice? Or is there some divine, ethical standard? God points out that this ambiguity was in itself the very essence of Job's trial (61–61). God adds that, "It had to seem unmeaning to have meaning" (63).

In a sense, Job places us on the cusp of an old philosophical conundrum: can God make a stone so heavy he cannot lift it? The answer appears to be yes. If God is infinite, he can make something infinitely heavy. But if God is omnipotent, then there is nothing that God cannot do, including lifting the infinitely heavy stone. In philosophy we point out that if the conclusions are contradictory, the fault lies in the premises. That is to say, it's a bad question, for God himself cannot be God if he is self-contradictory. Some answers to some questions, then, lie beyond the scope of human reason. Such is the lesson God imparts to Job.[24]

Job is ready to grant this. His concern is not really with his reasoning capacity at all. What he is looking for is not some propositional Truth, but rather some understanding of reasons for events. In this way, Frost's Job resembles the biblical Job, intent upon evidentiary and experiential understanding. The genuine suffering lies in "not knowing."

God picks up this thread of the argument by saying that Job liberated him. Since the fall of humanity in Eden (71–72), God himself has been in bondage to the Mosaic laws he imposed. The forfeits and rewards, curses and blessings of that law, although biblically understood as covenantal, are revealed here as a sort of police state ethics. Such is the danger of any covenant. By the wager in heaven, and Job's enduring it, God is returned to his throne. But he is also freed from having to give reasons (105–6).

Thyatira is not so easily persuaded. Indeed, she shouldn't be. It's a pretty impoverished argument that Frost's God advances here. Thyatira recounts how she cared for Job while he suffered (there is no biblical record of that), and that it was only reasonable that God should care for his made creature also. She accuses God of a petty tyranny, "All You can seem to do is lose Your temper / When reason-hungry mortals ask for reasons" (135–36). She makes it clear that she is not asking for some wide-ranging system of philosophical proofs, as Plato would have it (137–40), but rather "scraps of palliative reason."

At that point Job, saying that Thyatira always manages to get in ahead of him, picks up his argument. What was it all about? he wonders. What was the point? God asserts that his only claim is Truth, but that Job helped him demonstrate where truth lay. It is a matter of a spiritual discipline where humanity learns its "submission to unreason." Peter Stanlis is one of the few critics to have perceived this fundamental crux of the Masque. In "Robert Frost's Masques," Stanlis pinpoints Frost's conflict with national certitude in the modern age:

Perhaps nothing could be more antithetical than the philosophy of modern secular man, with his faith in reason, and Frost's satire on reason based upon a theology which derives from Old Testament religious orthodoxy. Where the modern rationalist makes man's reason supreme and simply eliminates God as irrelevant to his temporal or spiritual salvation, Frost exalts the omnipotence of God's arbitrary justice and makes man's reason appear peevish and impotent by comparison.[25]

One hesitates, perhaps, at Stanlis's use of the word *exalts*, simply because it is something implied behind the scenes of this Masque. At this point, Frost's Job is busy untangling a confusing webwork of suffering and power, justice and omnipotence, skepticism and purpose.

We do see at this point that truth is not so much categorical as it is existential; that is to say, we apprehend it not through categories of reason but through experience. The problem for Job, and for Frost we should add, is why those experiences so often have to be ones of suffering. Cued by God's "submission to unreason," Job engages his longest speech in the poem in which he begs for God's "beforehand" reason. He longs for the purpose of the design— "the artist in me cries out for design" (261)—and not what theologians concoct *ex post facto*. What satisfaction, Job wonders, can a God get in laughing at how badly humans "fumble at the possibilities" (275). Not until Job's cynical wife joins in with taunts and jeers, does God reveal something of the great wager with Satan in heaven—something the biblical Job knew nothing about.

In lines 331–33, Job thrusts one of his satirical barbs, targeting the chief irony of the poem:

> 'Twas human of You. I expected more
> Than I could understand and what I get
> Is almost less than I can understand.

As human creation, it is impossible for him to understand the mind of divine Creator. It is like studying one individual index finger and concluding that I now understand all of humanity. Conversely, to try to place the divine wager in terms that a Job could understand is to reduce it to the merely trivial. In his article "Robert Frost's Masques Reconsidered," Heyward Brook has argued that this is the essential point of the whole poem. The play is an elaborate satire of humanity's effort to capture God, and if the play makes God appear ludicrous it is simply to reveal the ludicrousness of finite efforts to probe the infinite. Such a view, though, does not fully account for the entrance of Satan—at God's beckoning. Here is an agent for evil, and the appearance of Satan introduces a separation between agency and permission that Job had not been fully aware of before.

With Satan's entrance Thyatira is jarred fully awake. This is more to her liking. Enough with the boring theology, as she searches for her Kodak camera to capture the three luminaries on film. It is, of course, the supreme absurdity—the great cosmic trio captured by technology. Thyatira badgers Satan mercilessly as she tries to get him to pose as *she* wishes—"No—no, that's not a smile there. That's a grin" (404). After Thyatira's pestering of Satan (she even asks for one of his prime apples), God feels compelled to explain Satan's diaphanous appearance—like a wasp here—and his lack of speech. Just as God himself has been stripped of personality and his divine godhood in the use of rational categories about him, Satan has been stripped of person-hood by "church neglect / and figurative use" (424–25). Like the technology of Thyatira's little Kodak, the modern church flattens the reality and divinity of God and the reality and power of Satan. The necessary consequence is a portrait of humanity standing alone and bereft of any significant meaning beyond its own being. Abandoned to the confines of its own rational scrutiny, humanity continues to search "out far and in deep," but sees only the surfaces below which the ultimate mysteries lie.

Which is precisely where this Masque ends. Human reason is altogether insufficient to understand God; indeed, to understand humanity itself. Satan is reduced to figurative use, a metaphor for a sort of indwelling evil inherent in the human condition. The tensions are self-consuming, ending in a final futility as the cynical Thyatira poses her three characters for her photograph and says, "Now if you three have settled anything / You'd as well smile as frown on the occasion" (464–65). The Masque ends in nearly perfect ambiguity and inconclusiveness. If you three have settled anything? It doesn't appear so—unless what has been settled is the insufficiency of human reason. Whatever the case, we may as well smile as frown. We can't do much of anything one way or the other.

From Reason to Mercy: Head to Heart

While *A Masque of Reason* grows out of one of the longer, and certainly the theologically most complex, books of the Old Testament, *A Masque of Mercy* grows out of one of the shortest biblical books, *Jonah*, with a very straight-forward, explicit theme. Both books share similarities, of course, which undoubtedly drew Frost's attention. Neither is properly a history, although each is situated at an indeterminate moment in Jewish history. Nor is either one properly a prophecy, although prophetic elements, such as Jonah's three days in the belly of the fish resembling Christ's crucifixion and resurrection, have been extrapolated. Both books are highly parabolic, and serve as rich ground for remythologizing theologians. Perhaps the most powerful similarity between both books is the revelatory quality. But in each case, unlike other revelatory books in the Old Testament, such as Daniel among the prophetic works or Deuteronomy among the legal books, Job and Jonah share revelation about a theme on human living, on the ethical values humanity requires to live at peace in this world.

While dates for the life of Job are indeterminate, placed virtually anywhere in the second millennium before Christ, Jonah may be fairly accurately dated as the first half of the eighth century B.C. His contemporaries included Amos and Hosea. The historical situation for Israel was dominated by the threat of Assyria. The book narrates a single prophetic mission, that of Jonah to Nineveh. Its theme is the prophet's human desire to prophesy bitter destruction upon "that wicked city," and his growing understanding of the ethics of mercy that must be extended to those very people. Thereby, Jonah sets a pattern for Israel (and humanity) itself: that God is concerned with all of creation, not just with a select few.

The story is familiar. When God tells Jonah to go to Nineveh and "preach against it," Jonah flees from the task aboard a ship. During a tempest at sea, the crewmen cast lots to see who the troublemaker is. When the lot falls on Jonah, and he agrees with the placement, he is cast overboard and swallowed by "a great fish," where he remains three days and three nights. From inside the fish, Jonah prays a prayer of deliverance, after which the fish vomits him up on dry land. When God reiterates his command, Jonah marches off to Nineveh, preaching destruction against it if the people don't repent. By this point, he would rather enjoy seeing fire and brimstone wash down in heavenly torrents to destroy the city. But an odd and unexpected thing happens. The people do repent. The peevish Jonah walks back into the desert to seethe for a while. He wanted justice. The Ninevites were wicked; they deserved a cosmic blast of vengeance. This is no place for the tenderness of mercy. That is, until Jonah needs it himself. In the searing heat, God causes a vine to grow up to shade Jonah. Then he permits a worm to attack it. Jonah is left shelterless in the scorching sun and wind. The parable is insufficient for the angry Jonah. God explains it pointedly, telling Jonah that his mercy in shading Jonah with the vine differs not at all in quality from his mercy in delivering the 120,000 inhabitants of Nineveh. Quantitative assessment of mercy is always secondary to the ethical quality of the act itself.

In structure and theme *A Masque of Mercy* may be considered of one piece with *A Masque of Reason*. In her careful study of relationships between the two, "A Man in Front of His God," Paola Loreto traces Frost's pattern in comparison to Ben Jonson's "spectacle of strangenesse," or the *antimasque*. In each the problems and turmoil of the antimasque are resolved in the *masque*, disorder achieves harmony, discord is supplanted by a ruler. Loreto observes that:

The two masques can be taken together as one dramatic piece. *A Masque of Reason* can be interpreted as an antimasque representing the disquieting doubt that there is no motivation for the heap of misfortunes God sent to Job, a man who had always been exemplary for his integrity. *A Masque of Mercy*, then, should be seen as the *masque* proper, whose function is to dispel the impression that the world is dominated by chaos and to restore man's faith in divine justice. In the masque, though, man's idea of God's justice is corrected. Man's merchant mentality is done away with and replaced with God's freely given mercy.[26]

Loreto isn't the first to suggest the antimasque/masque configuration. Heyward Brook made similar claims in "Robert Frost's Masques Reconsidered," but Loreto takes us to the point where rational order dissolves in a chaos that calls for a desperate corrective. The issue here, then, is what ethical guidelines Frost can forge out of the chaos to lead humanity into order.

Frost's *A Masque of Mercy* translates us to a modern day spiritual desert of the city of New York. Instead of seeking refuge aboard ship or under the vine, Jonah Dove (the Hebrew "Jonah" is translated as *dove*) seeks refuge in a bookstore kept by the odd couple, Jesse Bel[27] and the Keeper, presumably a pun on both the shopkeeper and also Cain's cynical response to God after murdering Abel, "Am I my brother's keeper?" (Gen. 4:9). Jesse Bel, however, tells us that the name came about from Keeper's mother's time in the Brook Farm community, Transcendentalism's idealistic experiment in socialism. The fourth character, Paul, represents of course the principal New Testament theologian, and he speculates that the book of Jonah may be the first instance in literature prior to his own to be specifically about mercy (375–77). Frost's *Masque*, however, moves at least at two levels—the conflict between divine justice and mercy but also the conflict between human justice and mercy at the political and social levels. The first conflict is carried between Paul and Jonah primarily; the second between Paul and the social liberal Keeper. Throughout the play, even when he is simply lurking in the dusty background of the bookstore shelves, Paul seems to be a central figure.

The play opens with Jonah, yet once again, fleeing God. He had been scheduled for a prophecy performance in New York, but at the last moment his courage failed him and he fled. Thus he is introduced as The Fugitive. Once he introduces himself by his right name, however, he also introduces the vexing problems that caused him to flee. He no longer trusts God to carry out his threats against an evil city. In fact, he "can't trust God to be unmerciful" (115). The difficulty for Jonah lies in the illogical fact of God's mercy. Jonah fears that mercy absolves the consequences of human sin. The redemptive acts of God don't make sense because they counteract "Anything we once thought we had to be" (315).

A large degree of what "we once thought we had to be" to Jonah's mind lay in the Mosaic Law, and represents also the modern misunderstanding of that law as a rigid accord of laws and punishment for violation. In fact, such was never the case in the covenantal form of the Suzerain treaty which God gave them. God reveals himself as a Lord of love, desiring the well-being of his people, and giving them the laws so that they could live in a loving relationship with him. This understanding clearly prevails in modern Judaism also, but seems to be missed or ignored by many other traditions. Jonah, in this case, represents those many others. Thus, when Paul asks him how he would want God to be other than merciful, Jonah responds, "Just, I would have Him just before all else" (363). But this is an impossibility already shown as such in *A Masque of Reason*. "Just" according to what and whose standards?

Dallas Willard, professor of philosophy at the University of Southern California, has in his book *The Divine Conspiracy* made observations that indirectly throw considerable light upon Frost's ethics. Willard's argument comes to bear upon Frost's examination of the ethics of justice. The view that has dominated the twentieth century, Willard says, is that "our culture holds reality to be limited to what can be discovered by scientific observation and exploration."[28] The consequence is a belief that scientific laws make everything intelligible, including ethical propositions and moral values. But of course naturalistic or scientific laws cannot exercise force in these domains for the simple reason that "There must be certain 'initial conditions' before the laws of science can explain anything. In their 'explaining,' those laws have to have something from which to start. And they obviously do not explain the existence or nature of those very conditions that must be in place before they can explain *anything*."[29] Nor, we might add, can such laws explain justice or mercy, the issues of this poem.

Jonah's complaint sets up the compelling philosophical drama that will center to a large extent upon Jesus' Sermon on the Mount. Paul introduces it by stating that "Christ came to introduce a break with logic / That made all outrage seem as child's play" (475–76). The Sermon on the Mount, he says, "'Twas lovely and its origin was love" (479). Here is the radical departure from reason, and the spiritual counter to divine justice seen merely as laws.

Keeper argues, and one can imagine that he does so with a magnificent sneer, that the Sermon is a "frame-up," its high ideals assuring universal failure so that we will be "Thrown prostrate at the Mercy Seat for Mercy" (485). The Sermon, he argues, is "a beautiful impossibility" (493), an "irresistible impossibility" (493), because it gives us such lovely ideals that no one can attain. For Keeper, the Sermon is an impractical absurdity. Beauty without essence.

Precisely because of that, it is an absurdity and beauty apprehended only by faith, not by reason. Paul argues that "Mercy is only to the undeserving" (500). Mercy is not earned, or it is not, by definition, mercy. This is the simple truth that Jonah and Keeper have failed to see. The argument, however, creates a slight shift in Jonah's point of view. Instead of looking backward as the Fugitive, he begins to look forward, "You ask if I see yonder shining gate, / And I reply I almost think I do" (530–31). In his response, Paul nicely defines this as a conversion, "Yes, Pilgrim now instead of runaway, / Your fugitive escape becomes a quest" (534–35). The key line of this passage occurs when Jonah exclaims "I'm all turned round" (548). The Latin root for conversion, *conversio*, literally translates as "to turn around."

But where does Jonah turn to? Not back through the outer door. Rather, he has to find his way through the cellar door, into the darkness, down a stairway he can't even see. The passage represents an existential leap of faith, daring the unknown. Paul points out, however, that it is the only way Jonah can prostrate himself before the cross. As Jonah admits that his need for justice has faded before his need for mercy (625–26), he steps toward the door.

As he does so, the door slams before him and Jonah crumples on the floor.[30] Aware that justice was all he ever had, all he ever pursued, he pleads for mercy while he too fades away like the justice he had built his life upon. The death of Jonah may be understood in two ways. Crumpled by justice, he is untouched by mercy. Or, mercy has overcome the justice he had built his life upon. But the inconclusiveness about Jonah is less important than the effect of his passing upon the other characters. They now confront the essential ethical issue: How then shall we live?

Keeper, accepting Jesse's earlier stated belief, declares that we have to live by courage, which, he points out, derives from the heart. Fear emanates from the soul. In this sense, then, courage is an act of fidelity, holding to beliefs even when fears attack those beliefs. Courage is also, it should be pointed out, a cardinal virtue in Frost's own code of ethics. Perhaps it is not surprising then that the poem ends with a deeply personal tone from Keeper and Paul.

Both have been powerfully affected by the night's events. Kneeling by Jonah's body, Keeper confesses that

> I can see that the uncertainty
> in which we act is a severity,
> A cruelty, amounting to injustice
> That nothing but God's mercy can assuage.
>   (710–13)

Our very lives, in which we are forced by courage to make choices and act upon them, are injustice—simply because we have no certain knowledge of

the outcome of those choices and acts. Hence the huge significance of courage. Courage not only acts *against* fear; it also acts *in* the fear of uncertainty.

Paul's final statement also bears a fascinating twist, particularly in the
light of one of Frost's stated beliefs. Paul picks up Keeper's argument that we
have to confront the fear deep in our souls that our courageous sacrifice is not
the best we have to offer, and may not be acceptable in "Heaven's sight." But
Paul has already established in his discourse about the Sermon on the Mount
that such ambiguity inevitably comprises the human situation. We cannot
attain mercy *or* perfection of our own right. Therefore, Paul insists that the
only prayer worth offering is this: "May my sacrifice / Be found acceptable
in Heaven's sight" (724–25). The sacrifice is one's life courageously lived; the
acceptability of that sacrifice is an act of mercy on Heaven's part.

At about the time *A Masque of Mercy* was being written (although Anna
K. Juhnke points out that the three early versions of "To Prayer I Think I
Go" are also pieces of the poem),[31] Frost wrote G. R. Elliott that "My fear
of God has settled down into a deep inward fear that my best offering may
not prove acceptable in his sight" (*Selected Letters* 525). The concern similarly arose through Frost's friendship with Rabbi Victor Reichert. The Rabbi
had written a scholarly study of Job, and their discussion frequently focused
upon biblical issues. While visiting Reichert in Cincinnati on 10 October
1946, Frost agreed to give a few remarks at the Rockdale Avenue Temple. His
remarks were based upon Psalm 19:14:

> May the words of my mouth and the
> meditation of my heart
> be pleasing in your sight,
> O Lord, my Rock and my Redeemer.

According to Lawrance Thompson, "RF later told Reichert that the service
helped him find precisely the ending he wanted for *A Masque of Mercy*"
(*Selected Letters* 555). In a 1953 letter to Reichert, the subject was still on
Frost's mind, this time because he wasn't sure that his poetic idea had a
biblical grounding: "Do you want to tell me where in the Bible if at all the
idea occurs as a prayer that our sacrifice whether of ourselves or our property
may be acceptable in His sight? Have I been making this up out of nothing?
You know how I am about chapter and verse—somewhat irresponsible some
would say" (*Selected Letters* 555).

If that concern helped Frost find the conclusion to his poem, however,
the idea is also enacted in deed. Keeper has the final words. He reiterates his
concept of courage of the heart battling against fear of the soul. Thereby he
also affirms his kinship with Jonah. But he also concedes to Paul the necessity

of laying Jonah's body before the cross in an act of mercy. The act responds to Keeper's earlier taunting of Paul about three crosses: star-crossed, mercy-crossed, or evil-crossed (440). The allusion works in several directions. The three crosses figure those on Golgotha at the crucifixion. Star-crossed love derives from *Romeo and Juliet*, a play where love breaks through all logic. The mercy-crossed derives from the act of Christ's crucifixion itself. Evil-crossed is the insistence upon justice, the fact that there had to be a crucifixion at all. It is fitting then, that as Keeper moves to take Jonah's feet to lay him before the cross, he says, "Nothing can make injustice just but mercy" (738). His very bending to Jonah in itself shapes an act of mercy.

Many readers see the mercy/justice conflict, which Frost calls "the pain of opposing goods exactly" (*Selected Letters* 466), unresolved in the poems. The change in Keeper, however, where he does in fact become My Brother's Keeper, suggests a resolution based upon love and mercy. In fact, one of the few other readers to consider this theme to be the fundamental continuity between the two *Masques* is Peter Stanlis. In "Robert Frost's Masques and the Classic American Tradition," Stanlis argues that human reason is insufficient to unravel life's moral mysteries, but that *Mercy* provides the alternative by affirming God's love as the basis for hope and faith.

The primary assumption of the poems is that reason has failed as a normative guide for right actions. Justice, however, is conceived by the characters of the poems as a rational category as opposed to an individual act or quality such as grace, forgiveness, love, or mercy. "Justice" is a legal term that attempts to be all-encompassing for the widest body of people possible. Else, of course, it is not justice but arbitrary whim. Indeed, all the characters' accusations of God's injustice fall precisely on that point: that it is arbitrary rather than absolute and normative. The problem is that when one's own reason cannot comprehend God's reasons, the human mind devises its own solutions to the conundrum of Justice/Injustice. We see several alternatives enacted in the *Masques*.

Job intemperately pleads for understanding from a God who insists that each person apprehends understanding existentially. Thyatira, whose role in the poem is too easily overlooked, represents the modern skeptic of all things supernatural. She often hides behind a thin, cynical sneer, ready to scoff at heaven and hell alike. She nicely shows how comfortable cynicism can be; she drifts off to sleep any time she wishes. But she also represents the modern age, cast in an ethical ennui.

In the case of Jonah we have the pleasure of watching a genuine transformation in character. Jonah enters as a frightened fugitive; he leaves like Bunyan's frightened Pilgrim, his eyes just glimpsing the Celestial City. Keeper too changes dramatically. Or, one might say, he finds the correct reasons for and proper understanding of his initial, cynical socialism. At first it is all anti-wealth and brittle railing against political injustice. At the end, as he bends to Jonah's body, he sees social justice as an act of love and mercy.

Although she has more lines than Thyatira, Jesse Bel is essentially a foil in this play. An alcoholic who preaches courage but can't practice it, Jesse drops into the background of the bookstore from where she makes her (often amusing) quips. Perhaps her most powerful line, however, occurs when she stands by the cellar door, which she has donated to Paul's use "To bring faith back" (566). One can almost imagine a plaintive wistfulness in her voice as she says, "Still what we need / Is something to believe in, don't we, Paul?" (567–68).

One finds change in Paul, too, and perhaps because of Jesse's plaintive question. He moves from titular Defender of the Word to an enactor of the Word. It is one thing to talk about Justice and Mercy; quite another to enact it. The fascinating thing is that the man seemingly without religion, the Brother's Keeper, New Deal Socialist, aides him in that transformation. It is very nearly, in fact, like a blending of two disparate sides into one, albeit slightly messy, whole.

Even though written relatively late in his career, the two *Masques* nonetheless represent a starting point for a consideration of Frost's ethics. The primary beliefs we glean from them are, first, that categorical rationalization is not a safe guide to ethical values, indeed may be inimical to them; second, that often confusing ethical values such as mercy, loving-kindness, and forgiveness are apprehended existentially, by an act of faith; and, third, that ethical values only become significant as they are acted upon. They are not merely abstract ideals, but concrete actions exemplified by Keeper moving to Jonah to carry him to the cross of mercy. If we find the Rationalist Ethic an unacceptable accounting for Frost's works, perhaps the Theological Ethic will provide clearer understanding.

NOTES

1. James Boswell, *Life of Johnson* (London: Oxford University Press, 1953, 1970), 561.

2. Benjamin Franklin, *The Autobiography* (New York: The Library of America, 1987), 1384.

3. David Hume, *An Inquiry Concerning Human Understanding* (New York: Bobbs-Merrill, 1955), 118.

4. Ibid., 138.

5. Ibid., 139.

6. Faggen, *Robert Frost*, 7–8.

7. Ibid., 8.

8. Ibid., 304.

9. Nathan Scott, *The Broken Center* (New Haven: Yale University Press, 1966), 11.

10. Robert Langbaum, *The Poetry of Experience* (New York: W. W. Norton, 1963), 16.

11. For a substantially detailed biographical accounting of "The Road Not Taken," see Larry Finger, "Frost's Reading of 'The Road Not Taken'" in the 1997 issue of *Robert Frost Review*.

12. William S. Doxey, "Whistling in the Dark: Robert Frost's Modernist Quest for Meaning," *West Georgia College Review* 23 (May 1993), 31.

13. Mordecai Marcus, *The Poems of Robert Frost: An Explication* (Boston: G. K. Hall, 1991), 231.

14. Reuben A. Brower, *The Poetry of Robert Frost: Constellations of Intention* (New York: Oxford University Press, 1963), 210.

15. Ibid.

16. Hall, *Robert Frost*, 40.

17. Peter J. Stanlis, "Robert Frost's Masques and the Classic American Tradition," *Frost: Centennial Essays III* (Jackson: University Press of Mississippi, 1974), 444.

18. Peter D. Poland, "Frost's 'Neither Out Far Nor In Deep,'" *Explicator* 52. (winter 1994), 96.

19. Beyond question, the most significant work in this area has been done by Alvin Plantinga, called by John Stackhouse, Jr., writing in *Christianity Today* (June 2001), "arguably the greatest philosopher of the last century."

20. Thyatira was one of the seven churches to whom Jesus dictated a letter through John in the book of Revelation. In general Jesus praises the church but he condemned a prophetess named Jezebel (see *Masque of Mercy*) who had led many people into idolatry, Satan-worship, and sexual immorality. A very helpful resource for following the allusions in the two poems is Laurence Perrine's "A Set of Notes for Frost's Two Masques."

21. Faggen, *Robert Frost*, 3.

22. John Robert Doyle, Jr., *The Poetry of Robert Frost: An Analysis* (New York: Hafner, 1965), 241. Frost's treatment of the nature of God in *A Masque of Reason* has elicited highly varied, sometimes diametrical, views. John Ciardi took the humanized God as one more sign that Frost had abandoned religion altogether. In "Robert Frost and His Use of Barriers: Man vs. Nature Toward God," Marion Montgomery turns the tables on humanity, arguing that the presumptive scene of God on the plywood throne actually incarnates humanity's failed understanding of God. In "The Bleak Landscape of Robert Frost," Roberta Borkat argues that "Frost is trying to show not man's misunderstanding of God, but God's lack of superhuman perfection" (458). Borkat's argument might be more persuasive if she had made such necessary distinctions as suprahuman versus superhuman: the latter, of course, God never claimed for himself.

23. This is not the only place in Frost's poetry where he struggles with a hidden God and the burning bush image (he also spoke occasionally of his poetry being hidden like God). In "Sitting by a Bush in Broad Sunlight," Frost asserts that:

There was one time and only the one
When dust really took in the sun;

And from that one intake of fire
All creatures still warmly aspire.

From the experience, Frost concludes, two things endure:

One impulse persists as our breath;
The other persists as our faith.

24. For a careful discussion of constraints upon God's power, see Nelson Pike, "Omnipotence and God's Inability to Sin."

25. Stanlis, "Robert Frost's Masques," 456.

26. Paola Loreto, "A Man in Front of His God, A Man in Front of Himself: The (Post) Modernity of Frost's *A Masque of Reason*," *Robert Frost Review* (fall 1999), 29.

27. The obvious biblical allusion for Jesse Bel is to the wicked Queen Jezebel of first and second Kings, although in the book of Revelation she is also depicted as an archetypal figure of evil, destroyed at the Second Coming. However, it is also possible that a very early run-in that Frost had with the poet and anthologist Jessie Belle Rittenhouse (1869–1948), may have played a minor role. In a letter to Sidney Cox in 1915, Frost halfheartedly dismissed the "temperate praise" in her review of *North of Boston* (*The New York Times*, 16 May 1915). But his full irritation erupts when he encounters her rejection of the rave reviews he had received in England: "The only nastiness in Jessie B.'s article is the first part where she speaks of the English reviews as fulsome. There she speaks dishonestly out of complete ignorance—out of some sort of malice or envy I should infer. Her anthology with the silly name [*The Little Book of Modern Verse: A Selection from the Works of Contemporaneous American Poets*] made a very bad miss in England" (Friendship 69).

28. Dallas Willard, *The Divine Conspiracy* (San Francisco: HarperCollins, 1998), 383.

29. Ibid., 383–84.

30. An interesting echo arises here from the poem, "I Years had been From Home" (J609), by Emily Dickinson, a poet whom Frost greatly admired. In the poem Dickinson imagines herself before the "Door" (of heaven), fearful to knock in case a "Face" should answer and ask her what her business was there. As such the poem is closely related to Dickinson's others, which use the poetic imagination to probe what lies beyond this side of life. Yet it intensifies here: "I laughed a crumbling laugh / That I should fear a Door." She reaches for the latch, trembling, "Lest back the awful Door should spring / And leave me in the Floor—." In Dickinson's poem, the narrator flees the house "like a thief." Jonah is unable to do so. All the doors to the outside are locked. Instead, the blow of the cellar door and the repulse "Crumple him on the floor" (518).

31. See Anna K. Juhnke, "Religion in Robert Frost's Poetry: The Play for Self-Possession," *American Literature* 36 (May 1964), 163. The poem "To Prayer I Think I Go," appears on pp. 130–31, 136, and 331 of *The Letters of Robert Frost to Louis Untermeyer*. The poem, which is not collected in *The Poetry of Robert Frost* but is included in its 1942 variant in *Collected Poems, Prose & Plays* (550), appears in variant forms, gathering lines through later versions. Common to each version is the image of going to prayer compared to descending a stair of self-abasement.

MARIE BORROFF

Another Look at Robert Frost's "Birches"

The reading of "Birches" I present in this essay[1] is founded on an interpretation of Frost's imagined world that I have argued for at length elsewhere and will summarize briefly here.[2] Frost's verse-parables, as I understand them, tell us that everything of value in human life derives from willed and well-intentioned encounters between human efforts and the resistance to them posed by the world. These encounters take place in three settings and involve three kinds of work. There is the primary work of manual labor: the pitting of human strength and skill against the weight and solidity of matter. There is the work of perception and thought: the endeavor to see what is present in reality, the world outside the self, and to accept the truth of what is seen, however reality and truth may fall short of wishful thinking. A third kind of work, akin to the second, is the endeavor to love the object of love, be it a life-partner, a friend, or something in the natural world, in and for itself. Beyond all these, evoked by symbolic suggestion, looms the work of the poet: the fashioning, in words, of new symbols for the pitching of the will "into commitments deeper and deeper" (786)[3] and the imposition of metrical patterns on the natural cadences of speech—Frost's "sentence sounds." Each kind of work yields its worthwhile product: a mowed field, a hard-won insight, a good marriage or friendship, a good poem. Each also has

From *Literary Imagination* 7, no. 1 (Winter 2005): 69–80. Copyright © 2010 by Association of Literary Scholars, Critics, and Writers.

its negative corollary in the form of loss: our encounters with the world wear us down, physically, mentally, and spiritually, and end by wearing us out.

As the order of the above topics implies, I consider the material realm, for Frost, to be primary and essential, preceding and giving rise to the abstract. In a late poem entitled "A Steeple on the House," he writes:

> A spire and belfry coming on the roof
> Means that a soul is coming on the flesh. (350)

The growth of a steeple-bush in the natural landscape, the raising of a steeple in the human landscape, and the dawning of spirituality in the human psyche are, for this poet, aspects of a single process.

The motif of upwardness in the passage I've just quoted is of great importance in the Frostian drama and appears there in many different forms, literal and figurative. It is often complemented by the downward pull of gravity or weariness to which the upward impulse must eventually succumb. Its presence is obvious in the early poem "Reluctance," whose speaker tells us that he has "climbed the hills of view,/ And looked at the world, and descended" (38). It plays a part in a later poem, "Two Look at Two," when the human partners, impelled upward by "love and forgetting," realize that they can climb no farther up the mountainside and are halted, as they turn back, by the appearance of another pair of partners: a buck and a doe (211–12). It takes a more trivial form (to give but one additional example) in "Fireflies in the Garden," whose titular insects, Frost says, "achieve at times a very star-like start. / Only, of course, they can't sustain the part" (225). And it goes without saying that the upward–downward trajectory is an essential element in "Birches."

It was "Birches" that Frost chose when asked, in 1933, to contribute a single poem to an anthology. He defended his choice by saying "I took it for its vocality and its ulteriority" (731).[4] By "vocality" I understand him to mean what I call "sound effects," and I shall have something to say on that subject later. "Ulteriority" calls for some preliminary discussion.

Frost said more than once that a poem was like a joke: to make the meaning of either explicit was to destroy its effect. In this opinion he resembles the speaker of his own "Mending Wall," who cannot, or does not wish to, explain to his neighbor what the "something" is that works against walls in spring:

> I could say "Elves" to him,
> But it's not elves exactly, and I'd rather
> He said it for himself. (40)

He liked to compare his poems to parables, citing, in his prose writings and at the end of "Directive," the passage in Mark 4 where Jesus says he speaks in parables to make his message inaccessible to those outside the kingdom of God, "that seeing, they may see, and not perceive; and hearing, they may hear, and not understand" (Mark 4:11–12).[5]

But there is more to "ulteriority" in Frost than the obscuration of messages, and this additional component is implied by his deceptively offhand statement that "[p]oetry is a kind of fooling that you got to get the hang of, and I go around playing that." He had just quoted the untitled couplet toward the end of *In the Clearing*: "It takes all sorts of in and outdoor schooling / To get adapted to my kind of fooling" (478).[6] He was not above leading his readers astray,[7] preventing them from sensing a hidden meaning by distracting their attention, as the speaker of "A Boundless Moment" leads his companion astray by telling him that a beech tree "clinging to its last year's leaves" in winter woods is called "the Paradise-in-bloom," before relenting and telling the truth (215–16). I have long been convinced that in "Mending Wall," Frost makes the question of whether or not to mend the literal wall so interesting, and presents both sides of it with such equal plausibility, that it monopolizes our attention, with the result that we fail to see the full importance of the figurative wall between two human beings that is the real subject of the poem. That wall separates an imaginative mind—the speaker's—from an unimaginative one—the neighbor's—and is clearly a wall that should be done away with if at all possible. The speaker tries to break through it, making a joke that falls flat in order to "put a notion in his head," but the neighbor's mind cannot get beyond the inherited saying he repeats verbatim. (For "speaker," we may substitute "poet"; for "neighbor," "reader.")

Ulteriority in Frost sometimes takes the form of an allusion—of language reminding those who have ears to hear of a specific text, beyond the poem, whose identity remains implicit. In "Hyla Brook," for example, when the speaker says solemnly that "This as it will be seen is other far / Than with brooks taken otherwhere in song," that is, the dried-up brook he has been talking about is quite different from the kind of brook that has been otherwise described in other poems, I think he is pointing at the celebrated prolixity of "*The* Brook" described by Alfred, Lord Tennyson, which, though men may come and men may go, babbles on copiously, as does the poem itself.

* * *

The classicist Helen Bacon has shown, in essays that can be highly recommended to anyone who wishes to look deep into this deceptively lucid poet,

how pervasively informed Frost's imagination was by the classical Greek
and Latin literatures he knew so well, and how often, and how silently, he
incorporated references to them in his poetry.[8] Two poems she discusses at
some length are "Wild Grapes" and "One More Brevity."

In "Wild Grapes," Bacon finds a sustained allusion to Euripides' *Bacchae*.[9] The plot of each involves a human being who rides skyward on a tree
and is brought back to earth, but the results are unlike: death by dismember-
ment for King Pentheus, safety and a kind of rebirth for Frost's little girl. The
girl, now a woman, reminisces before telling her story, dropping an additional
classical allusion as she does so. She says that she

> was come after like Eurydice
> And brought down safely from the upper regions;
> And the life I live now's an extra life. (183)

Bacon notes in this detail Frost's inversions of his classical source: Eurydice
was "come after" in the nether regions, not the upper, and she was not
brought back safely: the attempt to retrieve her was unsuccessful, so that she
failed to acquire the "extra life" of Frost's heroine.

In a more complicated, but cogent, interpretation of "One More Brevity,"[10] Bacon begins by recapitulating "the unlikely subject-matter" of the
poem, "a visit from a stray dog, a Dalmatian, who unexpectedly drops in to
[Frost's] Vermont cabin, spends the night, and vanishes the next morning"
(91). She remarks on what I see as another example of Frost's trick of keeping
our attention focused on the surface of the narrative: "the episode is described
in such an endearingly and doggily appropriate way that it scarcely seems
to need exploration" (91). In the analysis that follows, Bacon juxtaposes the
poet's opening reference to Sirius, the brightest star in the sky, with his ret-
rospective suspicion that the dog who had paid him a fleeting visit was none
other than an "avatar" of "the star itself, Heaven's greatest star" (434). She
then posits a series of links leading from the literal visitation to the figure of
Augustus Caesar as treated by Virgil in the *Aeneid*. She notes that the soul of
the murdered Julius Caesar was thought to have appeared at his funeral as a
comet, and that "Augustus, Caesar's adoptive son and successor, was saluted as
the son of a god, himself to become a god after death and to join his 'father' in
the sky" (93). In books 8 and 10 of the *Aeneid*, Aeneas is represented as prefig-
uring Virgil's contemporary, the emperor entitled Augustus, whose future victories, "his triple triumph of Actium, Dalmatia, and Alexandria" (95–96), are
represented on Aeneas's shield. There is a further connection between Sirius
and the month of August, which was named after Augustus: the "dog days,"
when Sirius is especially conspicuous, occur in that month. The name Frost

fancifully bestows on his visitor, "Gustie, Dalmatian Gus, that is," thus alludes both to the career of that emperor and to one of his celebrated victories.

It is fair to ask whether, granted the correctness of Bacon's interpretations, the covert presence of these classical texts enhances the meanings of the two poems, and if so, how. Bacon answers the first of these questions in the affirmative. She sees in both "Wild Grapes" and *Bacchae* a "contrast between true enlightenment and earthbound common sense that leaves no room for wildness and instinct" (89). And we may further note, in "Wild Grapes," the appearance of the same contrasting pair in the form of the mind and the heart, in the grown woman's concluding reflections, and her implied valuation of the latter over the former. The meaning of "One More Brevity" is more elusive. At the end of the poem, Frost refrains, with the reluctance we have already noted, from making explicit the message brought him by the canine avatar of ancient glory:

> A symbol was all he could hope to convey,
> An intimation, a shot of ray,
> A meaning I was supposed to seek,
> And finding, wasn't disposed to speak. (434)

Bacon says that "if Dalmatian Gus is really Augustus Caesar, then the undisclosed message for the poet must be something about the pain and struggle involved in trying to give social and political reality to a political ideal" (97). An additional inference seems justified from the lines preceding those just quoted: that the poet sees himself as vulnerable to the reproach of having failed to use his own creative powers to aid in that struggle (he thinks the "avatar" had perhaps favored him with a visit "to show by deeds he didn't resent / My having depended on him so long, / And yet done nothing about it in song").

To grant that the two poems are alike as instances of the same kind of ulteriority, and that their ulterior meanings are relevant to their ostensible ones, is not, however, to grant them equal stature in the Frostian canon. In "Wild Grapes," the speaker's reminiscent account of an experience that frightened her as a small girl holds our interest, and her concluding reflections on its significance are couched in language worth remembering. We respond to the drama with a seriousness that is in key with whatever memories of Euripides' *Bacchae* the poem may lead us to experience. I doubt whether, for readers of "One More Brevity," the combination of modern and classical materials works so well. For all the endearing and doggy appropriateness of Frost's account of the dog's arrival and bedding down, the incident has an inescapable triviality, and some of the speaker's comments on it have a self-conscious

cuteness that sort ill with invocations of Virgilian eloquence and the grandeur
that was Rome. A stray dog and an emperor posthumously elevated to divinity
make strange bedfellows. The poem ends unsatisfyingly, in indirection leading
to the above-quoted refusal on the poet's part to express whatever meaning
he found in it when recollecting it. Here, as perhaps also on other occasions,
we may tax Frost with having failed to heed his own dictum that "all who
hide too well away / Must speak and tell us where they are" ("Revelation" 28).

Thinking now about the superficial and possible ulterior meanings of
"Birches," I find that the boy's "play" as described in the poem fits Frost's
concept of work as I understand it: birch-swinging is an encounter in which
physical effort, abetted by an acquired skill, is pitted against the force of gravity. It yields a "product" in the form of a moment of triumph: the pleasure,
earned by the climb, of launching out at the strategic moment and riding
earthward "with a swish." The trick of pouring water slowly into a cup until
it rises above the brim without spilling over, to which Frost likens the boy's
painstaking way of climbing, seems a felicitous metaphor for the poet's
charging of his language with an import above and beyond its literal meaning
without letting it "spill over" into explicit statement. The third and last section
of the poem brings in the negative corollary of work, in Frost's world (and
ours): the wear and tear accompanying all effort, exemplified on the physical level by the vehicle of his simile, the tickling and scratching suffered by
one who bushwhacks his way through a pathless wood, and on the mental
level by the tiresome "considerations" that complicate and painfully thwart
our decision-making in life.

Each part of "Birches" is clear in itself; each makes good reading.
How—I trust that I may be allowed in this venue to raise so old-fashioned
a question—do the relationships among them contribute to the meaning of
the poem as a whole?

To begin with, the account early in the poem of what happens the
morning after an ice storm, in all the fullness of its visual and auditory
imagery, is surely longer and more elaborate than is needed for it to fulfill
its ostensible purpose: to flesh out the speaker's self-correcting statement
that ice storms, not boys, bend birches down to stay. What is more, it seems
to have been made deliberately conspicuous as a tour-de-force in which
just about everything in the poet's rhetorical bag of tricks is put to use.[11] Its
language is marked by a series of metaphors ("enamel," "crystal shells," "avalanching," "broken glass") as well as two extended similes (the heaps of ice
fragments on the ground make it seem "as if the inner dome of heaven had
fallen," and the birches bowed over by ice storms look like "girls on hands
and knees that throw their hair / Before them over their heads to dry in the
sun"). The lines exhibiting all this figuration display not only Frost's skill

in ringing the changes on the iambic pentameter norm, but also one of his most brilliantly sustained mimetic sound effects, in which we hear the sibilant consonants of "Soon the sun's warmth makes them shed crystal shells / Shattering and avalanching on the snow-crust." The passage is so blatant a display of poetic pyrotechnics that when the speaker blandly assigns it to "Truth ... With all her matter-of-fact about the ice-storm," it's all I can do to keep a straight face. Matter-of-fact, my eye. When I then ask what the implied opposite of truth is here, the answer that suggests itself is not "falsity" but "imagination"—that is, poetry. If, as our awareness of Frost's trickiness empowers us to do, we raise the question of an ulterior motive in these lines, the answer has to reside somehow in the fact that they bring to our attention his virtuosity as a poet.

Along with certain other readers, I find in the passage an additional sign of ulteriority in the form of an allusion to Shelley's "Adonais."[12] Surely the presence of the words "many-colored" and "glass" in the neighborhood of a reference to a "dome" that has fallen and broken into pieces points us toward Shelley's lofty declamation at the end of that poem: "Life, like a dome of many-colour'd glass, / Stains the white radiance of Eternity, / Until Death tramples it to fragments."[13] Woven unobtrusively into the language of the passage, the allusion exemplifies a characteristic mode of interaction in Frost, described by Richard Poirier as taking place "between 'voice' which is vernacular ... and 'voice' which is poetic, taken from the poetry of the past, Emerson or Wordsworth, Keats or Tennyson or Shelley."[14] I would only add that the former sounds directly in the inner ear, whereas the latter hovers in the knowledgeable reader's imagination.

A deliberate—one might even say brazen—divagation from the truth takes place when the speaker goes on, after talking about the ice storm, to indulge himself in fictionalized wish-fulfillment. Having begun the poem by saying that he "likes to think" a boy is responsible for the bowed-over birches he sees in summer woods, he returns to that preference and conjures up a boy to fit it, blandly spinning a realistic account of how the boy did what he knows no boy could have done.

The final section of the poem, the nineteen lines beginning "So was I once myself a swinger of birches," presents us with additional discrepancies between report and reality. I take it that the speaker's "dream" of going back to be a swinger of birches is merely that—he is far enough beyond boyhood to have lost the ability to maintain his poise while climbing a birch tree to the very top. Yet once he has expressed his wish to commit what Dorothy Parker called "temporary suicide" and afterwards come back to earth, and has affirmed that "Earth's the right place for love," he imagines himself as a swinger of birches and describes once again the physical actions involved.

How do these parts fit together, and how does the section as a whole comple-
ment the earlier sections of the poem?

My attempt to answer these questions will take as its point of departure some observations I have derived from an earlier study of the effects of
sound symbolism in Frost's poetic language, meaning by "sound symbolism"
the conspicuous repetition of the same or similar vowels and consonants.[15]
I identified in certain poems and passages what I called a "chanting voice,"
characterized, among other things, by such effects (134–35). The chanting voice proved to be associated thematically with Frost's notorious "dark
side," his dramatization of moments or episodes in which the central figure
confronts a literal or figurative threat of extinction (135). In a subgroup of
the poems that dramatize such experiences, the threatening agent is winter
snow and darkness; two important examples are "The Onset" and "Desert
Places." In these, the language describing what I call the "white nightmare" is
marked, in particular, by the repetition of sibilant consonants (135, 138). In
"The Onset," the "hissing" of the first heavy snow as it hits the bare ground
has menacing implications that are dispelled later in the poem in the image
of the "disappearing snake" of the April rill carrying off the melted snow of
the previous winter. As Frost imagines it, the snow that fills the natural landscape threatens the human agent within it not only with extinction but with
obliteration in the root sense of that word: the disappearance of the letters
traced by the poet on the page in a terrifying "blanker whiteness . . . / With
no expression, nothing to express" (138–39).[16]

If we accept these presuppositions, the ice storm in "Birches" can be
understood as symbolically posing a threat of death, reinforced by the sibilance of the language describing it and, for those who are aware of it, by the
allusion to the ending of "Adonais," with its exhortation to those who love the
soul of the departed poet to join him in death:

> Life, like a dome of many-colored glass,
> Stains the white radiance of Eternity
> Until Death tramples it to fragments.—Die,
> If thou wouldst be with that which thou dost seek!

In the final section of "Birches," the speaker confronts momentarily the possibility of his own death, and responds with an *absit omen*:

> May no fate wilfully misunderstand me
> And grant me half my wish and snatch me away
> Not to return.

"Earth's the right place for love" follows immediately, and, in turn, is followed immediately by "I'd like to go by climbing a birch tree." This last statement refers back to "I'd like to get away from earth awhile," specifying a method of achieving this separation. But "go" takes on, in context, the more specific meaning it has in playful allusions to dying like "It's a wonderful way to go," with reference, say, to death by chocolate. Descending to earth after climbing successfully to the very top of a birch tree—or, more generally, after successfully negotiating the trajectory of a life of laborious achievement—would also be a wonderful way to go.

I suggest that in the opening section of "Birches" we see the poet responding to the threatening implications of winter ice by a display of poetic powers. He simultaneously confronts, by covert allusion, one of his most important precursors in the classical canon of English poetry. But the allusion, like that to Eurydice in "Wild Grapes," works by inversion. Far from taking Shelley's pronouncement seriously, he demystifies and domesticates it, figuratively exchanging the grand cosmic perspective of "Adonais" for an earthbound one. Shelley's trampled fragments become "heaps of broken glass to sweep away"—clutter left on the floor as the result of some household mishap.

More profoundly, everything in the poem—indeed, everything in Frost—repudiates Shelley's impassioned summons to transcend the limitations of human life, with its invocation of the "sustaining Love" whose longed-for fires "consume . . . away the clouds of cold mortality." Not for Frost the Platonic "abode where the Eternal are," from which the precursor poet imagines the soul of Adonais beckoning. The right place for human beings is the world as we know it, the world in which all happiness comes from pitting ourselves against what is outside ourselves in any worthwhile form of labor we choose, including love and the writing of poems. In this world, those who strive upward in one way or another "toward heaven" must eventually yield to the downward pull of earth.

"Birches" shows us a man meditating on something he used to do as a boy, something that involved taking pains and rewarded him with happiness.[17] He himself, we infer, is far enough past boyhood to think occasionally of his own death, and to have experienced the world at times as a frustrating place where petty "considerations" hinder the free exercise of physical and spiritual powers.[18] When, at the end of his meditation, he thinks again of the playful work, or laborious play, of his boyhood, his description of it becomes an allegorical representation of the trajectory of life. It should be noted that in this second description of birch-swinging, the emphasis shifts from the climber's actions to the tree. Whereas earlier, it is the boy who is said to decide when he will fling out and enjoy his ride downward, now it is the tree which, when it can no longer bear the climber's weight, lowers him to earth. So, too, the human body, when the weight of life becomes too much for it, lets us down.

As for the pictorial detail of the "black branches" and "snow-white trunk" in the second description of the climb, it reminds me of something Eudora Welty once said. In her story "A Worn Path," the ancient black woman called Aunt Phoenix falls into a ditch while walking through the woods toward Natchez. Lying there, she goes into a trance in which she sees a hand offering her a piece of marble cake on a plate. When someone asked Welty whether the black and white of the marble cake was intended as a symbol of racial segregation, Welty replied, "No, it's just a recipe my grandmother made."[19] So I would say that the branches are said to be black, and the trunk white, because Frost knew that is what birch trees look like. And yet, having thought my way to the end of my interpretation, I also see that the detail works by keeping my attention on the tree rather than on the climber.

Frost wrote, in "Kitty Hawk," that

"Nothing can go up
But it must come down."
Earth is still our fate. (449)

But where, he might have asked, is the writing of poetry likely to go better—what better platform than earth could there be for the imagination's joyous upward foray against gravity in all its forms, an enterprise described nowhere in his poetry more movingly than in "Birches"?

Notes

1. Originally presented as a talk entitled "Steeple and Steeple Bush" at the Eighth Annual Conference of the Association of Literary Scholars and Critics on 19 October 2002.

2. See "Robert Frost: To Earthward," in *Frost: Centennial Essays II*, ed. Jac Tharpe (Jackson, Miss., 1976), pp. 21–39; "Robert Frost's New Testament: The Uses of Simplicity," in Borroff, *Language and the Poet* (Chicago, 1979), pp. 23–41; "Sound Symbolism as Drama in the Poetry of Robert Frost," *PMLA* 107 (1992): 131–43; and "Hay, Wild Orchids, and a Snake" and "Listening with the Imagination," videotaped lectures on *To Hear Their Voices: Chaucer, Shakespeare and Frost,* Yale Great Teachers Series (Florence, Ky., 1995; rpt. New Haven, n.d.).

3. Unless another source is specified, page numbers given for quoted passages refer to *Robert Frost: Collected Poems, Prose, and Plays,* ed. Richard Poirier and Mark Richardson (New York, 1995).

4. Cf. "The Constant Symbol," 786: "the chiefest [thing about poetry] is that it is metaphor, saying one thing and meaning another, saying one thing in terms of another, the pleasure of ulteriority."

5. In a talk entitled "On Taking Poetry," given at the Bread Loaf English School in 1955 (pp. 818–29), Frost said, "But this thing that I've brought up before here. I've quoted it, I think, in a couple of places, and it's always coming into my head: that these things are said in parable so the wrong people can't understand them and so get saved" (819).

6. *Interviews with Robert Frost*, ed. Edward Connery Lathem (New York, 1966), p. 161. In a talk at Bread Loaf entitled "On Taking Poetry," Frost made a similar statement: "I suppose a poem is a kind of fooling. . . . Of course, if the height of everything is fooling—God's foolishness—then poetry mounts somewhere into a kind of fooling. It's something hard to get. It's what you spend a good deal of education on—just getting it right" (818).

7. In a letter to Leonidas W. Payne Jr., Frost said he had been asked, "In my 'Mending Wall' was my intention fulfilled with the characters portrayed and the atmosphere of the place? . . . I should be sorry if a single one of my poems stopped with either of those things—stopped anywhere in fact. My poems . . . are all set to trip the reader head foremost into the boundless. Ever since infancy I have had the habit of leaving my blocks carts chairs and such like ordinaries where people would be pretty sure to fall forward over them in the dark. Forward, you understand, *and* in the dark. . . . It is my intention we are speaking of—my innate mischievousness" (*Selected Letters of Robert Frost*, ed. Lawrance Thompson [New York, 1964], p. 344). Cf. "I am not undesigning" (Letter to Thomas B. Mosher, ibid., 84).

8. The essays by Bacon that I have seen on this subject are as follows: "In- and Outdoor Schooling: Robert Frost and the Classics," *American Scholar* 43 (1974): 640–49; an "abridged and modified" version of an essay with the same title published in *Robert Frost: Lectures on the Centennial of His Birth* (Washington D.C., 1975), pp. 3–25; "For Girls: From 'Birches' to 'Wild Grapes,'" *Yale Review*, n.s., 67 (1977): 13–29; "Dialogue of Poets: *Mens Animi* and the Renewal of Words," *Massachusetts Review* 19 (1978): 319–34; "The Contemporary Reader and Robert Frost: The Heavenly Guest of 'One More Brevity' and *Aeneid* 8," *St. Johns Review* (Summer 1981): 3–10; and "Frost and the Ancient Muses," in *The Cambridge Companion to Robert Frost* (Cambridge, 2001), pp. 75–100.

9. See "Frost and the Ancient Muses," 83–90. Those who find my abbreviated versions of Bacon's interpretations unconvincing are urged to read the originals.

10. See "Frost and the Ancient Muses," 90–97; cf. "The Contemporary Reader and Robert Frost," 4–10.

11. The passage describing the aftermath of the ice storm (lines 4–24) was not, in fact, part of the poem as Frost first wrote it, though he added it before its first publication, in August 1915 in the *Atlantic*. John Evangelist Walsh, in *Into My Own: The English Years of Robert Frost* (New York, 1988) quotes Frost as saying, "some forty years after the fact," that "Birches" was made up of "two fragments soldered together so long ago that I have forgotten where the joint is" (25). If my interpretation of the poem is correct, the description adds to it a profundity it otherwise would have lacked. For its date of composition, see n. 17, below.

12. See, e.g., Jeffrey Meyers, *Robert Frost: A Biography* (Boston, 1996), p. 138, and W. D. Snodgrass's note on his poem "Albert Speer" in *The Norton Anthology of Modern Poetry*, 2d ed., ed. Richard Ellmann and Robert O'Clair (New York, 1988): "Compare Robert Frost's 'Birches' . . . I . . . wanted this passage's recollection of Shelley's 'Adonais' and all its idealism" (1163). It is amusing to find that, in a lecture at the Browne and Nichols School, Frost, having described how poets freshen their

language by "fetching" words out of their places, quoted the passage from "Birches" and asked, "I wonder if you think I fetched that word dome too far?"—without, of course, revealing his actual source (*Collected Poems, Prose, Plays* 697).

13. Quoted from *The Norton Anthology of English Literature* 6th ed., ed. M. H. Abrams (New York, 1993) 2:730.

14. Richard Poirier, *Robert Frost: The Work of Knowing* (New York, 1977), p. 20.

15. "Sound Symbolism as Drama in the Poetry of Robert Frost," *PMLA* 107 (1992): 131–44. Further references to this essay will consist of page numbers in parentheses.

16. Cf. Frost's tribute to the destructive power of ice in "Fire and Ice" (*Collected Poems, Prose, Plays* 204). The theme of the death threat posed by a winter storm is given a delightfully comedic turn in "Wilful Homing" (310), which begins "It is getting dark and time he drew to a house / But the blizzard blinds him to any house ahead." The poem's descriptive language features a sibilance that becomes especially conspicuous in a reference to the "icy souse" of snow getting down the speaker's neck. It ends in a neat double entendre, with the observation that if the arrival of the traveler on foot is too long delayed, "to those concerned he may seem a little late."

17. It should be noted that the phrase "swinger of birches," used twice in the final section of the poem, has an honorific ring by virtue of its grammatical form (compare "So I too used to swing birches once"). That is, it seems to express an action central to the identity of the person bearing it, as does the epithet *hippodamos*, "tamer (or breaker) of horses," in Homer, rather than an incidental way of behaving. Cf. Auden's line "Sad is Eros, builder of cities," in "In Memory of Sigmund Freud."

18. The poem need not, of course, be interpreted as autobiographical, but it is worth pointing out that Frost wrote it in late July 1913, when he was thirty-nine. See Walsh, *Into My Own*, 115.

19. Kate Bogan, "Southern Graces: Eudora Welty, 1909–2001," *Times Literary Supplement* (3 August 2001): 12.

KENNETH LINCOLN

Quarreling Frost, Northeast of Eden

> It takes all sorts of in and outdoor schooling
> To get adapted to my kind of fooling.

When Robert Frost talked about pinning syllables on a sound-curve as hanging garments on a clothesline, or playing tennis with the metric net up, he wasn't just fooling. You could tie the sleeves and pant legs together, he added, no benefit to the clothes. Cracker-barrel card perhaps, he did study Latin and Greek at Harvard, taught the classics, and believed in formal distinctions over free verse. "Instead of Rah Rah Rah Radcliffe," Frost says in the twenty-fourth of his forty-eight notebooks published by Harvard's Belknap Press in 2006, "I cheer 'Iambics forever!' Tell the I Amb Jehovah said." There are rules of nature and tested rhyme traditions, the gravity of use and the uses of proven norms. On this score the Yankee pundit aligned with Modernist traditions of individual talent.

Verse has accentual rhythms, and Frost tied iambic cadence to music and dance—"the straight-crookedness of a good walking stick," he added from his woodsy rambles—grains and knots and growth rings that tense the line and torque it and give poetry the burly resilience of human speech, only more so. "Write with the ear to the speaking voice," he advised in his forty-fourth notebook. "Seek first in poetry concrete images of sound—concrete

From *Southwest Review* 93, no. 1 (2008): 93–111. Copyright © 2008 by Kenneth Lincoln.

153

tone images." The ear may be the best of poets, he argued, but its cut and concision are whetted by the mind, its edge honed by hand. *Scythe* and *axe* were the writer's favorite farm tools—consonants with aspirant thickness and soughing vowels, sounds that say physically what *characters* they are. Uncommon craft and common use, Frost reached below Wordsworth's median, the working classics of time-worn texts, *The Odyssey* through Shakespeare, the Book of Job through Hardy, Aeschylus through Yeats. "The best thing to be said of the classics is that they have been good enough to survive," he wrote in his twenty-ninth notebook.

"Rub your finger on a smooth surface so as to make it 'catch' and vibrate enough for a 'note'": the poet wrote in notebook nine, "just so the speech rhythm on the verse rhythm." Run the handled adz of speech across the grain of metric pattern to resonate what Frost termed "the sound of sense," irregular inflections against regular tone patterns, he added to John Bartlett in a letter that tacked a Preface to his collected poems, "The Figure a Poem Makes." Made by hand crafted human care, the poem cuts an acoustic figure in time and space. The lost generation's *il miglior fabbro*, Ezra Pound, who got Frost's first books published and reviewed in London, held in the *ABC of Reading* that "Rhythm is form cut into TIME, as a design is determined SPACE."

In living rhythmic figures the poet must connect with locally hewn time and space. The writer's tears flow through the reader's eyes, the poet's surprises startle his audience awake. "Reality," he said coolly looking upriver, "is the cold feeling on the end of the trout's nose from the stream that runs away." And the poet's currents ran contrary to expectation, as with his home farm's "West-Running Brook." The mantra "Dark Darker Darkest" courses through the forty-eight notebooks like the River Styx, and his frosty temperament, poetics, and patrilineal heritage hovered around the dew point. Like a "piece of ice on a hot stove," Frost imaged by way of his surname, the poem rides through reading "on its own melting," natural as winter rime pebbling at sunrise or spring sleet warming to rain. The lyric passage of crystal to fluid in a talk-song—metric pattern flowing to narrative usage, dramatic sound measuring to aesthetic sense—is the same for love's tremor through the body, the poet said, "a momentary stay" against the confusion of time begging grace from eternity. There is no sentimental lint on this man's pant leg. He did not claim to save mankind, only to humor his reader against false assurance. "I learned to laugh when I was young," he jotted in his nineteenth notebook, "And all my life the habit clung."

A "lover's quarrel with the world," the poet said fetchingly of his work, a commitment neither side can back out of, but argues passionately with Sophoclean recognition of wedded differences. The down-under roots of words and things tell all, as Pound argued of *paideuma*. "(Poetry is a deep indwelling.)" Frost jotted in notebook four. No thematic hobbyhorse or Trojan nag of theory will carry a reader through the old man's rocky pastures. "Not that meter, though the meter is much and not that tone though the tone is more," he insisted in the nineteenth notebook, "and not that meter and tone together are enough. There must be cadence cadence cadence." Cadence or cadenza, as the Latin-versed poet well knew, comes from *cadere*, to "fall," and where the poet's foot, voice, heart, and thought rhythmically fall determine most everything in Frost's post-Edenic verse. You have to get down and walk word-by-word through his song-lines, for better or worse, what has served for ages as careful listening and close reading. "Words that have been mouthed like a common tin cup," he advises in the eighth notebook, "chasing a drop of quicksilver around a plate with pinches." We take his hand and read the sage on his own terms. "Think a poem out," he says in the forty-seventh notebook, "or feel it out."

Frost's poems dramatize *character* in New England, and Edenic missteps pattern all of his great work in a Calvinist land where the Bible and *Paradise Lost* were essential reading in every parlor. "In Adam's fall We sinned all," he quipped of Milton's Puritan pessimism in his twenty-sixth notebook. "We haven't had a chance from the day Eve ate that rotten apple." From reversed falling feet and gapped line breaks, to thematic undertones and after-echoes of ideas, to cadenced decrescendos and the end-reaches of time, what Frost called *abruption*, literally a sudden breaking off or miscarriage (*abruptio placentae*), underlies the surprises, break-ups, and dark mysteries of the poems. Warning against "death by jingle," he defined poetry as "that good in human nature which can never become habit" (notebook forty-seven). Consider the classic monologues on birches, walls, and apples as three post-paradisiacal ages of a young, middle-aged, and old Adam in the Northeast Kingdom. "Poetry is a fresh look and a fresh listen" (notebook forty-five). Then allow Eve to share the stage in playing out the New England fall of an ill-fated marriage through personally witnessed home burial.

Climbing to Cross Purposes
It was a thing of beauty and was sent
To live out its life like an ornament.
—"A Young Birch"

The boy climbing birches far from village games is a man looking back at Eden, literally nostalgic "delight." The tensile trees of a lost paradise bend left and right across the darker forest backdrop, and he'd like to think a boy has been swinging the branches, but not so gravely physical as an ice storm. "Often you must have seen them," he breaks the steady blank verse layout mid-line, as the folksy appeal to boyish delights is backlighted by the "shattering and avalanching" crystal shells of chill fancy that "the inner dome of heaven had fallen." Winter apocalypse and summer nostalgia, contrary revelations of things to come, or just another storm? Frost twists in the crosscurrents of having things more ways than one.

Pulp for toothpicks and firewood, the slender young trees "never right themselves" again, even if lonely men fantasize birches years later trailing branches and leaves on the ground "like girls on hands and knees" drying their hair in the sun. Frost buries an Adamic key in picturesque birch—erotic Eve to a dominant Adam or supplicant to a dour Jehovah? Pre-Puritan or post-Edenic, the poet's images don't settle into allegorical road signs, rather they tendril the undergrowth to keep the elect reader puzzling the dark woods. "Fun playing with tales from the Bible. Inexhaustible book," Frost jots in notebook thirty-one. "Only danger is if people aren't brought up on it a poet can't track on it." The Calvinist New World promises a scouring search for truth through an old-stone savage landscape, as the poet told 1937 graduating Oberlin students: "And the thing New England gave most to America was the thing I am talking about: a stubborn clinging to meaning,—to purify words until they meant again what they should mean." Frost harbors an obdurate purism, then, a scouring labor of love to clean up the language and make it real from the roots down. "Puritanism had that meaning entirely: a purifying of words and a renewal of words and a renewal of meaning." How go about this deep cleansing in a poem?

The speaker rights the unrhymed, enjambing pentameter walk of Renaissance blank verse: "But I was going to say when Truth broke in / With all her matter of fact about the ice storm." The Truth of Nature proves feminine, he lets slip, interruptive of a boy's pranks the way Mother Nature corrects an errant son who would *subdue* his father's trees, conquering their stiffness "one by one." High jinx in paradise, the ensuing lines throw the regular metrics off-line with trochaic spondees and an unsettling anapest: "Then he flung outward, feet first, with a swish, / Kicking his way down through the air to the ground." Is this a little boy's bout against God the Father, climbing the forbidden Tree of Knowledge and flinging his mortal weight out and down like some seraphic acrobat returning to the ground where the girls spread their floral hair in the sun? "Bundle of toothpicks for kindling," Frost noted a practical use for birches in notebook nine. Again personal reminiscence reminds "you"-the-reader of transgressive youth in steady iambic pentameter: "So was I once myself a swinger of birches. / And so I dream of going back to be."

A world-weary Adam would regress to the delights of Eden, but how? He'd like to "get away from earth awhile," then come back and start over, not expiring, he hastens to add, no Fate "snatch me away / Not to return."

Tone is all at this point, understatement a laconic troll under the bridge of understanding. "Earth's the right place for love: / I don't know where it's likely to go better." Indeed, the thin edge of human sense wedge, the graveled ballast necessary for poetic torsion—where else but earth could we love woods, walls, and dividing paths? How we say the words affects how we mean to live in reality. "Poetry lives in the tenor of the sentence" (notebook eight). The vernacular grounding of aerial fancy steadies the boy's climbing and coming back, poetic flight girdered more or less in blank verse and no-nonsense righting of fanciful sensibilities dependant on earthly sense, what Williams termed "the ground sense necessary" in his burial poem "Tract." Reading Wordsworth by way of Aristotle, Frost noted in his thirty-first notebook, "nothing comes down from above but what has so long since come up from below that we have forgotten its origin." He was fed up with the term *nature poet* and preferred kinship with a natural scientist's "fresh noticing" of grounded details. "All is observation of nature (human nature included) consciously or unconsciously made by our eyes and minds developed from the ground up. We notice traits of nature—that's all we do." The poet advised being careful with the word "natural—with all words in fact. You have to play the words close to the realities. And the realities are from below upward and from outside inward."

If New England Adam has to live out his years northeast of Eden, surviving by the sweat of his brow though he holds *dominion* over all, he wants to be standing on the earth, not beneath it. "My growing suspicion is that practically all is from down up and from out in" (notebook thirty-one). Make no heavenly mistake, this fallen place is right for love, and it's hard to come up with a "likely" alternative. *Like* is always a trip word for Frost: it's potentially misleading as a simile that can't quite nail down what he's talking about, but has to glance off. A "snow-drop" dimpled spider, a heal-all "like a froth," and dead moth wings "carried like a paper kite"—all appallingly white as deadly similes in the protective discoloration or camouflage of "Design." On the other hand, likening is so humanly colloquial in local speech—the failing struggle to say what you mean and mean what you say—that "like" can't be abandoned. A stutter in the forward progress of syntax, slightly off the mark of the telling image, a substitute filler—*like* isn't exactly what we'd like to say, but speakers settle for it when they can't find the right word. It's become a less literate speech marker among the young.

We incline toward truth, then, fancy things a slant way, since exact words fail, and speakers try to imagine a world scrimmed through faulty likenesses. "I'd like to go by climbing a birch tree," the poet muses in steady iambic rhythm a foot short, "And climb black branches up a snow-white trunk / *Toward* heaven, till the tree could bear no more, / But dipped its top and

set me down again." This is hard spondaic work trying to escape earth's gravity. The diction thickens and meter tendons against easy ascension, the black
branches line-striped like stark pages against the snow-white trunk of God's
ladder. The key word "*Toward* heaven" is capitalized and italicized across the
line break. Let the poet incline toward eternity, get high as possible poetically,
challenge God up the laddered-cross, but then swing out and back down
safely to earthly lines, as a boy bending birches in the pre-walled garden.
Pound's 1913 Parisian crowd of "Petals on a wet, black bough" lies not far
from the poem's genesis, but Frost ducks the vatic for the vernacular terres-
trially basing his mortal vision. Adam would do it all over again, "good both
going and coming back," as long as his second chance is not aborted by a tran-
scendent end to things. He's a mischievous player, a boy too far from town for
baseball, and he hedges his bets against eternal rapture by marking his stance
on earth and his steps poetically. "A Play no matter how deep," Frost noted in
the nineteenth notebook, "has got to be so playful that the audience are left
in doubt whether it is deep or shallow." It's all right for the poet to recall that
boys will be boys, and to get all the fun you can out of the game, but always
remember there's a lot more coming and going, many miles to travel, years
to bear up the forested road to heaven. After all that, who knows. "Forgive,
O Lord, my little jokes on Thee / And I'll forgive Thy great big one on me."

Holes in Folk Sayings

I'm all for abruption. There is no gift like that of suddenly turning
up somewhere else.
                              —Frost to Louis Untermeyer, May 24, 1916

"Mending Wall" raises another homey matter, since by now Adam has a
neighbor. Eve's back at the house with the kids, and *paradise* is a "walled
garden" whose boulders are going feral. Rather than climbing trees toward
heaven, a more wizened Adam has some repair work to do. "Something
there is that doesn't love a wall," he inverts syntax to begin colloquially and
obliquely with his namesake, the New England "frost-heave" that abrupts
regular lines in roads, walls, and landscapes. "Something there is" is a trochaic bump that drops, then rises iambically on a rhythmic line with no
particulars until love hits the wall of negative inversion, *doesn't*. But who
loves walls anyway? Isn't the verb a bit overdone, out of place, not quite
right for wall fanciers? Well, yes, but that's the way the language works, or
doesn't work, in its sidling attempts to name things likely human like love.
Counterarguments, or "talking contraries," as Frost liked to say, are Socrati-
cally necessary to advance understanding. Love is a big word encompassing a
lot of things, so walls and all things human are fair game. Indeed, but what

doesn't love walls then? The linchpin to the line, dead center, is the negated verbal action of *doesn't*: "That sends the frozen-ground-swell" under the wall spilling the rocks "And makes gaps even two can pass abreast." An abruptive spondee underlies "makes gaps" crucial to open passage, two-by-two, as though the animals could return to the Ark through naturally occurring cracks in Eden's walls. Still, what's missing in these opening lines? *Does* is negated by *not* and contracted into *doesn't* where the elided "o" syntactically gaps the walled line. "The sentences are a notation then for indicating the tones of the Oh's," Frost noted of Shakespearean intonation. "Omit the O's and the sentences still indicate the tones. All good sentences indicate tones that might be said in Ohs alone or in the Ohs with the (same) sentences" (notebook twelve and see the extended remarks on interjective Ohs in the forty-fifth notebook, "the brute noises of our human throat that were all our meaning before words stole in").

What's missing—the naught of things—may be a shadowy sign of Nature's gravity and entropy, an abruptive design of a Maker's disruptive play through connective divisions. Dickinson calls her nerve gap "Zero at the Bone," but Frost is more furtive, less histrionic. *Something* may be the way things are or would be without man's meddling, the unwalling of post-Edenic expulsions, the original Proto-Indo-European *ar-* "connectings" of art and nature, as in arm, arc, arch, ardor, and articulate. Such are the tenuous bonds between Adam and his domain, the neighborly amblings of one man into another's property. Crossings: all contracted into a very American verb of resistance, *doesn't*. No kings or taxes, liberty or death, *Non serviam*, don't tread on me. Good poetry in Frost's hands turns on such small subtleties and large contraries, no less than Dickinson's perceptions bend with certain slants of light (in notebook seventeen he mentions assigning his students Dickinson to read and memorize). "All beauty may come from the way context is woven to make stress certain on one particular word" (notebook four). Frost charges a critic to "put his finger on the place / Matrix most of poem" (notebook nineteen). And he could as well spoof his own lines in notebook forty: "Something there is that doesn't love a wall / Something there is that does and after all."

Hunters plunder the land and their yelping dogs break walls chasing rabbits, a human kind of nonsense no less than poking holes through poetic lines. Regardless of the agents—dogs, elves, or frost-heaves—the walls come down and the men meet in springtime to rebuild the barrier separating them. "We keep the wall between us as we go." It's a curious kind of neighborly work, endemic to New England's hard-scrabble temperament where distance is critical to crusty connection—clearing the land of rocks crucial to homesteading when Indians once foraged freely among the stones in the woods.

This "outdoor game" comes to little more than habitual spring ritual, but here the mischief moves our Yankee guide to question walls between his pre-lapsarian apple and the neighbor's post-lapsarian pine trees (pining evergreen blues). What are we walling in and out, he quizzes the other of their compulsive spring mending, but "like an old-stone savage armed" a darker paternal saying oddly dictates New England ritual: "Good fences make good neighbors."

Wait a minute, what's wrong here? Consider the real gap: fences have holes and are *not* walls. Folk sayings may be riddled with mischief. In rebellious America a father's strictures should never be completed by blind obedience. "Pity for bastard embodied in law of inheritance," Frost says in the seventeenth notebook. Maybe we should think deeper about these inherited words and things and gaps. Walls are connective divisions, no less than bark and epidermis, and we rub up against others to join our differences. The land may be divided into private parcels, but Nature holds wild sway in common, the frost-heave a rolling underground abruption to possessive pattern. No less so, trochees overturn iambs in a poetic line, or dactyls and anapests add abruptive tensions to blank verse regularity. Public choice is abutted by maverick chance. Our democracy, after all, is contingent on private rights made public, one among many, shared individualism the common birthright.

So why do good fences make good neighbors? Like doors, windows, and gates they let the light through, allow for passage back and forth. Fences acknowledge differences without denying common bonds. Good walls, a bit more Yankee obdurate, could do likewise naturally, given the neighborly gaps that join two men in springtime, if at all. *Doesn't* it make a contrary kind of sense? And so we "go behind" our "father's saying" at times to question the ancestral Word, to riddle reality, to aerate village wisdom, to parse inheritance in a new land. How Americans connect through division may keep our house in union, as the frost-heaves of season, temperament, and time keep us honest to our father's contestable legacy of one among many.

Laddered Darkness

And if you're lost enough to find yourself
By now, pull in your ladder road behind you
And put a sign up CLOSED to all but me.
Then make yourself at home.
                    —"Directive"

What happens to an aged Adam after apple-picking in the fall of the Fall, that is, post-Edenically when he begins to question eternity anew for real? The man is working class, picking apples life-long by the sweat of his brow, and his long ladder interminably sticks its dyadic prongs *through* the tree of life. He's no longer a boy climbing up and out of the sky, or a landowner quibbling gaps in inherited folk arguments, but blue-collar Jacob wrestling the Angel of Death, seven accents of opening struggle enjambed across three of secondary release. "My long two-pointed ladder's sticking through a tree / Toward heaven still." Up the long ladder, the Irish say, down the short rope, lethally knotted. Surely one acquainted with the night, the insomniac Frost almost outlived all his family and friends. Late in the game the poet-narrator still hasn't made it home, to heaven, or back to Eden. The double-ll end-rhymes echo incessantly, rhyming fall with fill, still, cellar, well, fell, all, and will, slant-rhyming bough and now with off and trough, break and ache, much, harvest, and touch, earth and worth. It's too much sound work for an aged everyman. "But I am done with apple-picking now," Adam says tired of one thing after another, and drowses on his ladder, only to be haunted Hamlet-fashion ("to be or not to be") by looking into an iced mirror darkly, "through a pane of glass" at the strange "world of hoary grass." He's not Whitman rooting up-trail in leaves of grass. The world has been too long and too much with him, and he's dropped lower than Wordsworth would ever go, as Frost said.

The old man lets the cataracted ice-trough window drop and shatter. His broken-line nightmare of hallucinatory apples falling into a cellar bin prefigures a final fall off the ladder, metaphor notwithstanding. "For I have had too much /" he says in stilted iambic trimeter, "Of apple-picking: I am over tired / Of the great harvest I myself desired." The first-person pronoun cries triply through the diphthong, ai-ai-ai, bending under its mortal weight. The pentameters stumble broken backed across line breaks, the end-rhymes ossified or slanting off-voweled across lines (much, picking, overtired, harvest, desired, touch). The "great harvest" cannot be handpicked, only offered in a discard pile of bodily sacrifice. "For all /," the line gaps like a crack in a stone drain, "That struck the earth /" it staggers on in dimeter, all are trashed in the "cider-apple heap," poor substitute for sacrament. "One can see what will trouble /," the old man topples broken-lined in heavy anapests for all, "This Sleep of mine, whatever sleep it is." Indeed, as with stopping by woods on a snowy evening in absolutely regular blank verse: snooze and you lose. Freezing to death "with miles to go before I sleep" is one way to go without thinking at the winter solstice, unminding the savage dark of frosty woods, "the Hour of Lead." Falling asleep off the ladder toward heaven, perhaps a homely birch stripped of its black-and-white bark, poses equal mortal hazard.

Where to turn? Though he's hibernating for winter, the woodchuck "could say whether it's like his / Long sleep," the falling man muses, "Or just some human sleep." The time warp choices: sleep through winter and wake in

spring, or "just" fall humanly asleep for good. Frost has buried a native joke at
the monologue's end. How much wood could a woodchuck chuck, goes the
folk riddle, if a woodchuck could chuck wood? The joke is it can't. The hibernating woodchuck, named from Algonkian Cree *wuchak* or *weejak*, is a lowly
marmot and couldn't beaver down a birch if its life depended on deforesting
Eden. Chucking wood is not Adam's option. Likewise, the tree of Life contains heartwood of death, the Cross debates a promise of afterlife, and Jacob's
ladder grounds itself in a fixed wrestling match. Frost the feisty non-believer
has his fun with Calvinist fundamentalists. "It is like the greatest jest, but I
can find no record or sign of God's having ever laughed anywhere," he wrote
in the thirty-third notebook. "Comedy is pagan. The solemn hush of tragedy
at the end is the beauty of Christianity."

No heavenly Tree without a Fall to hell, no challenging God without
mortal Expulsion, no climbing our Father's ladder to the Rapture. "I like a
mystery that can't be solved," he wrote in his fifteenth notebook, "and best
of all mysteries a deed the motive of which remains a mystery." Something
there is, the syntax inverts to the twisted metric step, that doesn't love a
religious false answer or easy likeness. We'd *like* to be born-again in the
New World, would *likely* face stony obstructions all over again, and *liking*
to live forever, die for good. Whether we wake again like the woodchuck
seems a diversionary misnomer, a *like* that *doesn't* promise much of a heavenly loophole.

His and Hers: Grievous Reasons
. . . in sorrow thou shalt bring forth children; and thy desire shall be
to thy husband, and he shall rule over thee.
—Genesis 3:16

Home burial of a couple's firstborn may be the most painful labor a man
can do. Helpless witness through an upstairs window seems a woman's
most grievous nightmare. God didn't say things would go easy. The man
works to bury his sorrow; the woman buries her postpartum shock in grief.
Frost's darker sentiments were indeed Sophoclean, as he jotted in the eighth
notebook, "Let man not bring together what God has put asunder." Adam's
curse is to father and work toward the future, Eve's sorrow to birth and
nurture the past—they bear an ache of mortal weight, according to Scripture, the all-too-human burden of sinful reason. "Never again would birds'
song be the same," Frost elegizes Eve's wayward voice elsewhere in Adam's
woods. "And to do that to birds was why she came." Temporally theirs is an
ancient tragedy of fated free will in a fallen garden. What can he do but do
what must be done; what can she do but want otherwise? The narrative has

drawn a Western blue-line through millennia to a New World Eden drag-
ging us back through the Fall all over again.

Frost knew these things up close, losing his four-year-old son Robert Jr.
to *cholera infantum* in 1900. His wife Elinor bore the losses of six children in
all, suicide, despair, and madness among the family tragedies. To his chagrin
the old stoat Robert Sr. almost survived them all. He was depressive and
overbearing, savagely masculine and boorishly American, but a hard-scrabble
scribbler all the same; and he made an honest living, more or less, writing
burly verse on a rough-cut plank and holding forth for New England villagers
whose history was aboriginal slaughter, witch burnings, Revolutionary par-
ricide and Civil War fratricide, backwoods incest, shed idiots, cruel winters,
crop failures, and Industrial Depression. "America the Lummox of Nations,"
he scribbled in his twelfth notebook, cursing the gifted tragic regression of
Adam's émigré Expulsion:

> . . . cursed is the ground for thy sake; in sorrow shalt thou eat of it
> all the days of thy life;
> —Genesis 3:17

"Home Burial" unfolds as a domestic contretemps. Both still-life drama and
stairway dance, the poem begins "He saw her from the bottom of the stairs /
Before she saw him." Male visual intrusion, a voyeuristic kind of patriarchal
privilege, replicates inversely what she has been doing upstairs—observing
him. Both characters watch each other like vultures circling rancid prey, and
she is just a bit ahead of him. Both are conversely wedded in how they deal
with grief, he a man of working cognition, she a woman of laboring sorrow.
The poem marries grief with reason, Joseph Brodsky feels, mind mating
heart in wedded *agon*.

The man is initially looking up from the bottom of the stairs, in the
lower position of Jacob looking up at the Angel, or Joseph staring at Jesus on
the Cross. Regressively, she's looking over her shoulder beginning to descend,
shifting down into her skirt, then up again for one last fearful glimpse,
Eurydice weaving away to Dis. All is contrapuntal, the two locked into a
deadly *pas de deux*.

He starts up the stairs toward her asking what she sees "From up there
always?—for I want to know." He *wants* to know, he *will* know, or so be
damned. She pivots and sinks toward him, her face registering numb terror.
He repeats his intrusive will to know what she sees, "Mounting until she
cowered under him," clearly gender domination, not so subtle sexual innu-
endo, submission her only defense, indeed the carnal origin of the tragedy just
interred. "I will find out now—you must tell me, dear," he says imperatively,

tagging on the diminutive endearment with the afterthought of a brute who mumbles "scuze me" after he shoves his date into a doorway ("much character," Frost notices in notebook seventeen, "is shown in a person's way of saying excuse me humorously carelessly"). She little resists his shouldering up the stairs, her neck stiffening ever so slightly in the silence. For she knows the "Blind creature" can't see what she sees, but at last he murmurs the fatal "Oh" and yet another desolate "Oh." He's not overly responsive, and she still cannot believe that he takes in her charnel vista. "What is it—what?" she now insists, and he says just that he sees now, nothing else. He who usually says everything cannot say just *what* he sees. She persists in maternal disbelief and demands that he "Tell me what it is," as they reverse lead roles like cardiac arrest dancers who can't find a coupling rhythm.

It is but a window frame, a terrible window framing *his* family graveyard—three slate stones and one marble slab he is "wonted to," memorials "Broad-shouldered" on the side hill. And yet not the stones, but the fresh-earth "child's mound" crowns what he sees that she sees obsessively. "Don't, don't, don't, / don't," she stutters across the line break, and we begin to see that he does now see what she can't stand to see. "Don't" serves as the terrible sinew between them all along—her refusal of his entreaties, his insistent advances sealing her violated horror over conception and a resulting child's death, *don't* contracting the double o's of do not.

So she withdraws under his arm on the banister and surreptitiously slides downstairs, coiling with silently menacing accusation that causes him to say haltingly twice before he knows what he's asking, "Can't a man speak of his own child he's lost?" One beat less than the blank verse of this monotonal, pentametric encounter, one integer less than the marriage can stand—one word not enough or spondaic tetrameter too much from a noisy husband who cannot fathom his wife's wordless grief. His measure is off, his tone deaf. She desperately grabs for her hat, rejects needing second thought, rushes for the freedom of air outside the stifling house, frantic to "get out of here." An old story: a man's intransigent heady intelligence, a woman's emotional panic to be free of his all-too-rational heaviness. The adamantine weight of mortal time and the earth itself drags all down to existential hell.

"Amy!" he implores her by familiar name, "Don't—don't go." Doubly negative, don't go elsewhere, listen to me, then balking, "I won't come down the stairs." He thinks he's reversely in charge at the top of the conjugal stair-ladder, and he fixes "his chin between his fists." The man's doubled hands say everything knuckled around his tightened voice, and she knows he doesn't know how to see or to ask in the right manner. He has the wrong words, the wrong voice, the wrong gestures. The husband does speak anyway, stupidly, tragically: "There's something I should like to ask you, dear." His is a school teacher's tact beneath the gallows. How "dear" is his obtuse refusal to see her side of grief, to deny her irrational need to look back at their loss, her panic to abandon him and his ways, her unassuageable desperation to join another in her grief? Fingers on the latch are her only reply to his helpless entreaty for help in how to ask.

He repeats the futile defense, that his words are nearly always offensive to her sensibilities. A man can't be manly with "womenfolk," he mutters half unheard, but must "keep hands off / Anything special you're a-mind to name." And that's just it: his words are not hers "a-mind," though Adam named everything in the Garden and held *dominion* over all, ribbing and naming her too. He can't get the right tone of voice, and she is inordinately poor in his house, and she has no mind of her own among his things or words or ways.

Then he says it all in a way that torques the common bond of love into a wretched oxymoron, a double bind of non-possessive covet that seals his fate in her exit. It's the unbridgeable chasm between his and hers: "Though I don't like such things 'twixt those that love. / Two that don't love can't live together without them. / But two that do can't live together with them." His and hers, mine and yours, inside and out, bondage and freedom, language and silence, presence and absence. The wedded contraries are endless and they boil down to his will and her won't. *E pluribus unum*—separately or in common? "Not as a woman weeps:" Frost charged his own gender, "but as a man—against his nature and against his will" (Notebook nine).

He pleads with her, his tone shifting from willful to frustrated, to complaining, to plaintive, "Don't—don't go. / Don't carry it to someone else this time." Ahh, another audience down the road, an outsider, a sympathetic listener uncensored by the marital gag rule. "Tell me about it if it's something human," he begs of the indefinable (perhaps not at all human) the *other* in the estranged *Id*. "Let me into your grief." He wants in, she keeps him out, come-hither rejected by locked-out and get-lost. The conjugal bed is no-man's land, emotional mis-carriage the crime.

The man tries a different tack from pleading. He's not so much unlike others, he reasons sophistically, as her distance makes him out to be. She may be overdoing it a little, he needles her. "What was it brought you up to think it the thing," he circles her hauteur, "To take your mother-loss of a first child / So inconsolably—." He would make her grow up his way, draw her out rationally and reason away grief, adding "in the face of love" almost as a footnote to their loss. Whose love or face, and why inconsolable? Who loves what in this war of breaking wills? She will *not* let go, and he *will* know what she denies him by gendered upbringing—a mother's love that supersedes a father's justice, the Virgin Mary's sacrifice overreaching Joseph's suspect

patriarchy. In the face of tragedy men reason, women grieve. And now she
accuses him of sneering, which he vehemently denies, though he sounds like
a judge at his own hanging and quickly takes offense, reversing himself and
offering, moreover threatening, to "come down to you," adding indignantly,
"God, what a woman!" With Adam's surly impatience he can't help repeat for
a third time that it's come to this: "A man can't speak of his own child that's
dead." A terribly vernacular double negative—he can't speak of what he can't
have, his own firstborn son. Notice that "lost" has been replaced by "dead," the
end-stop of his finite sorrow. She fills in around and goes beyond his stunted
grief-love with bottomless sorrow.

The woman feels that he can't speak properly of the dead child because
he doesn't know how to grieve fully beyond self-justifying, doesn't know how
not to speak of unspeakable things. He thinks and works without feelings,
having dug "his little grave" by hand, making the gravel "leap and leap in
air, / Leap up, like that, like that." Sympathy wavers. A bystander can only
imagine her fitful repetitions in the shock of loss, her obsessive-compulsive
retracing the incontrovertible fact and inconsolable grief as the man buries
their firstborn—her scurrying from bedroom to hall window, down and back
up the stairs, stopping and starting through her sobs and stony reticence. She
watches him digging like a vole eyeing a badger, and when he at last rumbles
into the kitchen with his earth-stained shoes and soiled spade leaned against
the wall, she cannot stand his cloddish everyday chatter, concluding irrevoca-
bly that she does not know this man she once married and to whom she bore
a child. His only defense is the dying sneer of the damned, "the worst laugh I
ever laughed," Adam's derisive curse in Expulsion, *risus sardonicus*.

And she goes on repeating his self-damning words about a graveyard
birch fence rotting in the wet earth, all the while he ignored "what was in
the darkened parlor," her manner room of sorrows and shelved *Paradise Lost*
and Bible. And in the monologue she knows she's alone with her grief, that
from birth to sickening death, "One is alone, and he dies more alone." It is
interesting that she's reduced by custom to speaking of "One" as "he," herself
in his shadow, Eve still victimized by Adam's patrilineally cursed language.
It's a village conspiracy. Neighbors mouth their concerns and return to normative patriarchal living, she laments, while the grief-stricken women cower
alone with their losses. "But the world's evil," she concludes with Calvinist
stigmata. "I won't have grief so / If I can change it. Oh, I won't. I won't!" Amy,
whose name derives from French for *beloved*, is grievously countering Yahweh's Adamic fetters: *Amy* cries *I am* too and *won't* submit. Eve's convulsive
sorrow denies the routine of going on, the custom of forgetting loss, the logic
of overcoming birth-sacrifice. Like Lot's wife she will look back forever. This
estranged woe-of-man voices the other side of the agony between will and

not, a feminine *won't* seeded in the disobedient apple (notebook thirty-one records that "I cant and wont" are the "most desperate mood of all"). Hers is the anorexic *will not* that cancels unwanted entry from Frost's heretical "God the Seducer" in his notebook, rejects fleshly sustenance, survives closer to the bone on more of less, and says she's through with Daddy.

He still doesn't get it. "There, you have said it all and you feel better," he humors her weeping. Close the half-open door, the man commands, "You won't go now." He's negating her will again, oddly asserting her *won't*, as he was "wonted to" the family plot framed by the window. Her heart's gone out of this little tantrum, the husband cajoles, why keep at the nonsense? He makes his worst gaffe yet. And then abruptly comes *his* second epiphany out the window: "Amy! There's someone coming down the road!" My God, dear, what if a third party heard or saw us now? he reasons in fear of the public domain, their irreconcilable differences become common knowledge. Her grief is private witness through the framing windowpane, his horror is public opprobrium, from the road, inner life crossed with outer legions. After all, it is *his* walled garden, and she came *after* birthing in sorrow with his spawn rib now buried in the dank earth, and oh dear people do talk.

But she sees differently, hears another witness coming, perhaps a different angel, maybe a seductive demon, but certainly someone other, anyone else. She is, after all, his wo-man. "*You*—oh, you think the talk is all," she rejects his schoolish blather, canceling the contrapuntally rigged dialogue. Who is this dark figure coming down the road, fate, death, God? "Burglar, banker, father," another New England woman poet said of the Almighty and closed her door on all suitors, including her immediate family. Frost's Eurydice greets the oncoming shadow of Dis or Pluto, the dark underground stranger. "I must go—/ Somewhere out of this house. How can I make you—". Strangely enough, even self-destructively, she resorts to his mode of willing the unwilling, "How can I make you—," in order to get free, anywhere but here, the need to flee overriding the domestic obligation to stay.

And he is terrifyingly measured in his rage: "If—you—do!" Finally all is em-dash monotone, monosyllabic fixity in his voice, male authority asserted over the feminine wilds of intemperate time and space. Obtuse spondaic violence poses a motion-stopping threat of what he will do if she does go. Orpheus futilely demands obedience of Eurydice as she opens the door wider to go outside, to disappear down winter's lethal rabbit hole, to run off heedless with a dark other. "I'll follow and bring you back by force. I *will!*—" So he says. Neither Christian nor Greek paternal God has come back yet with the run-away goods, though their grief-song keeps burbling through the woods.

As from the beginning, male and female lifelines counter each other with the do's and don'ts of love, the wills and won'ts of mortal choice: his family will against her need to be free, his reason against her grief, his logic against her feeling, his language against her muteness, his body against her wake. Buried back home, his and hers will never be theirs or ours, grievous reasons of difference rooted deep in the mortal earth with an unforgiving God's final Words.

> In the sweat of thy face shalt thou eat bread, till thou return unto the ground; for out of it wast thou taken: for dust thou art, and unto dust shalt thou return. And Adam called his wife's name Eve; because she was the mother of all living.
>
> —Genesis 3: 19–20

> Doubting her presence, Orpheus, filled with fear,
> And anxious too a lover's eyes to cheer,
> Looked around. That instant, backward borne, she fled. . . .
>
> —Ovid, *The Metamorphoses*, Book 10

Chronology

1874	Born on March 26 in San Francisco to William Prescott Frost Jr. and Isabelle Moodie Frost.
1885	After the death of his father, Frost moves to Lawrence, Massachusetts, with his mother and sister.
1892	Graduates from Lawrence High School with his covaledictorian and future wife, Elinor White. Attends Dartmouth College for a few months.
1893	Take first teaching job (eighth grade) in Methuen, Massachusetts. Works in the Arlington Mill in Lawrence.
1894	"My Butterfly," Frost's first published poem, appears in *The Independent*.
1895	Marries Elinor Miriam White.
1896	First son, Eliot, is born.
1897–99	Attends Harvard as an undergraduate.
1899	Daughter Lesley is born.
1900	Eliot Frost dies. Another son, Carol, is born. Family moves to a farm in Derry, New Hampshire.
1900–10	Farming and teaching at the Pinkerton Academy in Derry.
1903	Daughter Irma is born.

1905	Daughter Marjorie is born.
1907	Daughter Elinor Bettina is born; dies in infancy.
1911–12	Teaches psychology at New Hampshire State Normal School in Plymouth.
1912–15	Resides in England with Elinor and their four children. Writes and farms in Buckinghamshire and Herefordshire. Meets Ezra Pound.
1913	*A Boy's Will* published in London.
1914	*North of Boston* published in London.
1915	Moves to farm in Franconia, New Hampshire. Frost's two books are published in the United States.
1916	*Mountain Interval* published. Elected to the National Institute of Arts and Letters.
1917	Begins teaching English at Amherst College.
1919	Moves to new farm near South Shaftsbury, Vermont.
1920	Cofounds the Breadloaf School of English at Middlebury College.
1921–23	Poet in residence at the University of Michigan.
1923	*Selected Poems* and *New Hampshire* are published.
1923–25	Professor of English at Amherst College.
1924	Receives Pulitzer Prize for *New Hampshire*.
1925–26	Fellow in letters at the University of Michigan.
1926	Resumes teaching at Amherst College.
1928	*West-Running Brook* published.
1929	*A Way Out* published. Robert and Elinor move to Gully Farm in Bennington, Vermont.
1930	*Collected Poems* published.
1934	Daughter, Marjorie Frost Fraser, dies.
1936	*A Further Range* published. Serves as Charles Eliot Norton Professor of Poetry at Harvard University.
1937	Second Pulitzer for *A Further Range*.

1938	Elinor White Frost dies. Frost resigns from Amherst College.
1939	Enlarged *Collected Poems* published. Awarded the National Institute of Arts and Letters Gold Medal for Poetry. Buys farm in Ripton, Vermont, for a summer home.
1939–42	Serves as Ralph Waldo Emerson Fellow in Poetry at Harvard.
1940	Son Carol commits suicide.
1942	*A Witness Tree* published.
1943	Receives third Pulitzer for *A Witness Tree*.
1945	*A Masque of Reason* published.
1947	*Steeple Bush* and *Masque of Mercy* published.
1949	*Complete Poems* published.
1957	Travels to England, where he is honored at Oxford and Cambridge universities and the National University of Ireland.
1958	Appointed Consultant in Poetry to the Library of Congress.
1961	Reads "The Gift Outright" at the inauguration of President John F. Kennedy. Lectures in Athens and Jerusalem.
1962	Visits Moscow as a guest of the Soviet government. Meets privately with Premier Khrushchev. *In the Clearing* published.
1963	Awarded the Bollingen Prize for poetry. Dies on January 29 in Boston.

Contributors

HAROLD BLOOM is Sterling Professor of the Humanities at Yale University. Educated at Cornell and Yale universities, he is the author of more than 30 books, including *Shelley's Mythmaking* (1959), *The Visionary Company* (1961), *Blake's Apocalypse* (1963), *Yeats* (1970), *The Anxiety of Influence* (1973), *A Map of Misreading* (1975), *Kabbalah and Criticism* (1975), *Agon: Toward a Theory of Revisionism* (1982), *The American Religion* (1992), *The Western Canon* (1994), *Omens of Millennium: The Gnosis of Angels, Dreams, and Resurrection* (1996), *Shakespeare: The Invention of the Human* (1998), *How to Read and Why* (2000), *Genius: A Mosaic of One Hundred Exemplary Creative Minds* (2002), *Hamlet: Poem Unlimited* (2003), *Where Shall Wisdom Be Found?* (2004), and *Jesus and Yahweh: The Names Divine* (2005). In addition, he is the author of hundreds of articles, reviews, and editorial introductions. In 1999, Professor Bloom received the American Academy of Arts and Letters' Gold Medal for Criticism. He has also received the International Prize of Catalonia, the Alfonso Reyes Prize of Mexico, and the Hans Christian Andersen Bicentennial Prize of Denmark.

CLEANTH BROOKS was a professor at Yale University. For several years he was coeditor of *The Southern Review*. His work includes *The Well Wrought Urn*; *Understanding Poetry*, with Robert Penn Warren; and *A Shaping Joy: Studies in the Writer's Craft*.

EDWARD J. INGEBRETSEN is an associate professor at Georgetown University, where he also is director of the American studies program. His publications include *Robert Frost's Star in a Stone Boat: A Grammar of Belief* and *Maps of Heaven, Maps of Hell: Religious Terror as Memory from the Puritans to Stephen King.*

GEORGE F. BAGBY is a professor at Hampden-Sydney College. He is the author of *Frost and the Book of Nature.* His work has appeared in various journals as well as in *On Frost.*

LEWIS KLAUSNER has been an adjunct assistant professor at John Cabot University in Rome. He also has taught at the University of Utah in Salt Lake City.

JOHN HOLLANDER is an emeritus professor at Yale University. He is general coeditor of *The Oxford Anthology of English Literature.* His critical books include *The Poetry of Everyday Life* and *Rhyme's Reason*; he also has published many books of his own poetry.

DAVID HAMILTON is a professor at the University of Iowa, where he has directed the MFA program in literary nonfiction and edited *The Iowa Review.* He is the author of *Textualities: Essays on Poetry in the United States,* a collection of poetry, and *Deep River: A Memoir of a Missouri Farm.*

RICHARD J. CALHOUN is an emeritus professor at Clemson University. For many years, he was editor of the *South Carolina Review*, where he established a special issue on Frost for each spring. He is a past president of the Frost Society. He has published books on poets and for several years reviewed contemporary poetry for *American Literary Scholarship.*

JOHN H. TIMMERMAN is a professor at Calvin College. In addition to his book on Frost, he has written on T. S. Eliot, Jane Kenyon, and other writers. He also has written devotional books and other Christian texts, as well as short fiction and creative nonfiction.

MARIE BORROFF is an emeritus professor at Yale University. She is the author of *Language and the Poet: Verbal Artistry in Frost, Stevens, and Moore* and *Robert Frost's New Testament: Language and the Poem.* She also has published poetry and is a translator.

KENNETH LINCOLN is a professor at the University of California, Los Angeles. He was chairman of the country's first interdisciplinary master's program in American Indian studies. He is the author of *Native Poetics* and other works and also has written novels, poetry, and personal essays.

Bibliography

Bock, Martin. "Frost's 'The Oven Bird' and the Modern Poetic Idiom." *The Texas Review* 7, nos. 1–2 (Spring–Summer 1986): 28–31.

Borroff, Marie. "Sound Symbolism as Drama in the Poetry of Robert Frost." *PMLA: Publications of the Modern Language Association of America* 107, no. 1 (January 1992): 131–44.

Brodsky, Joseph, and Seamus Heaney, Derek Walcott. *Homage to Robert Frost.* New York: Farrar, Straus and Giroux, 1996.

Cady, Edwin, and Louis J. Budd, ed. *On Frost.* Durham: Duke University Press, 1991.

Charney, Maurice. "Robert Frost's Conversational Style." *Connotations: A Journal for Critical Debate* 10, nos. 2–3 (2000–2001): 147–59.

Evans, David H. "Guiding Metaphors: Robert Frost and the Rhetoric of Jamesian Pragmatism." *Arizona Quarterly* 57, no. 3 (Autumn 2001): 61–90.

Faggen, Robert, ed. *The Cambridge Companion to Robert Frost.* Cambridge; New York: Cambridge University Press, 2001.

Fleissner, Robert F. *Frost's Road Taken.* New York: Peter Lang, 1996.

Frattali, Steven. *Person, Place, and World: A Late-Modern Reading of Robert Frost.* Victoria, B.C.: University of Victoria, English Literary Studies, 2002.

Frost Annual. *South Carolina Review* 22, no. 1 (Fall 1989): 33–119.

Frost, Carol. "Frost's Way of Speaking." *New England Review: Middlebury Series* 23, no. 1 (Winter 2002): 119–33.

Galbraith, Astrid. *New England as Poetic Landscape: Henry David Thoreau and Robert Frost.* Frankfurt, Germany: Peter Lang, 2003.

175

Giles, Paul. "From Decadent Aesthetics to Political Fetishism: The 'Oracle Effect' of Robert Frost's Poetry." *American Literary History* 12, no. 4 (Winter 2000): 713–44.

Hadas, Rachel. *Form, Cycle, Infinity: Landscape Imagery in the Poetry of Robert Frost and George Seferis.* Lewisburg [Pa.]: Bucknell University Press; Cranbury, N.J.: Associated University Presses, 1985.

Hatch, James C. "The Pastoral of Limits in Robert Frost." *Genre: Forms of Discourse and Culture* 40, nos. 1–2 (Spring–Summer 2007): 81–104.

Heaney, Seamus. "Above the Brim: On Robert Frost." *Salmagundi* 88–89 (Fall 1990–Winter 1991): 275–94.

Ingebretsen, Edward J. "Love's Sentence: Domesticity as Religious Discourse in Robert Frost's Poetry." *Christianity and Literature* 39, no. 1 (Autumn 1989): 51–62.

Jandl, Nathan J. "A Two-Pointed Ladder: Balancing the Ambiguities of Metaphor and Environmental Engagement in Frost's Poetry." *Robert Frost Review* 18 (Fall 2008): 103–23.

Jost, Walter. "Lessons in the Conversation That We Are: Robert Frost's 'Death of the Hired Man.'" *College English* 58, no. 4 (April 1996): 397–422.

———. *Rhetorical Investigations: Studies in Ordinary Language Criticism.* Charlottesville: University of Virginia Press, 2004.

Kearns, Katherine. *Robert Frost and a Poetics of Appetite.* Cambridge; New York: Cambridge University Press, 1994.

Kilcup, Karen L. *Robert Frost and Feminine Literary Tradition.* Ann Arbor, Mich.: University of Michigan Press, 1998.

Kjorven, Johannes. *Robert Frost's Emergent Design: The Truth of the Self In-between Belief and Unbelief.* Oslo [Norway]: Solum Forlag; Atlantic Highlands, N.J.: Humanities Press International, 1987.

Lakritz, Andrew M. *Modernism and the Other in Stevens, Frost, and Moore.* Gainesville, Fla.: University Press of Florida, 1996.

Lloyd-Kimbrel, E. D. "A Condition of Complete Simplicity: Poetic Returns and Frost's 'Directive.'" *Robert Frost Review* (Fall 1991): 7–17.

Marcus, Mordecai. *The Poems of Robert Frost: An Explication.* Boston: G.K. Hall, 1991.

Mauro, Jason Isaac. "'The More I Say I': Frost and the Construction of the Self." *Arizona Quarterly* 57, no. 2 (Summer 2001): 93–115.

Monteiro, George. "History, Legend, and Regional Verse in Frost's 'Directive.'" *New England Quarterly* 75, no. 2 (June 2002): 286–94.

———. *Robert Frost & the New England Renaissance.* Lexington: University Press of Kentucky, 1988.

Morton, Colleen. "The Role of the Imagination in Creating: Or, Transforming Environment in Robert Frost's Poetry." *Mount Olive Review* 8 (Winter–Spring 1995–1996): 127–37.

Murphy, James. "'A Thing So Small': The Nature of Meter in Robert Frost's 'Design.'" *Modernism/Modernity* 14, no. 2 (April 2007): 309–28.

Oehlschlaeger, Fritz. "Fences Make Neighbors: Process, Identity, and Ego in Robert Frost's 'Mending Wall.'" *Arizona Quarterly* 40, no. 3 (Autumn 1984): 242–54.

Oster, Judith. *Toward Robert Frost: The Reader and the Poet.* Athens: University of Georgia Press, 1991.

Pack, Robert. *Belief and Uncertainty in the Poetry of Robert Frost.* Hanover, N.H.: University Press of New England [for] Middlebury College Press, 2003.

Phillips, Siobhan. *The Poetics of the Everyday: Creative Repetition in Modern American Verse.* New York: Columbia University Press, 2010.

Poirier, Richard, ed. *Robert Frost: The Work of Knowing.* Stanford: Stanford University Press, 1990.

Regan, Stephen. "Robert Frost and the American Sonnet." *Robert Frost Review* 14 (Fall 2004): 13–35.

Richardson, Mark. "Robert Frost and the Motives of Poetry." *Essays in Literature* 20, no. 2 (Fall 1993): 273–91.

Rotella, Guy. "Frost and Invitation." *Robert Frost Review* 15 (Fall 2005): 35–49.

———. *Reading & Writing Nature: The Poetry of Robert Frost, Wallace Stevens, Marianne Moore, and Elizabeth Bishop.* Boston: Northeastern University Press, 1991.

———. "Robert Frost: Slacker." *Robert Frost Review* 18 (Fall 2008): 63–84.

Sheehy, Donald. "Pastoral Degenerate: Frost and Rural Sociology." *Robert Frost Review* 16 (Fall 2006): 18–30.

Sheehy, Donald G. "(Re)Figuring Love: Robert Frost in Crisis, 1938–1942." *New England Quarterly* 63, no. 2 (June 1990): 179–231.

Stanlis, Peter J. *Robert Frost: The Poet as Philosopher.* Wilmington, Del.: ISI Books, 2007.

Trachtenberg, Zev. "Good Neighbors Make Good Fences: Frost's 'Mending Wall.'" *Philosophy and Literature* 21, no. 1 (April 1997): 114–22.

Wilcox, Earl J., ed. *His "Incalculable" Influence on Others: Essays on Robert Frost in Our Time.* Victoria: English Literary Studies, University of Victoria, 1994.

Wolosky, Shira. "The Need of Being Versed: Robert Frost and the Limits of Rhetoric." *Essays in Literature* 18, no. 1 (Spring 1991): 76–92.

Acknowledgments

Cleanth Brooks, "Frost and Nature." From *Robert Frost: The Man and the Poet*, edited by Earl J. Wilcox. Copyright © 1990 by UCA Press.

Edward J. Ingebretsen, "'If I Had to Perish Twice': Robert Frost and the Aesthetics of Apocalypse." From *Thought* 67, no. 264 (March 1991): 31–46. Copyright © 1992 by Fordham University Press.

George F. Bagby, "'Assorted Characters.'" From *Frost and the Book of Nature*. Copyright © 1993 by the University of Tennessee Press.

Lewis Klausner, "Inscription and the Burden of Judgment in 'Directive.'" From *Studies in Romanticism* 34, no. 4 (Winter 1995): 569–82. Copyright © 1995 by Boston University.

John Hollander, "Robert Frost's Oven Bird." From *Sewanee Writers on Writing*, edited by Wyatt Prunty. Copyright © 2000 by Louisiana University State Press. Reprinted by permission of the author.

David Hamilton, "The Echo of Frost's Woods." From *Roads Not Taken: Rereading Robert Frost*, edited and with an introduction by Earl J. Wilcox and Jonathan N. Barron. Copyright © 2000 by the Curators of the University of Missouri.

Richard J. Calhoun. "'By Pretending They Are Not Sonnets': The Sonnets of Robert Frost at the Millennium." From *Roads Not Taken: Rereading Robert Frost*,

179

edited and with an introduction by Earl J. Wilcox and Jonathan N. Barron. Copyright © 2000 by the Curators of the University of Missouri.

John H. Timmerman, "Rationalist Ethics." From *Robert Frost: The Ethics of Ambiguity*. Published by Bucknell University Press. Copyright © 2002 by Rosemont Publishing and Printing.

Marie Borroff, "Another Look at Robert Frost's 'Birches.'" From *Literary Imagination* 7, no. 1 (Winter 2005): 69–80. Copyright © 2010 by the Association of Literary Scholars, Critics, and Writers.

Kenneth Lincoln, "Quarreling Frost, Northeast of Eden." From *Southwest Review* 93, no. 1 (2008): 93–111. Copyright © 2008 by Kenneth Lincoln.

Index

A

"Acquainted with the Night," 63,
     101, 105–106
"After Apple-Picking," 4–5, 9
Age of Reason (Paine), 113
"The Aim Was Song," 82
"All These Birds" (Wilbur), 75–76
American Apocalypses (Robinson), 25
American Enlightenment, 112
animism, recurrent, 41, 50–51, 56n2
apocalyptic themes
     Christian, 29, 31
     in "Design," 25, 27–28
     fears of termination, 33
     life compared to poetry, 26
     rewriting of, 32
     sources of, 29
     textual secrecy, 26
Arnold, Matthew, 9
astronomy and Frost, 53–54, 115
"The Auroras of Autumn" (Stevens),
     1
Autobiography (Franklin), 112
"Autumn Refrain" (Stevens), 76

B

Beyond Formalism (Hartman), 59
"Birches"
     chosen by Frost for "ulteriority,"
          142
     figures of speech and, 146–147
     ice storm as death threat, 148–149,
          152n16
     individuality of, 8
     The Onset and, 148
     poet meditates on boyhood
          pleasure, 149–150, 152nn17–
          18, 156–157
     Shelley's "Adonais" allusion in,
          147, 148, 149
     sound symbolism in, 148
     ulterior meanings of birch
          swinging, 146
     wish fulfillment in, 147
birds, poetical, 74–75
Bloom, Harold, 1–8
"Bond and Free," 47
"A Boundless Moment," 143
A Boy's Will, 4, 7
Brad McLaughlin ("The Star-
     Splitter"), 49, 115
Brave New World (Huxley), 112
The Broken Center (Scott), 116
"The Broken Drought," 94
Brook, Heyward, 129
"Bursting Rapture," 25, 29–30, 31

C

"A Cabin in the Clearing," 5, 7
Christmas tree, 124
classical texts, 144–145
climbing to cross purposes, 155–158

181

"Closed for Good," 47

Coleridge, Samuel Taylor, 74

"Come In," 13–14, 21, 76

Complete Poems, 25, 121

Comus (Milton), 122, 123

The Conduct of Life. (Emerson), 2,
    3, 6

"The Constant Symbol" (essay), 96,
    119

correspondences, doctrine of, 43–44

craftsmanship of Frost, 95, 99, 109,
    150

D

Dante, 66–67, 72ni7, 86, 87–88

"'Deeds that Count': Robert Frost's
    Sonnets" (Evans), 98

"The Deserted Village," 87

"Design"
    apocalyptic themes of, 25, 27–28
    high-quality dark sonnet, 101
    individualism of, 8
    metaphorical characters in, 5, 47
    most explicated sonnet, 106–107

"A Dialogue of Self and Soul"
    (Yeats), 68

"Directive"
    attention given to, 1, 8, 59–60, 70
    biographical reading of, 4, 69–70,
        72n15
    children's playhouse and, 63–64
    confusion in, 68
    Dante and, 66–67, 72n7
    elitist posturing in, 70
    Emerson's "Illusions" and, 6–7
    inscription genre and, 59
    laddered darkness, 160–162
    language used in, 62–63
    last lines compared to
        Wordsworth, 65–66
    as lesson in being skeptical of
        poetic fictions, 64
    Mark 4:11–12 reference, 66, 143,
        151n5
    as reply to Eliot, 87, 92

The Divine Conspiracy (Willard), 133

"Divinity School Address"
    (Emerson), 1, 113

Drake, Joseph Rodman, 75

E

Eliot, T.S.
    Dante as source for, 87–88
    "Directive" as reply to, 92
    on Frost, 94
    Frost and, 14, 89
    Frost's quarrel with, 94
    Sweeney Agonistes, 17–20

Emerson, Ralph Waldo
    Bloom on, 1–8, 55
    "Divinity School Address," 1, 113
    enthusiasm for geology role, 52
    "Illusions" (essay), 6–7
    Nature, 26, 42, 43, 44, 46
    "Power," 2, 4
    "Uriel," 1–2, 3, 7–8

epitaphs of poets, 60–61

"Etherealizing," 100, 108–109

European Enlightenment, 112

Evans, Oliver H., 98

F

Faggen, Robert, 114–115, 124

"The Fall of Rome" (Auden), 14–20

"The Fear," 37

Field Guide to North American Birds,
    82

"The Figure a Poem Makes" (essay),
    26, 96

figures of speech, 47–48

"Fire and Ice," 25, 29, 30–32

"Fireflies in the Garden," 142

"For Once, Then, Something,"
    35–36, 39n12, 49–50

Franklin, Benjamin, 112

Frost, Elinor (wife), 102, 106, 117,
    127, 163

Frost, Lesley (daughter), 72, 89, 90,
    127

Frost, Robert

concern about own talent, 28
confessions to Thompson, 68, 70, 72n15
on definition of a poem, 95–96
family tragedies of, 163
longevity of, 32
move to England, 117–118
nature linked to humanity by, 11–13, 17, 23–24, 51–52, 114–115
negativity of, 3–4, 5
status at midcentury, 93–94
status at millennium, 94–95, 109
See also Eliot, T.S.; Emerson, Ralph Waldo; Poe, Edgar Allan; style of Frost; Wordsworth, William; Yeats, William Butler; titles of specific works

G
"The Generations of Men," 49
Genesis, quotations from, 162, 163, 168
God, rationalist thought on, 114

H
Harmon, William, 87
Hartman, Geoffrey, 59, 60
holes in folk sayings, 158–160
"Home Burial," 37, 69, 162–168
Human Understanding (Hume), 113
Hume, David, 112–113
humor/satire, 108, 109
Huxley, Aldous, 112
"Hyla Brook"
  conflict with past and present memory, 63
  Emersonian poem, 101
  extra line added to, 109
  irregular rhyme scheme of, 105
  obscure reference to "The Brook," 143
  prosopopeic nature of poetry and, 59–60

I
"Illusions" (essay) (Emerson), 6–7
"In Harmony with Nature" (Arnold), 9–10
inscription genre, 60–61
Interviews with Robert Frost, 115
In the Clearing, 5, 143
"In Time of Cloudburst," 52
"Into My Own," 102–103
"Iota Subscript," 71
"It Is Almost the Year Two Thousand," 16, 25, 29, 93

J
Jesse Bel (A Masque of Mercy), 137
Job (A Masque of Reason), 2–3
Johnson, Samuel, 112
Jonson, Ben, 131
"A Journey from Patapsko to Annapolis" (Lewis), 74–76
Judaeo-Christian tradition, 29

K
Keats, John, 74
"Kitty Hawk," 28, 150
Kjorven, Johannes, 119

L
laddered darkness, 160–162
Langbaum, Robert, 116, 121
Lanier, Sidney, 75
"The Lark Ascending" (Meredith), 74
"A Leaf Treader," 21–22, 42
"Leaves Compared with Flowers," 42–43
"The Lesson for Today," 66–67
"Letter to The Amherst Student," 28
Lewis, Richard, 74–75
Life Studies (Lowell), 109
"Lines Left upon a Seat in a Yew-tree" (Wordsworth), 61–66, 67, 68
"A Lone Striker," 41
"A Loose Mountain," 53

Loreto, Paola, 131–132
Lowell, Robert, 109

M
"A Man in Front of His God"
 (Loreto), 131–132
"Maple," 49
masque as dramatic form, 122–123
A Masque of Mercy
 Frost's finding conclusion to,
  135–136
 from *Jonah*, 130
 mercy/justice conflict and, 136
 in modern-day New York City,
  132
 "My Brother's Keeper" in, 54–55,
  136
 opening of play, 132–133
 placement in *Complete Poems*,
  121
 primary assumption of, 136
 Sermon on the Mount and,
  133–134
 similarities of both masques,
  130–132
 story of Jonah, 131
 structure and theme of, 131
A Masque of Reason
 Eliphaz and, 125
 ending with ambiguity, 130
 Job's conversation with God, 2–3,
  126–129
 placement in *Complete Poems*, 121
 publication of, 122
 Satan's entrance, 129–130
 tension running throughout Frost,
  124–125
 Zophar and Bildad enter with
  advice, 125–126
masques of Frost
 on mysteries of humanity, 123,
  138n19
 similarities of both masques,
  130–132
Maxson, H.A., 97, 104, 107–108

"Mending Wall," 46, 142–143,
 151n7, 158–159
Meredith, George, 74
Milton, John, 122
miracles, remythologization of,
 113–114
"The Mocking-Bird" (Drake), 75
"*The Mocking Bird*" (Lanier), 75
"The Most of It," 75
Mountain Interval, 5, 118
"Mowing," 9, 100, 108, 119
"My Brother's Keeper," 48, 54–55,
 136
mythologizing in poetry, 73–74

N
Nature (Emerson), 26, 42, 43, 46
"The Need of Being Versed in
 Country Things," 10–13, 63
"Neither Out Far Nor In Deep,"
 123, 124, 125
"Never Again Would Birds' Song Be
 the Same," 81–82, 106
New Hampshire, 34, 91
"New Hampshire," 10, 59–60, 87,
 90, 91
"The Nightingale" (Coleridge), 74
North of Boston, 4, 118
notebooks
 "In Adam's fall We sinned all" (on
  Milton), 155
 "lover's quarrel with the world,"
  154
 "Poetry lives in the tenor of the
  sentence," 157
 publication of, 153
Notebooks (unpublished), 121
"Nothing Gold Can Stay," 9, 25, 29

O
"Once by the Pacific"
 based on childhood fear, 103
 as dark sonnet, 101
 humanity in, 37
 nature as presence, 41, 51

rhyme scheme of, 98, 102
"One More Brevity," 144–146
"The Onset," 32–35
The Onset, "Birches" and, 148
"On Taking from the Top to Broaden the Base," 52–53, 54
On the Sonnets of Robert Frost (Maxson), 97
The Ordeal of Robert Frost (Richardson), 94–95
"Our Doom to Bloom," 25, 29
"Our Hold on the Planet," 52
Our Place Among Infinities (Proctor), 115
"The Oven Bird"
  "The Aim Was Song," 82
  American poet-teacher, 82–83
  analysis of by Maxson, 104
  Auden's invoking of Frost, 83
  Field Guide to North American Birds, 82
  grammar of birdsong and, 79–80
  literal and figurative falling, 78–79
  opening a puzzle, 77
  ornithology of bird, 76–77, 82
  phonological patterning of, 78
  questioning by bird, 80–81, 82
  say-song of, 81
  sounding analyzed, 77–78
  text of, 77
  traditional nature sonnet, 100

P
Paine, Thomas, 113
"A Passing Glimpse," 51
"A Patch of Old Snow," 47
Philosophical Essays (Hume), 113
"The Planet On the Table" (Stevens), 67
Poe, Edgar Allan, 29, 38n8
The Poetry of Experience (Langbaum), 116, 121
"Power" (Emerson), 2, 4
"A Prayer in Spring," 9

The Prelude (Wordsworth), 50
Proctor, Richard, 115
Psalm 8, 24
"Putting in the Seed," 107

Q
quarreling Frost, northeast of Eden, 153–168
  overview on notebooks, 153–155
  climbing to cross purposes, 155–158
  his and hers: grievous reasons, 162–167
  holes in folk sayings, 158–160
  laddered darkness, 160–162

R
"Range Finding," 9
rationalism, 111
rationalist ethics, 111–140
  overview, 111–112
  behind the masque, 121–124
  experience of unreason, 124–130
  Frost in context of, 117–121
  head to heart, 130–137
  in historical context, 112–116
Reichert, Victor (rabbi), 135
"Reluctance," 142
The Yale Review, 123
rhyme scheme of quatrains, 86
Richardson, Mark, 95
"The Road Not Taken"
  ambiguity in text of, 117
  analysis of by Maxson, 120–121
  irregular line prosody of, 119–120
  origin of, 118
  simplicity of deceptive, 37
  "The Sound of Trees" and, 118–119
  as superb pastoral poem, 119, 121
Robert Frost (Thompson), 118
Robert Frost and the Challenge of Darwin (Faggen), 114
Robert Frost's Emergent Design (Kjorven), 119

"Robert Frost's Masques and the
    Classic American Tradition,"
    (Stanus), 122
"Robert Frost's Masques
    Reconsidered" (Brook), 132
Robinson, Douglas, 25
"The Rock." (Stevens), 1
romanticism, expiration of by 1900,
    111

S
"Sailing to Byzantium" (Yeats), 74
Santayana, George, 111, 117
"Scorn Not the Sonnet," 96
Scott, Nathan, 116
"A Servant to Servants," 37
"Sitting by a Bush in Broad
    Sunlight," 54, 57n15
skepticism of Frost, 114
sonnets
    best of Frost's, 101
    difficulties of writing, 96
    Frost on, 98
    Frost's variants on, 98, 100, 102,
        108–109
    humor/satire in, 108
    Italian, 101
    list of Frost's, 100
    rhyme scheme of, 102
    "Scorn Not the Sonnet," 97
    usual conception of, 99
    Wordsworth's influence, 97
"Spring and All," 87
"Spring Pools," 9
Stanlis, Peter J., 122, 136
"A Star in a Stoneboat," 5
"Stars," 53
"The Star-Splitter," 49, 115
Steeple Bush, 4
"A Steeple on the House," 142
Stevens, Wallace, 1, 67, 76
"Stopping by Woods on a Snowy
    Evening"
    ambiguity of, 92
    Bloom on, 7

as companion to "The Onset," 34
Dante's influence on, 87–88
definition of man implied by,
    22–23
Echo and, 85–86
Eliot and, 87–88, 92
familiarity of, 85
Frost's anecdote on, 89–90
Frost's "saying" of, 88–89
publication of, 91
as radical revision of "New
    Hampshire," 91
style of Frost
    anxiety and, 33–34, 39n11
    iambic cadence, 154
    irony of view of nature, 114–115
    melodrama and cosmic despair,
        30
    mysteries of humankind, 116
    posturing, 32–34
    simple yet profound beauty, 37
    tense ambiguity of, 115
    use of like, 157–158
    verse parables interpreted, 141–
        144
Sweeney Agonistes (Eliot), 17–20

T
"The Tables Turned"
    (Wordsworth), 82–83
"Take Something Like a Star," 54
textual secrecy, 26
"Their Lonely Betters" (Auden), 83
"The Silken Tent," 106
"The Sound of Trees," 118
Thomas, Robert, 118
Thompson, Lawrence (biographer),
    10, 68, 70, 72n15, 90, 118
Thoreau, Henry David, 43, 46, 49
"Time Out," 48–49, 57n12
"To Earthward," 9
Top 500 Poems (Harmon), 87
"Tract" (burial poem), 157
"Tradition and the Individual
    Talent" (Eliot), 87–88

"Tree at My Window," 44–45,
    50–51, 56n8
"The Trial By Existence," 7,
    123–124
"Two Look at Two," 10–11, 142
"Two Tramps in Mud Time," 4, 9

U
ulteriority, explanation of, 143,
    151n6
"Uriel" (Emerson), 1–2, 3, 7–8

V
"The Vantage Point," 104–105
verse parables, interpretation of,
    141–144, 151n5

W
The Waste Land (Eliot), 87–88, 92
Welty, Eudora, 150
"West-Running Brook," 49

Whitman, Walt, 1
"Why Wait for Science," 100, 108–109
Wilbur, Richard, 75
Wilde, Richard Henry, 75
"Wild Grapes," 144–145.130
Willard, Dallas, 133
"The Wood-Pile," 2, 9, 64
"Wordsworth, Inscriptions, and
    Romantic Nature Poetry,"
    (Hartman), 60–61
Wordsworth, William
    influence of, 50, 97
    inscription genre and, 61–62
    "Lines Left upon a Seat," 61–66,
        67, 68
    The Prelude, 50
    "The Tables Turned," 82–83
"A Worn Path" (Welty), 150

Y
Yeats, William Butler, 16–17, 68, 74